From Army to Indiana University to Texas Tech . . .
from explosive news headlines to ESPN's reality show
Knight School . . . from making lifelong enemies of players
and colleagues to unrivaled NCAA victory . . . here is the
full story of college basketball's winningest coach,

BOB KNIGHT

"This is the truly authoritative 'Beyond the Brink' book on Bob Knight,
a meticulously reported and powerfully rendered expose that Bob
Knight and his supporters NEVER wanted told. Every disturbing detail
is on the record and it's as fascinating as it is frightening. Steve Delsohn
and Mark Heisler's biography promises to make even the most ardent of
Knight Kool-Aid drinkers ask themselves the question they've avoided
at all costs: Do the ends really justify the means with this coach?"
                    —Adrian Wojnarowski, *New York Times* bestselling author of
                                            The Miracle of St. Anthony

"College basketball meets *One Flew Over the Cuckoo's Nest*."
                    —Bill Reynolds, author of *Cousy* and *Fall River Dreams*

"Evenhanded and in-depth reporting brings clarity and truth to a situation that's long been debated by Knight supporters and detractors."
                    —*Publishers Weekly*

"A hard book to put down."

                    —*The Advocate* (Baton Rouge, LA)

This title is also available as an eBook

BOB KNIGHT

THE UNAUTHORIZED BIOGRAPHY

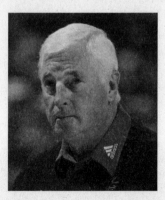

Steve Delsohn and Mark Heisler

POCKET BOOKS
New York London Toronto Sydney

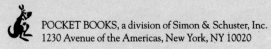

POCKET BOOKS, a division of Simon & Schuster, Inc.
1230 Avenue of the Americas, New York, NY 10020

Originally published in hardcover in 2006 by Simon & Schuster, Inc.

Library of Congress Cataloging-in-Publication Data

Delsohn, Steve.
Bob Knight : the unauthorized biography / Steve Delsohn and Mark Heisler.
p.   cm.
1. Knight, Bobby. 2. Basketball coaches—United States—Biography. I. Heisler, Mark.
II. Title.
GV884.K58D45 2006
796.323092—dc22
[B]
2005056342

ISBN-13: 978-0-7432-4348-3
ISBN-10:   0-7432-4348-X
ISBN-13: 978-0-7434-6267-9 (Pbk)
ISBN-10:   0-7434-6267-X (Pbk)

This Pocket Books trade paperback edition January 2007

10 9 8 7 6 5 4 3 2 1

Designed by Dana Sloan

Manufactured in the United States of America

For information regarding special discounts for bulk purchases,
please contact Simon & Schuster Special Sales:
1-800-456-6798 or business@simonandschuster.com

For Mary Kay, Emma, Hannah, and Grace

—Steve Delsohn

To my everythings, Loretta and Emily

—Mark Heisler

CONTENTS

Introduction   1

ONE: **Bobby: Orrville and Columbus, 1940–62**   9

TWO: ***Enfant Terrible:* Cuyahoga Falls and Army, 1962–68**   27

THREE: **A Farewell to Arms: Army, 1968–71**   53

FOUR: **Sheriff Bob: Indiana, 1971–72**   71

FIVE: **Glory Days: Indiana, 1972–76**   87

SIX: **Our Man in San Juan: Indiana and Puerto Rico, 1976–79**   107

SEVEN: **The Book of Isiah: Indiana, 1979–82**   129

EIGHT: **The View from Olympus: Indiana and Los Angeles, 1981–84**   151

NINE: **Not Going Gently into That Good Knight: Indiana, 1984–87**   177

TEN: **The Honeymooners: Indiana, 1987–93**   207

ELEVEN: **Dinosaur: Indiana, 1993–99**   237

TWELVE: **Twilight of the Hoosiers: Indiana, 2000**   273

THIRTEEN: **The Lion in Lubbock: Texas Tech, 2001–**   309

Acknowledgments   333

BOB KNIGHT

My poetry, my rhymes, were written by a man who, having seen something of war, is more impressed with the manly virtues it engenders than the necessary and much exaggerated horrors attendant upon it. They are offered to the public in the hope that they may help to counteract the melancholy viewpoint of many of our poets who write of the great wars.

We should not dwell on sorrow that these slain in battle have died, but rather be thankful that they have lived . . .

As for the kind of remarks I make, why sometimes I just, by God, get carried away with my own eloquence.

—Gen. George S. Patton

INTRODUCTION

*I guess maybe people are attracted or whatever to a no-bullshit
guy who tells people to shove it up their ass when he thinks it's
appropriate.*

—Bob Knight
Esquire, March 1988

Appearances to the contrary, he doesn't tell everyone that. The surprising thing about Bob Knight, who isn't known for his warmth, is how warm he is and how funny; that despite being one of the most widely condemned figures on the American sports scene, he has so many friends who are as fiercely loyal to him as he is to them.

If no one really knows him outside his inner circle, the surprise is how large it is, including so many of his fellow coaches who bless his name for saying the things they dare not, and almost all the players who survive his four-year Hell Week.

It's another closely guarded secret how caring he is. His appearance with Ryan White, the Indiana schoolboy with AIDS who was shunned by his community, and his devotion to Landon Turner, his former player, who was paralyzed in an auto accident, are rare instances when Knight let the public see his better side. He can be as endearing as scary. It is impossible to dislike him if he likes you, which is one reason he got away with so much.

Of course, if you add up all his friends, his peers, and the former players who revere him, and add the entire state of Indiana plus all the Texas Tech fans, it's still a statistically insignificant percentage of the world's population, the rest of which sees an entirely different Bob Knight.

* * *

It was always up to Knight which side of the line you fell on. That was the point. Andy Andreas, the coach at Cuyahoga Falls High School who met Knight when he was 21 and gave him his first job coaching the jayvees, said, "Bobby could be very charming or he could be a horse's ass. But *he* made the decision, and he made it in a split second."

Everyone has seen the intimidating, glowering Bob Knight who rages up and down the sideline, fuming at referees, grabbing his players by the most convenient uniform or body part. He was 6-5 and weighed 210 pounds when he was young and trim, but no matter how big he got, he always seemed bigger. Radiating aggression, with the lightning flashing in those dark eyes, an angry Knight was a sight no one forgot.

"Bob has this look that I refer to as a look to kill," says former Indiana University athletic director Clarence Doninger. "I've been the recipient of it. I've watched him do it to others. And if you are the recipient of it, you're scared shitless."

The fear he inspired lay at the heart of Knight's legend. He raged openly, as when he was photographed grabbing Jim Wisman's jersey in 1976 with an expression so furious it looked like he was about to devour Wisman. It was no secret; it was more like theater, with the entire nation watching. Knight's story is as much about the society that forgave him for so long, until the wins-to-incidents ratio dropped low enough for him to be finally held to account.

For all the storms Knight called down on his own head, he had such a bang-up time being Bob Knight that he couldn't bear to give it up. In 1981, when Knight was 40, *Sports Illustrated*'s Frank Deford wrote a sympathetic profile called "The Rabbit Hunter," which Knight liked so much that he kept a copy in his desk. Deford echoed the hope, often voiced by Knight's friends, that he would learn to tell the important issues, or elephants in this metaphor, from the trivial ones, represented by the rabbits. So many people latched on to Deford's metaphor, it soon became a cliché, as did the assertion that Knight would reenact the fall of Woody Hayes, the Ohio State football coach whose career ended when he hit an opposing player. That comparison got such wide circulation that Hayes himself told Knight not to repeat his mistakes.

Given decades of warning, it should have been easy to avoid Hayes' fate, but when the time came to choose, Knight wanted to stay exactly who he was. He loved blasting away at the rabbits and watching them scamper away until all he could see was their furry tails.

He actually brought a shotgun to practice once, in 1993 after his team was upset by Butler. He often blew up just for fun. Assistant Coach Jimmy Crews told of a time when Knight walked into Assembly Hall before a practice with his staff, regaling them with one of his stories. As soon as he got into the arena, he broke off and began yelling at his players who were warming up, continuing all the way across the floor to the door leading to the basketball offices. As they went through the door, Knight turned back to his assistants and without missing a beat, picked up the story where he had left it.

Knight insisted he never lost control but he was moody in the best of times and beyond consolation in the worst, which was when a chair could be thrown, a throat could be grabbed, or, according to two of his players, he could use the word "nigger" in a tirade directed at Isiah Thomas.

In the end, the problem wasn't as much Knight's behavior as his refusal to be held accountable. Even as he apologized, on those few instances when higher authority made him, he would insist he had only gone too far in the service of a worthy cause, like correcting the Big Ten's officiating. No matter what he did, anything less than complete support from his friends or the IU administration amounted to betrayal.

Coaching brought out the best in him—his passion, his intelligence, his toughness—but it also brought out the worst. Given the extremes in his behavior and his insistence on being true to himself and himself only, he spent his storied career riding for a fall.

Knight always sensed what he risked; he just couldn't imagine that he wouldn't prevail. On the wall of his office in Assembly Hall, he kept a framed quote by Gen. George Patton: "You have to be single-minded, drive for only one thing on which you have decided. . . . And if it looks as if you might be getting there, all kinds of people, including some whom you thought were loyal friends, will suddenly show up doing their hypocritical God damndest to trip you, blacken you, and break your spirit."

"Pretty dark," Dave Kindred, one of Knight's best friends in the press, once told him.

"And true," replied Knight.

Under fire, Knight presented lavish defenses with orchestrated testimony from all around him—players, assistant coaches, IU officials, friends, admirers in the press. He inspired reverence, hatred, but most of all, fascination. Mark Montieth, who covered him for the *Indiana Daily Student* and went on to work for the *Indianapolis Star*, said whenever three writers from anywhere in the state got together, sooner or later the talk turned to Knight. When Knight coached the 1984 Olympic team, which was only together for five months with Knight on his best behavior, three writers comparing notes found they had all been dreaming about him.

Knight conceded nothing, mounting his indefatigable defenses as the number of controversies reached double figures and kept climbing, which was pushing coincidence. Everyone lives in his own reality, but Knight's was like an adjoining planet. Nevertheless, for 29 years an entire state of the union lived in his world. Knight being Knight, he was only surprised when he couldn't get the other 49 states to fall in line, too.

Knight kept alive a fading tradition of tyranny. In 1954, when Texas A&M football coach Bear Bryant took his boys to a brutal preseason camp in Junction, Texas, Knight was entering Orrville High School where Bill Shunkwiler, the football coach he revered, was apt to grab him by the face mask.

For years, Knight's players regarded his regimen as he did, as tough love. Indeed, 25 years after Bryant conducted his experiments in heat exhaustion, Isiah Thomas was still getting paddled at St. Joseph's, the nice Catholic high school in the suburbs he bussed to every day. "Jeff Hornacek's dad, Jack, was the dean of students," says Thomas. "Every day I was late, I had to drop my pants and he would give me the paddle."

No one fought Knight harder than Thomas, but Isiah not only forgave him, he became one of his foremost loyalists. When Knight let them—after they had completed the course and moved on—his players loved him back. A macho culture is all about fathers and sons. Knight had issues with his own father, and it produced the angriest, most demanding, but ultimately caring, surrogate dad his surrogate sons could imagine.

"Being around Knight is like going to your parents' house for Christmas," wrote Jack Isenhour, one of his first players at Army. "You revert to child-player status and I'd no sooner call him 'Bob' to his face than call my mother 'Louise.' He's 'Coach' and although I'm in my mid-50s now, I'm still scared of the son of a bitch."

Knight's players never stopped wanting to please him or dreading his displeasure. Many years later, Thomas was asked if he could tell how much Knight cared for him in the end.

"I don't even know if he likes me," says Thomas, laughing.

Competition warps behavior but Knight wasn't merely competitive. It was more like his life or his manhood was on the line every day, which left no time for niceties. To Knight, basketball was like Carl von Clausewitz's definition of war, a continuation of policy by other means.

Of course, it wasn't just basketball. Knight's intensity and sense of mission extended to anything he happened to be doing.

"We're fishing on Madison River and going along having a good day," says Kohn Smith, one of his assistants in the '80s and a frequent hunting and fishing partner. "It was kind of tough, not real good, but it's a real slick river in the middle of Montana. And all of a sudden all these trout start feeding in a frenzy on the top, you know, we'd been waiting for it all day.

"So, I'm fishing there above it. Madison is real rough and rocky and you can't hear because of the fast water, it's almost like in a rapid. And he's about 50 yards below me and all of a sudden I hear this blood-curdling yell. . . . I turn around and well, hell, he's way down the river, just screaming. And I look and all I can see is the top of his hat as it goes down in the river.

"Well, you know, you stumble out and you get up. And he lets into

a tirade of cuss words I'd never heard in my life. You know, for five minutes, just screaming and yelling, madder than heck. He has to peel off all
of his clothes, dump his waders out, hang his clothes up on a tree.

"And all this time I'm catching fish. Every time I catch another, he
starts into another tirade and starts into another tirade. Every time I'm
catching a fish, it just pisses him off because he's on the bank, having to
sit out, basically. I had to turn my back to him and kind of giggle to myself. Now, anybody else, you'd say, 'Hey you dumb shit, way to go.' And
you'd laugh at each other, you know. But man, if you'd turned and
laughed at that, holy hell, you might lose your life. . . .

"Say you're hunting birds in Montana. Now, everyone else doesn't
give a dang or doesn't care, but at the end of the day he can tell you how
many coveys of hens that we got up and how many shots that he
thought he had that were good shots, and how many he missed. . . . I
don't ever think he's totally relaxed because anything like that can set
him off. I mean, he can be out in the deer and squirrels and all of a sudden his reel breaks or his rod breaks and it'll send him off."

Knight attacked golf, his other passion, with the same fervor. Bob
Hammel, the sports editor of the Bloomington *Herald-Telephone*, was
with him and assistant coach Dave Bliss one day when Knight broke
every club in his bag but his four-wood and putter by the ninth hole.
When Knight then knocked his tee shot down the middle of the fairway,
Bliss said, "Well, I'll say one thing, your four-wood's fighting for its life."

Knight was a star among stars. He treasured relationships with John
Havlicek, Bill Parcells, Jack Nicklaus, Tony LaRussa, D. Wayne Lukas,
Sparky Anderson, Johnny Bench, Dick Schaap, and Howard Cosell, as
well as his oft-consulted college of cardinals, the coaching greats Pete
Newell, Hank Iba, Clair Bee, Red Auerbach and Joe Lapchick. Knight
met presidents Gerald Ford, Ronald Reagan, and George H. W. Bush and
shot birds alongside King Juan Carlos of Spain, but when he found himself in the Soviet Union on a fishing trip with his idol, Ted Williams, in
1991, it was as if God had summoned him to heaven to visit.

There he was, Bobby Knight from Orrville, Ohio, whose parents had taken him to Cleveland for ball games where he had gotten chills just watching the Splendid Splinter step into the batter's box, fishing alongside him like an equal. They were equals! For all his aura, Williams was a guy's guy just like Knight was, always skirmishing and testing the people around him. Knight would write in his autobiography that there were few other moments in his life when he was more aware of how far basketball had taken him.

Like Williams, who said his goal was to walk down the street and have people say, "There goes the best hitter who ever lived," Knight wanted to be the best coach who ever lived. In both cases it was true, or close to it.

Knight won three NCAA titles, 11 Big Ten titles and 854 games by the start of the 2005–06 season, putting him 25 behind Dean Smith's all-time record, and he did it with relatively modest talent. UCLA's John Wooden coached ten NBA All-Stars and Smith coached eleven at North Carolina; Knight coached one, Isiah Thomas. There were wiser coaches and there were certainly less self-destructive coaches but, pound for pound, there may have been none better.

"Sure, Indiana doesn't cheat," said former Texas coach Abe Lemons, "but you have to realize that guy could pick up five sons of bitches off the street and win."

Knight's virtues were ritually trotted out whenever he got in trouble, so his graduation rate and the fact that he didn't cheat became another cliché. Nevertheless, his program really was special. As Steve Alford, who suffered as much from Knight's wrath as anyone who stayed four years, wrote in his book, *Playing for Knight*:

> *An Indiana player should be sensitive. Coach frequently invited handicapped people or learning disabled children to our practices. Without Coach saying anything, we always made a point of going over and spending some time with our guests, making them feel welcome and appreciated. Coach wanted players who would do that instinctively, without being asked.*
>
> *An Indiana player has to be responsible. We always made that point in the strongest way to recruits: We can't cut class, we don't*

get favors from professors, nobody pays our parking tickets and no-
body will bail you out if you get arrested.

And finally an Indiana player has to be able to play for Coach
Knight.

Player after player Knight had screamed at and manhandled wound up coming back to Bloomington in the summer. Other coaches who were gentler envied the devotion Knight inspired. Outsiders couldn't see that, but that was who Knight was, too.

Robert Byrnes, an IU professor of Russian history, once told Kindred that Knight was "the greatest teacher I have ever seen." Byrnes just wished someone could persuade him, "You can be intense and demanding and you can do it without the vile, unspeakable language and without the rude and barbarous behavior.

"I just hope it can be done before somebody or something drives Bobby out of the job," Byrnes said. ". . . I come away from his practices— I'm almost embarrassed to use the word—I come away inspired."

Across the state line, people sneered at the bumpkins for selling out to this tyrant, but Indiana wasn't the only place where winners who embodied questionable values were romanticized. It happened from New York, which sat at the feet of the bully George Steinbrenner, to California, where Al Davis carpetbagged his way up and down the state. This wasn't just Indiana. This story could have happened anywhere.

ONE

BOBBY

Bobby has got so much. . . . He doesn't cheat. He doesn't drink. He doesn't even chase women. But for some reason, he thinks he has been a bad boy and no matter how successful he becomes, he thinks he must be punished.

—IU assistant Roy Bates
to SI's Frank Deford

I can remember my mom saying time and frigging time again, "Just remember, somebody has to lose." And my rejoinder has always been, "Why should it be me?"

—Bob Knight
Playboy, March 2001

From the beginning, he was different.

Robert Montgomery Knight, the only child of the local freight agent on the railroad line and the second-grade teacher at Walnut Street Elementary, was the best athlete in Orrville, Ohio, but every hamlet has its local stars who grow up to teach phys ed or sell real estate. Bobby was the one who would attain the greatness they had all dreamed about. Almost from the day he was born and the cry that became his first complaint, he went his own way.

His father, Pat, grew up on an Oklahoma farm and went to work on the Nickel Plate Railroad, which brought him to this little town of 5,000 in the northeast corner of the state. To Bobby, born when Pat was in his 40s, his father was a Gary Cooper figure, upright, low-key, princi-

9

pled, and determined, "the most honest man I have known," and "the most disciplined man I ever met."

The son took pride in his father's flinty virtues, and he told everyone the same stories, which became the standard starting point in published profiles of his life. Pat never earned more than $8,000, never had a credit card, owned three cars his whole life, and paid cash for them. He took out his only loan to buy their $22,000 house and paid it off in four years by giving up his hobbies. Knight said his dad never tipped, "because he always said, 'Nobody ever gave me a tip for doing anything.'"

However, there was a distance between father and son that was difficult to bridge. Pat was so hard of hearing, Bobby had to yell to be understood, and it was easier just to co-exist. Pat worked long hours and didn't go to Bobby's games. They shared a passion for fishing, but that was something a father and a son could do together in silence.

Pat was already 43 and Hazel 38 on October 25, 1940 when Bobby was born. Pauline Boop, their next-door neighbor, says both parents acted even older than their years. The one who seemed the youngest, Boop says, was Hazel's mother, Sarah Henthorne, who lived with them.

"There was always this terrible barrier between [Bob] and his dad because his dad's hearing was so bad that he was almost deaf," says Boop. "His mother did not drive a car and his father was mostly working. But his grandmother drove and she always took him places. And she was just the sweetest woman. She was a perfect gem."

John Flynn of the *Louisville Courier-Journal*, one of Knight's first press confidants, wrote that Knight used to call Mrs. Henthorne "mother." She doted on him, letting him win when they played board games because she couldn't bear to see how upset he got when he lost. Hazel Knight herself once noted, "I think he was closer to his grandmother than he ever was to me or his father."

Nevertheless, Bobby said his mother, whip-smart and inclined to speak her mind, was his biggest influence. Bruce Newman, who interviewed Hazel years later when he wrote for the *Indiana Daily Student*, remembers her as "sort of typically Midwestern, old school, a bit schoolmarmish and forbidding in ways. She was gracious enough to let a college kid come into her house and talk to her for an hour, so she wasn't mean or anything. But I don't remember her as being a particularly warm person."

"He gets that dry sense of humor from his mother," says Kathy Harmon, who was Kathy Halder when she dated Bob in high school. "His mother was—you just had to know her, you know. She just had that real dry, talked kind of slow, sense of humor. And she was fun, but I don't know—I mean, they built a new house when they were in high school. It was a two-bedroom house—one for his grandmother, one for his mother and father, and he had a room off the kitchen. And later, it was turned into a laundry room. But, I mean, you would have thought that with having a son, they'd build a three-bedroom house, but they didn't. . . . Like, it was at the end of the kitchen and there was a wooden folding door that folded across there, and his bed was actually a daybed.

"His father and mother, that I can remember, never, ever saw Bobby play a game of basketball. . . . I took his grandmother to a couple of games and she saw a couple of games but that was it. It was just—it was a different family. I mean, he loved his mother and his father, but I think his grandmother pretty much raised him."

Says Norman Douglas, then Knight's best friend: "His father probably did work 10 to 12 hours a day because any time we went to his house, his dad wasn't there. When he was there, I do remember his father was hard of hearing. In fact, that added to the humor on occasion. There were some things that happened that he was oblivious to and that would crack us up because he's just sitting there, staring off into space, not knowing anything happened. But I think Bob felt very close to his dad. And his father was very strong-willed, there's no doubt about that. I think Bob picked that up from him, where right is right and wrong is wrong, and gray isn't in this household."

As soon as Bobby could get the ball up to the hoop, he began shooting baskets with Pauline Boop's husband, Don, a dentist everyone called Doc. The Knights and Boops lived in such close proximity, Pauline says she used to cook bread in her kitchen just 20 feet from the room where Bobby slept. Before Doc Boop's death, he told John Flynn that Bobby's "grandmother and I came close to raising him," noting, "I guess I shouldn't say this, but I believe that them always letting him win had some effect on him. He was an average boy, very intelligent, mind you, but I didn't notice anything until he got into high school. Then his temper started showing up. It grew in college and I don't think it has abated yet."

Flynn often repeated the story about Mrs. Henthorne letting Bobby win to keep him from getting upset. To Flynn, like Doc Boop, it explained a lot.

The way Knight remembers it, his childhood was idyllic and Orrville a great place to grow up, filled with Norman Rockwell characters. Nevertheless, he wasn't an ordinary child. He liked to hang out with the grownups, who, in turn, liked to hang out with him.

"Bob had a lot of adult friends," says Norman Douglas. "Most of us didn't have that. We all knew each other's parents and their friends, but our friends were each other. Bob had this set of adult friends that he spent a lot of time with."

Almost all of them were his coaches, who had time for him and shared his love of sports. In *Knight: My Story*, he ticks off their names gratefully, thanking them in detail for everything they did, starting with Frank Mizer, who ran the local beauty parlor and started a baseball team Bobby played on when he was nine.

He was ambitious and industrious, even if he was the one who decided where his ambitions lay and what he would work at. He got good grades effortlessly and read voraciously. When the library would compile a list of its top readers, he wrote, it would always be nine girls and him. He devoured the Chip Hilton books, written by the famous basketball coach Clair Bee, the John R. Tunis baseball books, and the Hardy Boys mysteries.

Starry-eyed Bobby hung on every word of Jimmy Dudley's Cleveland Indians radio broadcasts and George Walsh doing Kentucky Wildcat basketball. Small-town kids once listened to the sound of trains at night; Bobby listened to the crackling voices doing play-by-play on radio and dreamed of brightly lit stadiums. As he wrote in his book, "My lifelong status as a hero worshipper started in those days."

As an eighth grader, he was a 6-1 forward who averaged 29 points with a line-drive shot he wasn't bashful about taking. At Orrville High, the varsity basketball coach, Jack Graham, jumped him to the varsity as a freshman.

"He got broken in pretty good by the upperclassmen," says teammate Warner Harper, a senior who stuck up for the 15-year-old Knight. "They gave him a very rough time. They kind of ganged up on him at practice. They would do little things like throw an elbow and he would get mad. A couple times it almost broke into a fight. Then he got past that. I talked to him one day and told him he had to dish something back out. And Knight started to do that. Then everything was all right."

Bobby handled the hazing without complaint. In his autobiography, he says only that starting as a freshman is "never easy." Kathy Harmon says she could tell it bothered him but he wouldn't talk about it. "He was one of those people that kept everything pretty much inside of him," says Harmon. "I would confide in him but he didn't confide in me. I don't think he confided in his parents either. Maybe his older cronies, the guys he hung out with, but I don't think so. I think he kept his problems to himself."

At Orrville, Bobby was an end on the football team and such a good hitter on the baseball team, he could even stand up to Dean Chance, the young fireballer from nearby Wayne County High who would pitch eleven seasons in the major leagues. Bobby lived for basketball, though, and everything else in his life, like girls, ran second or farther back.

"It was a weird kind of relationship until we were sophomores and juniors in high school because basketball was everything," says Kathy Harmon. "You never saw him anywhere that he didn't have a basketball in his hand. And it wasn't like every Saturday night you saw him. Because if there was a basketball game somewhere, he went. He was consumed by it."

Knight was as brash as he was intense. Kathy Harmon says he didn't lash out at other people but was hard on himself. "Like if he had a bad game," she says, "he was really—well, you just didn't—I knew better than to even approach him after the game. . . . He was, you know, he just didn't like himself."

In Knight's sophomore yearbook, Harmon wrote a note to the "English brain," telling him to "watch the temper." Even in a good mood, Knight was such a cutup in class, Pauline Boop says they almost kept him out of the National Honor Society, although he wound up as the president of the group. In his senior yearbook, he appears in a photo with the other members of the honor society, glowering into the camera.

"There were teachers who thought he was arrogant," says schoolmate Bob Shonk. "I don't think he did it maliciously, but he tried to make a joke of things in class and they sometimes didn't appreciate it. He got into trouble more than once. The teachers would throw him out of class or ask him to go down to the principal's office."

Fortunately, Graham, the basketball coach, was patient with Bobby, who required a lot of patience. "Knight would speak up to Graham in front of us, they would get into it and Graham would throw him out of the gym," says Warner Harper. "But the relationship between Knight and Graham was strong."

In Knight's sophomore year, he was the star of the team, averaging 19 points as the Red Riders went 8–11. He averaged 25 the next year, but missed four weeks with a broken foot; the team wound up 5–13. Yearning to get back, he tried to go out and shoot with his foot in a cast and broke several of them.

That year, 16-year-old Bobby wrote an autobiography for a school project. He called it, "It's Been a Great Life (So Far)." He said he wanted "to go to college, to join the ROTC and to do my service hitch after I graduate. When that is over, I hope to become a basketball coach."

In Knight's senior year, he and his teammates were on a bus to a football scrimmage, batting around a blown-up condom when someone knocked it up to the front where the coach, Bill Shunkwiler, sat. Tabbing Knight for it, Shunkwiler stomped on the flying rubber and proceeded to keep Bobby on the field in the sweltering heat for every play of the entire scrimmage, on offense and defense.

"He was on the field the whole doggone day," says Shunkwiler. "And no one said a word about it. Didn't say anything about that bouncing prophylactic. But the team knew that I knew who blew it up and bounced it. And I just let it go. That's how we disciplined. He played every play that we had in the scrimmage. Then we scrimmaged again the next day and I made him do the same thing.

"The longer you'd go out without water, the tougher we thought you were. Something else we did, which we would probably all go to jail for now, was to grab you by the collar of your shoulder pad and drag you down to the ground. Sometimes you'd grab a mask. You'd shake the mask but never physically beat up a kid. We did have hands-on explanations."

Knight didn't complain and, years later, he would never understand why anyone else would. To Bobby, tough love was love nonetheless.

Shunkwiler was a particular favorite. The leathery older man always had time for Bobby, who would go over to his house and pepper him with questions about coaching. Sometimes Shunkwiler took him scouting with him.

Unfortunately for Knight, Jack Graham, the basketball coach he liked so much, left before his senior year. Graham was replaced by Bob Gobin, who had no experience in varsity sports and just wanted all the boys to participate. When Knight scored 40 points in a scrimmage against Wadsworth, he said Gobin told them, "We won't have that happen again."

Knight was devastated. "I had worked hard to get ready for that senior year," he wrote. "No kid ever worked harder at basketball." Knight wasn't intimidated, though. He argued with Gobin until he was kicked off the team and the townspeople had to come running to Bobby's aid.

"The school board got into it," says Roy Bates, the basketball coach at nearby Wayne County High School, who would one day join Knight's Indiana staff. "Of course, Bob had a lot of friends around town who didn't like it, either. So, they had quite a row in the community. He was only 17, 18 years old, and then the adults took it up and he's in the middle of it."

Fearing Bobby would lose any chance of getting a basketball scholarship to college, his father took him next door to talk it over with Doc Boop. Boop and Bobby then went to see Gobin. They made a deal: Bobby would be suspended for one game and Gobin would try harder to win.

That was the first in a lifetime of controversies. As Knight notes in his book, "Being right and being quiet has never been a combination I was good at."

Bobby averaged 20.6 points as the Red Riders went 11–9 and made the state playoffs. He graduated from Orrville that spring and went out into the great, wide world that didn't know what it was in for.

Knight had several scholarship offers, all but one from midsized schools like Bowling Green or Miami of Ohio. Jack Graham urged him to choose one of those, where he thought Knight would be sure to play a lot. Doc Boop drove Bobby around the state, checking them out.

Ohio State, which represented the major leagues, hadn't scouted Bobby, but Boop was a graduate of the OSU dental school and knew some people in the athletic department. He sent game films of Knight to Columbus, which were forwarded to the freshman coach, Fred Taylor. Taylor was intrigued and invited Knight to visit.

It was the spring of 1958 and the Buckeyes were on the verge of something big. On an outing at Merrybrook Stables outside Columbus, Knight met his fellow recruits: Jerry Lucas, John Havlicek, and Mel Nowell, who would form one of the greatest freshman classes in the era before freshmen were eligible.

People had been talking about Lucas since he was in grade school. His fame had mushroomed when he led tiny Middletown High to 76 straight wins and state titles in his sophomore and junior seasons. Like everyone in Ohio, Knight grew up with Lucas's legend. Knight went to Cleveland Arena to watch the Single A finals in 1956 but couldn't get a ticket for the Double A finals, in which the sophomore Lucas led Middletown to victory. In 1958, when Middletown's run ended in the state finals at Ohio State's St. John Arena, Knight was there, watching on a recruiting visit.

At that spring outing at Merrybrook Stables, Knight played with Lucas, Havlicek, Nowell, and two more big-name Ohio high school players, Bud Olsen and Gary Gearhart. Since Olsen and Nowell would eventually play in the NBA, this group included four future pros, two of whom would be Hall of Famers.

Knight was thrilled to be on the same court. He knew he wasn't on the same level as Lucas but no one else was, either. The 6-2 Nowell, a hotshot from Columbus, was a superior athlete, and the 6-5 Havlicek was a gazelle, but Knight thought he was good enough to find his own niche. It just wouldn't be the one he wanted.

It was as if his entire college career was set up to break his heart.

Knight started on the celebrated freshman team, which played only two games all season, against the varsity, which was now coached by Fred Taylor. Both of the games were closed to the public. Living up to their hype, the Buckeye freshmen won both, with Lucas getting over 40 in each.

Lucas played center with Nowell and Gearhart at guard and Havlicek and Knight at forward. Knight could make his line-drive shot if he was open, but he had trouble defending and rebounding. As Havlicek, one of his closest friends on the team, put it, "He just wasn't an individual who could jump over the rim and snatch rebounds or put the stops to a guy."

Nevertheless, Knight's Dennis-the-Menace personality was no less commanding than it had been in Orrville. He was no longer the star but he was still the life of the party. Teammates called him "Dragon," after he bragged about riding with a biker gang with that name. Knight said some of them were such bumpkins, they believed it for a while. Kaye Kessler, who covered the team for the *Columbus Dispatch*, says no one believed it for a second. "There weren't any street gangs in Orrville," Kessler says. "In fact, they were grape crushers. Orrville is the home of Smucker's Jelly."

The Ohio State freshmen were called "The Fabulous Five" and there was talk among Buckeye fans that they would all start as sophomores. However, the returning players the next season included junior guard Larry Siegfried, who had averaged 19 points as a sophomore and would go on to average double figures over seven seasons with the Celtics. Another holdover, junior forward Joe Roberts, would play three NBA seasons.

Lucas, Havlicek and Nowell became three-year starters. Siegfried and Roberts got the other two starting jobs in 1959–60, with Knight buried on the bench. With so much talent, everyone had to make sacrifices and it was hard all around.

"I was bitching and moaning," says Siegfried, relegated to playmaker as a junior after leading the team in scoring as a sophomore. "Hell, I quit 450 times. We were all struggling with our roles because there was so much talent on that team."

Says Kessler, "Nowell was always pissed off because Lucas was getting all the headlines and Siegfried was always griping and they'd come to our rooms when we were on the road and gripe because they weren't getting enough publicity. Remember, all of these guys had been huge scorers in high school."

Knight had been a huge scorer himself, but now he was a long way from Orrville.

"Bobby had this impression that he was going to be with us," says Nowell, the Buckeye most offended by Knight. "But, when we became varsity, Bobby didn't get a spot in the starting lineup. And not only did he not get a spot, there were several other people that would get in before him. There was the starting five and there were the next few players who would get right in at practice and work with the starting five. And then there was a term that was used—'all you others'—as in, 'All you others go down to the other end of the floor.' I think Bobby was in all you others a few too many times, and that certainly made his life feel pretty uncomfortable."

In Knight's autobiography, he notes diplomatically that he was "kind of a pain in the ass . . . not outwardly but inwardly." Actually, he did nothing but complain. Taylor was once quoted as calling him "the brat from Orrville," although he denied it, but there was no more doubt that Knight was a brat than that he was from Orrville. Taylor's assistant, Jack Truitt, says Knight vowed to transfer 84 times, once after every game in his career.

"Bobby used to pout all the time because Fred didn't play him much," says Kessler. "He used to sit at the end of the bench and piss and moan. And Fred would often make Bobby sit right beside him. He said, 'If you're going to pout, you're going to do it beside me.'"

Big Ten teams were run-and-gun outfits, emulating the famous Hurryin' Hoosiers of Branch McCracken, but Taylor, who was making his debut at the varsity level, wanted to emphasize defense. He had spent time over the summer with California's defense-minded Pete Newell, the coach of the defending national champions, who had generously shared his thoughts and schemes.

Defending was a problem for Knight, who was passionate but slow. His sophomore year, he often lined up against Roberts, who was bigger at 6-6 and so athletic, he jumped right over him for rebounds. Knight set about whittling him down to size.

"He had the temper, yes," says Roberts. "If you fouled him or if he fouled you, he was ready to go to war. He was just a feisty guy. But one day he fouled me so bad I went to him and told him, 'You better guard Havlicek today because I'm not taking that.'"

Years later, when Taylor was retired and doing TV commentary at an IU game, someone asked him what kind of defensive player Knight had been. Taylor walked out 15 feet from the basket along the baseline, pointed to the floor and said, "Right here was where he would foul guys. He'd either shove them out of bounds or foul them but they weren't getting by."

A new era dawned in Ohio State basketball, which had lived a quiet existence until the fall of 1959. Before the Fabulous Five, the athletic program and the state revolved around Hayes' football teams, which was the way Woody intended to keep it. As far as the basketball coaches were concerned, AD Ed Weaver existed to rubber stamp Hayes' demands, while they had to justify every penny they spent.

"When it came to money, Woody could do whatever he wanted to and Fred had to meet a tight budget," says Taylor's assistant, Jack Graff. "Fred was jealous of Woody because he had so much control."

"Fred had an intense dislike of Woody Hayes," says Howard Nourse, another OSU player. "I don't know whether it was born out of jealousy but he moved the basketball offices from being besides the football offices to the extreme opposite side of St. John Arena on the administrative floor. He moved them as far away from the football offices as possible. He made no bones about it."

The basketball team hadn't won a conference title since 1950, but its time was coming. Led by the great sophomores, Lucas, Havlicek and Nowell, the Buckeyes went 21–3, won the Big Ten, then stormed into the NCAA Finals, routing Western Kentucky, Georgia Tech, and NYU in the tournament by an average of 19 points.

Nevertheless, they were underdogs in the Finals against Pete Newell's defending champion Cal Bears, the nation's top-ranked team. The game was at the Cow Palace in San Francisco, where Cal often played and rarely lost, having won 45 of its last 46 games there.

Undaunted, the Buckeyes shredded Newell's defense, making 16 of their first 19 shots and romping to a 75–55 victory. All five starters—Lucas, Havlicek, Nowell, Siegfried, and Roberts—were in double figures.

Knight, who scored six points in the first tournament game, didn't score another the rest of the way. For his sophomore year, he averaged just 3.7. Still, he had been part of a championship team and he had two more years to make his mark, or so he thought.

Knight was 19 that spring, and his life was changing. Two months after the NCAA Tournament, he came home to Orrville for the weekend, went out, and returned to find his grandmother sitting in her favorite chair with her hat and coat still on. She was 82 and just back from shopping. He thought she was just napping, until he realized she wasn't asleep.

"He came tearing over to my house," says Pauline Boop. "I don't know if he said, 'Grandma is dead,' or 'Something is wrong with Grandma.' But, as big as I was, and I was real pregnant, I went over to his home and we took her out of the chair and laid Mrs. Henthorne on the floor and tried to call the emergency squad. And she had died.

"Several days after the funeral, I still hadn't delivered, and he asked me if I would go to the cemetery with him, which was in Akron. And I did. He never mentioned Mrs. Henthorne's name again."

Everyone knew how close they had been. Townspeople said Mrs. Henthorne had been feeling poorly for a while but hung on until the basketball season ended and Bobby could come home.

Knight had broken up with Kathy Harmon in their senior year in high school when she tired of his preoccupation with basketball. After his first year at Ohio State, he began dating another local girl, Nancy Falk, who had been a year behind at Orrville High, where Harmon remembers her as "very popular and really cute."

Nancy later told John Feinstein that Knight walked up to her at the swimming pool where she was lifeguarding and announced, "Well, now that you're grown up, would you like to go out?" She said yes. The rest of Knight's time at Ohio State, Nancy would drive the 50 miles to Columbus to see him and, a year after he graduated, they would marry.

Before Knight's junior year, two of the players who had been ahead of him, Joe Roberts and Dick Furry, had graduated, giving Bobby hope he would start at forward. Instead, the job went to senior Richie Hoyt.

"Bobby hated not playing," Fred Taylor said. "Which is exactly what you want. You want kids who want to compete and that's just what Bobby was. But he was very blunt about thinking he should play more, and there were times when that was difficult for me and for him."

"I don't know how many calls I got [from Knight]," Doc Boop told John Flynn. "One day Fred even called and said, 'If you don't come get this kid, I'm going to kill him.' Fred always had a problem getting Bobby to play the defense he wanted."

Nor was Knight's strong-willed mother, Hazel, going to hold still for this. "I saw a couple letters that she sent Fred Taylor," says assistant Jack Graff. "She said that your best basketball player, you're sitting him on the bench. And that wasn't true at all. We'd kind of laugh about it. We agreed what we were doing was right. And it's tough to criticize when you're winning that way."

Coming off their NCAA title, the Buckeyes seemed to be on the verge of a dynasty, going 24–0 in the regular season and rolling through their first three games in the NCAA Tournament. After they beat Kentucky by 13 in the regional finals, Adolph Rupp called them "truly great." In Kansas City for the Final Four, they beat Jack Ramsay's St. Joseph's team by 26 to advance to the finals against Cincinnati.

No one gave the Bearcats a chance. They were a surprise entry, in their first season without the great Oscar Robertson. Their new coach, Ed Jucker, had slowed them down since he didn't think they were good enough to run as they had with Robertson. One of the Kansas City papers joked that the Bearcats checked out of their rooms and left Kansas City after winning the semifinals. Even Jucker worried they "might be the victim of another blowout."

Jucker was just hoping to keep it close long enough to give his players a chance to get over the notion the Buckeyes were invincible. To everyone's surprise, the Bearcats and their tough defense kept it close all the way.

With 1:41 left, Cincinnati led, 61–59. Ohio State fans were curling into the fetal position when a little-noted junior named Bobby Knight came off the bench to make the biggest hoop of his life, tying it, 61–61.

"Knight got the ball in the left front court and faked a drive into the middle," says Jack Truitt, "then crossed over like he worked on it all his life and drove right in and laid it up. That tied the game for us. And Knight ran clear across the floor like a 100-yard dash sprinter and ran right at me and he said, 'See there, coach, I should have been in that game a long time ago!'

"I said, 'Sit down, you hot dog. You're lucky you're even on the floor.'"

No one scored again in regulation, but the Bearcats went on to shock the Buckeyes, winning 70–65 in overtime. Siegfried threw a towel over his head and cried through the trophy presentation. Havlicek and Knight wandered the streets of Kansas City afterward, disconsolate.

Knight had averaged only 4.4 points as a junior, virtually what he had as a sophomore, but off the floor he was the straw that stirred the drink. From the time he joined the varsity, Kessler, the beat writer, considered him "the biggest character on the whole ball club."

"Lucas was Mr. Perfect and Havlicek was Mr. Awed," says Kessler.

"John was awestruck about everything. Gearhart was quiet and Nowell and Roberts were the only blacks on the ball club and hung out together. Knight was just a prankster all the time. He was kind of fun-loving, but then there were periods of sullenness."

On a trip to New York, Kessler went with the team to a dinner at Mama Leone's. "Mama Leone's had this wine cellar where you could eat and all the wine and champagne was lined up right behind you," he says. "Well, Knight just heists one of those bottles of champagne. He always did those kinds of things. This was Knight. He was a gangster and he had that snide little smile, which he still has today."

Knight wasn't any more serious as a student, but he was so intelligent he cruised through four years without effort, graduating with a degree in history and government with a 2.95 average, just under a B. "He'd borrow somebody's notes the night before a test and he would come out with an A and they would come out with a B or C," says Gary Gearhart.

Says Joe Roberts: "Bobby was almost a genius and he did not attend class with regularity. He ended up with A's and B's because he was really smart and because he absorbed a lot."

Knight fascinated his teammates and friends, as he always would. With Knight, no one ever knew what was coming. "Bobby was quite a split personality," said Havlicek. "There were times when we were good friends and then, like that, times when he wouldn't even talk to me."

"He could be very smooth and articulate when he wanted to be," says Nowell, "and he could be a person that you'd wonder, whoa, where is this coming from? Is this the same person?"

Knight entered his senior season in the fall of 1961 as a starting forward but lasted only two games before being recalled to the bench. This time, a junior named Doug McDonald became the starter.

"Senior year was very difficult for him," says Nowell, "because the truth is that a guy took his spot who Bobby probably expected to play in front of. But this guy was much better to play with because he moved the ball well, he was unselfish, he played defense and he was happy to be there. His name was Doug McDonald. He was only a junior."

If Knight hadn't known it before, he knew it now. This was how his entire college career would be: excruciating.

"It was terrible for him, really," Nancy Knight told John Flynn. "He wanted to play more than anyone can imagine. I would drive down from Orrville with his mom and dad to see the game and he would spend most of the time on the bench. Afterwards, he would tell me how much he hated it all. Then he'd cool off and spend the next three hours just talking about it."

Not that Knight's senior season was uneventful. In an early game at highly ranked Wake Forest, the Demon Deacon mascot, trying to pump the crowd up, cut into the Buckeyes' layup line. Knight punched him in the head. "That kind of set the tone for the game," said Havlicek. Ohio State won, 81–62.

The Buckeyes started 22–0 and clinched the Big Ten before losing a meaningless last game to Wisconsin. They were ranked No. 1 all season over Cincinnati, the defending champion, which lost twice. If anyone wondered who counted in Ohio, Governor Mike DiSalle announced at a banquet in Columbus that the Buckeyes deserved the top ranking.

As expected, Ohio State blew through the NCAA Tournament again, beating Western Kentucky by 16, Kentucky by 10, and Clemson by 16 on its way to a rematch against Cincinnati.

For the second year in a row, Cincinnati was the underdog. Few believed the Bearcats' 1961 victory had been anything but a fluke, rankling their players, who had to look up at Ohio State in the rankings all season.

This time, it wasn't even close. Cincinnati led by 18 points in the second half and cruised to a 71–59 win. Lucas, who had twisted his left knee against Clemson the night before, played with his leg taped like a mummy's, missed 12 of his 17 shots and scored 11 points in his last college game. Knight spent his last college game on the bench, despite a second half that was almost all garbage time.

The Fabulous Five had gone 78–6, with one NCAA title, three appearances in the Finals, and three Big Ten titles. They were 40–2 in the Big Ten but would be remembered as much for the promise they failed to realize. Knight started two games in his career, wouldn't be remembered for much of anything, and couldn't even manage a graceful exit.

It was a memorable basketball banquet that spring with the heralded class of '62 saying its good-byes. Lucas, who had had to bear the weight of all the expectations and disappointments, said it had been "the greatest four years of my life," and expressed his gratitude to Taylor. Knight, who had had to bear only his personal frustrations, gave a pointedly rueful speech.

"Bobby was very upset," Truitt says. "All the seniors speak at those things, you know? When he spoke, he wasn't thanking everybody and saying he had a great time and that kind of stuff. He kind of said he didn't have anything to be thankful for."

The Knights weren't done. After the banquet broke up, Knight and his mother, Hazel, confronted Taylor and the assistants.

"She was saying we had ruined her son," says Truitt. "That's exactly what she said. I guess she felt we'd ruined his confidence or whatever. We just stood there and listened. . . . I would normally let them say their piece and forget about it, but that one stuck with me."

If Knight left Ohio State angry at Taylor, he had learned a lot from him. Knight would one day say that it was Taylor, not Knight, who taught the Big Ten about defense.

Knight's own struggles on defense had only made him study it harder. No one knew fundamentals and techniques as well as he did, even if it wasn't enough in the face of superior athleticism. Truitt remembers walking by his room one evening when he was a freshman and watching him working on blocking out a bed post.

"We had just worked that day on blocking out on the weak side," says Truitt. "Knight was working on his footwork, putting his inside foot forward and then making a reverse pivot."

It would become accepted wisdom that Knight's college career drove him to the heights he reached. He once told *Sports Illustrated*'s Frank Deford, "You know why Havlicek became such a great pro? Just because he wanted to beat Lucas, that's why." As Deford noted, Knight was really talking about how badly he wanted to beat them both. Nevertheless, it's hard to imagine Knight averaging 15 points a game at Ohio State and turning out one bit different. It was just who he was.

"I think he came out of there saying, 'Goddammit, I'm going to prove I know this game,'" says Kaye Kessler. "He was sitting there on the bench pouting, frustrated that he wasn't playing but I think he was smart enough that he became a great student of a game. And I think he watched everything Fred Taylor did, starting with the clipboard Fred always carried."

Like Taylor, Knight would prepare meticulously, organizing practices to the minute. He adopted Taylor's philosophy of giving players roles according to their abilities, so shooters shot and rebounders rebounded—not that Knight would resemble Taylor much otherwise.

"Fred was somewhat distant when it came to communicating with players," says Gary Gearhart. "He was never good at talking to us one-on-one. I think that was one of the things Bobby picked up from him, to be more direct and communicative with players."

Did he ever.

TWO

ENFANT TERRIBLE

CUYAHOGA FALLS AND ARMY, 1962–68

*With the temperament he had, he was in the perfect envi-
ronment to start his career. Back then it was all guys.
There were no women. It was a macho place.*

*So, you know, when he yelled at us, it was just some-
body else yelling at us. "OK, who's chewing my ass this
time?"*

— Paul Franke, Army, Class of '70

*There was a time when calling him Jekyll and Hyde was
a compliment.*

— Nancy Knight

Every young coach has to start somewhere, no matter how far down
the line. In Knight's case, it was all the way down to the Cuyahoga
Falls High School junior varsity in Cuyahoga Falls, Ohio.

It would have been just a lark for him, if he had larks. He had a degree in history and government and was planning to go to law school, as
his father wanted him to do. To Pat, sports always seemed like children's
games. To his son, however, the law was sensible but not appealing. Five
of Bob's former teammates were off playing pro basketball and he wasn't
even sure what he was going to do when he grew up.

So he put off his legal career to try something close to his heart. As
he had said he would in "It's Been a Great Life (So Far)," he became a
basketball coach. So there he was, on the sideline, like so many of the
men he had admired, clipboard in hand like Fred Taylor. Of course, Taylor didn't break all of his.

27

*   *   *

No one ever took a jayvee job as seriously as Knight did, but that would be a key to his success. No one ever took anything as seriously as he did. If it wasn't the Big Ten or even the varsity, it was all the same to Knight, brimming over with emotion that needed an outlet. He had turned down a varsity coaching job at little Celina High in western Ohio because they wanted him to double as the line coach in football. Single-minded from the beginning, or even before he began, Knight told the Celina folks he wanted to be somewhere he could spend the whole year working on basketball.

Cuyahoga Falls, in the northeast corner of the state, had a lot going for it. With 2,500 students, it was one of the biggest schools in the state. Knight would also be the varsity assistant to Andy Andreas, one of the most respected coaches in the state. If Pat Knight thought his son was wasting his college education, Andreas was one more of those supportive father figures Bob collected.

"I would say that Andreas saw himself as Knight's mentor," says Gary Eiber, Knight's JV center and co-captain. "But he also seemed to look at Knight as almost a son. Andreas had a daughter, he didn't have a son. He and Knight had a strong relationship."

The players were thrilled to have him. Even a reserve from the great Buckeye teams was like a rock star who had been dropped into their midst.

"Living in Ohio, Ohio State was the university," says guard Tim Dudich, the other co-captain. "And at that particular time they had been to the Final Four for three straight years. Jerry Lucas was a legend. There was Siegfried, Havlicek, and Nowell. And there was Bobby Knight. We were truly excited to be getting someone with such a huge background at the college level."

They weren't as excited when they saw what he had in store for them. Knight's first practice at any school would always be memorable, starting with the very first one with the Cuyahoga Falls JV.

Knight turned 22 on October 22, 1962, the week he began preseason workouts, running his 15- and 16-year-olds as if they were the cross-country team. When practice started, they found there were worse problems than being out of breath as he outlined his football-style "suicide drill." With one of them on either side of the foul line, Knight rolled a basketball between them and they had to dive for it. The player who got it went to the back of the line, but the loser had to do it against the next player.

Knight said the trick was to dive at the other player, knock him backwards, then get the ball. Players learned another technique: Let their teammate get it first, jump on top of him and try to knock it loose. Otherwise, their teammates would be jumping on top of them.

Another drill obliged them to step in front of a teammate who was barreling at them to draw a charge, a tactic Knight helped popularize, although it wasn't popular with his young players at first. JV coaches were usually older men who approached coaching like teaching a phys-ed class, or young guys starting out who weren't sure of themselves. But, when it came to basketball, Knight always knew what he wanted and it usually had something to do with one player colliding with another.

He was a good teacher but an impatient, volatile one, and it didn't matter if his players were hardened Army cadets, gung-ho Hoosiers, or these tender shoots at Cuyahoga Falls. One day Knight's best player, forward Larry Vucovich, threw a bounce pass to a teammate who laid it in and, the next thing he knew, Knight was going ballistic.

"Knight starts going crazy," Vucovich says. "I'm out of the gym, I'm off the team, I'm kicked out of there. So, I go to the locker room and I still have no idea what I did, nor does anyone else, of course. So, then he just killed them at practice. And then I went into the coach's office later, this little office Knight shares with the other coaches.

"I say, 'Geez, Coach, I'm sorry.'

"He says, 'Okay, Vucovich, you can be back on the team. But don't you ever throw a bounce pass again!'"

Vucovich went home that night "still a basket case," but he figured out what Knight was doing, making a point by targeting one of his best players. The uniforms and the stakes would change but not the method. As smart and as dedicated as Knight was, it was the ferocity he brought to practice that put him in a league of his own. No opponent or game situation scared his players as much as he did.

"You know, it's interesting," says Vucovich. "Knight was intimidating, but in a game I never felt the least bit intimidated. In practice I sure was, but never in a game."

And heaven help them if it all didn't work the way he thought it should. Knight lost his coaching debut on a last-second shot, and the next day he put his players through a workout that was so long, parents called the school to complain.

"We stayed very late at night," says Eiber. "I can't recollect the exact time but it was several hours. Knight was not a happy camper. You can imagine—the first game he ever coaches and he loses."

They lost just two of their remaining fifteen for the season, the likes of which no jayvee team had ever seen.

"He never did anything violent, but the temper was there," says Dudich. "I think the first three or four games, he broke clipboards in half over his leg. Then I guess the fourth or fifth game, the manager gave him a rubber clipboard that didn't break."

Says Eiber: "Not too many coaches break clipboards over their knees to begin with. As far as being 22 years old, straight out of college, and in front of 3,000 people at a big high-school arena? Yes, Knight could lose it even back then."

What Knight did in front of 3,000 didn't compare to what he did when there was no one around. He was especially inclined to dramatic gestures at halftime, when, as Vucovich says, "He used to get pissed off and throw our tray of orange drinks against the locker room wall."

Even at 15 and 16, Knight's players had seen extreme behavior from coaches before, but it could be jarring to the rest of the student body. Years later, a Cuyahoga Falls student named Susan Wilkonson wrote the *New York Times*' Ira Berkow, describing how Knight used to "rant and rave" in the hallways. "One particular time, I had the misfortune of being in the hall when he was throwing a student up against a locker," wrote Wilkonson. "I couldn't equate this behavior with being in sports or being human. It scared me to death."

Knight's commitment knew no bounds, nor could that of his players. The 6-5 Eiber had bad hands and often felt the wrath of Knight, who had him squeeze a tennis ball all day and got permission from his teachers to let him do it in class. When Eiber kept dropping passes, Knight put him through his "fireball drill," firing a ball at him as hard as he could from close range.

"He only used it on two or three players," says Eiber. "And when he singled you out and did this to you, I guess you could have two points of view. One was that he was picking on you, and the other one was that he was trying to improve you."

One day, Eiber could stand the improvement process no longer and fired the ball back at Knight as hard as he could. Vucovich, who'd been doing the drill too, watched in horror.

"The ball missed Knight by three feet," Vucovich says. "It went all the way down to the other end and bounced behind the bleachers. I'm thinking, 'Eiber, you just got us both killed.' I look over at Eiber and his lower lip is vibrating, he's so afraid. Knight looks down where the ball went, looks back at Eiber and says, 'Eiber, that ball is worth more than you are. Now go get it.'"

The Tiger JVs went 13–3, but mere success was not enough. That would be another Knight trademark; nothing was ever enough. In one close game, they were trying to hold the ball with a one-point lead at the end, when Vucovich found himself so open in the corner, he took a shot. Fortunately, he thought, it went in, sealing the victory.

"Then I turn around to the guy who's been guarding me and we shake hands near the foul line," Vucovich says. "I turn around again and Knight is right in my face. He sprinted to where I was from the far end of the gym, he's three inches from my nose and he says, 'Vucovich, if I'd had a gun, you'd have never gotten that shot off!'"

Knight was in vintage form when they scrimmaged the jayvees at Orrville, his old high school, 45 minutes away. Cuyahoga, the bigger school, won handily but sloppily. Everyone knew what that meant.

"After it was over, nobody wanted to ride back with Knight," Vucovich says. "We're all trying to get in other cars because he's pissed. Well, as usual, he says, 'Vucovich, you're riding with me.' So I'm sitting in the front seat—and he drives about 90 miles an hour no matter where he goes—and he's yelling at me the whole way back. 'Goddamn you, you're not doing this, you're not doing that! Goddamn you guys, you're just not playing well!'

"You don't want to say to him, 'Yeah, but we murdered this team.' You don't want to say that at all. Because, of course, we beat these guys but Knight is extremely upset because we weren't mistake free."

The worst part of it was the sheer unpredictability. Rages blew up out of nowhere. So did moments when Knight was fun. When you expected the one, you often got the other. It was hell. It was great. It was exhausting.

Once Knight benched Dudich, his starting guard and co-captain, for an entire game. Before the next practice, Dudich's father walked up to Knight and asked why. With the whole team braced for the explosion, Knight patiently broke it down for Dudich's father, who was allowed to walk away unscathed.

"He explained why I wasn't playing, what I needed to improve, that this was a learning experience for me, and not to be down about it," Dudich says. "My dad was really impressed with him because he was willing to talk to him, willing to tell him what was going on. He wasn't above explaining to my dad."

It was an unforgettable season for the Cuyahoga Falls jayvees, although it was obvious Knight wouldn't be one of them for long.

"I enjoyed playing for him," says Vucovich. "He made an impact on my life and most of it good, quite frankly. Even though he picked on me, I always thought he was trying to make me better. He made me do things right, with discipline. But you also knew that he was moving up, that something was going to happen with this guy. He could not possibly be satisfied coaching 15-year-olds when he's as intense as he is."

Knight would count his year at Cuyahoga Falls as one of the most exciting of his life. When the varsity played Canton Lincoln, Knight suggested putting center Bob Forte at the high post and spreading the floor at the end. When it worked, Andreas told Knight that had been a really good idea.

Wrote Knight, 37 years later: "An assistant coach can live on a moment like that a long time."

Greater highs and lower lows awaited. One of the great coaching careers had begun, humbly, if not quietly.

In coaching, where opportunity is capricious, connections are all-important. So there was some self-interest involved when Knight took Andreas' advice and made up with Fred Taylor.

"Bobby and his mother weren't even talking to Fred when Bobby came to me as my assistant after he graduated," Andreas told the *Louisville Courier-Journal*'s John Flynn. "I knew Bobby and Fred were at sword's point and I also knew that it wasn't best for Bobby. So I advised him to make peace with his college coach and his alma mater. I told him if he was ever going to go anywhere in college coaching, he would need Fred Taylor's help."

The mild-mannered Taylor readily forgave Knight. In the spring of 1963, after Knight's year at Cuyahoga Falls, they were at the Final Four in Louisville, chatting in the lobby of the Brown Hotel, when Army coach George Hunter came over. Hunter was impressed by the dynamic young man. When Knight left, Hunter told Taylor that if Knight had a military obligation, he could get him transferred to West Point so he could serve it while assisting him and coaching the plebes.

Knight had finally reconciled himself to starting law school. Taylor had even called John Wooden, asking if he would take Knight as a graduate assistant while Bob attended the UCLA law school. As far as a grateful Knight was concerned, George Hunter's offer was all that kept him in coaching and out of the law. When school let out at Cuyahoga Falls, Knight enlisted in the Army and was sent to sweltering Fort Leonard Wood, Missouri, for basic training, before going on to West Point. His father, Pat, thought he had lost his mind.

"First of all, he couldn't understand why the hell you would go to college to be a coach," Knight told *Playboy*. "He didn't think you needed a college education to coach—never could comprehend that. But when I told him I was going to join the Army to coach at West Point, he really thought then he'd raised an idiot."

"So did I when, not more than a week after I had done it, Coach Taylor called and told me George Hunter had been fired at Army."

Taylor came through for Knight again, explaining the problem to Hunter's replacement, Tates Locke. Locke, another hard-driving young man from Ohio, knew of Knight and agreed to honor Hunter's offer. In August 1963, Private First Class R.M. Knight arrived at the United States Military Academy. Fifty miles north of Manhattan, the campus sat high and imposing on a bluff above the Hudson River. Knight was thrilled to be on the premises, with the cadets marching around the parade grounds and history oozing out of every crevice.

He arrived, driving through the main entrance at Thayer Gate, parked at the physical education building, and entered its gymnasium, which had carved into its stone portals:

UPON THE FIELDS OF FRIENDLY STRIFE
ARE SOWN SEEDS THAT
UPON OTHER FIELDS, ON OTHER DAYS
WILL BEAR THE FRUITS OF VICTORY.

The words were from General Douglas MacArthur, before he left his post as commandant for his own rendezvous with destiny in the Philippines. PFC Knight, who bled red, white, and blue and cherished the idea of athletic competition as a surrogate for war, was home at last.

Not that MacArthur was thinking about basketball when he wrote of "friendly strife." Generals had been suggesting that games were surrogate battles for centuries, as in the Duke of Wellington's claim about winning the battle of Waterloo "on the playing fields of Eton." However, in modern times, their war game of choice, and the Academy's specialty, was football, which had a martial air and, as in combat, pitted large teams in physical confrontations that played out over a great geographic area.

MacArthur had been the football team's student manager in 1902 and was a diehard fan ever after. He was so thrilled by Army's 38–0 rout of Navy in 1949, he cabled the West Point brass from his Tokyo headquarters: "From the Far East I send you one single thought, one sole idea, written in red on every beachhead from Australia to Tokyo: there is no substitute for victory." Fortunately for the nation, the humiliating loss had no lasting effect on the Navy.

Army was one of the game's greatest dynasties in the 1940s and 1950s. Coached by the renowned Red Blaik, led by Heisman Trophy winners Doc Blanchard (Mr. Inside) and Glenn Davis (Mr. Outside), the Black Knights won three straight national titles and went undefeated in five of six seasons from 1944 to 1949. They had another undefeated season as late as 1958, led by too-good-to-be-true Heisman Trophy winner Pete Dawkins and the famous "lonely end," Bill Carpenter. When they beat Navy, led by sophomore Joe Bellino, MacArthur wired Blaik, "In the long history of West Point athletics, there has never been a greater triumph," signing off with his now-familiar, "There is no substitute for victory!"

In the '60s, with college football exploding in popularity, it became harder for the service academies to compete at the elite level (the '58 Army team had averaged 210 pounds on the line). Nevertheless, Army remained a power, hiring Paul Dietzel away from LSU.

Basketball was still thought of in some quarters, like West Point, as a YMCA game. "When Tates took it over," Knight wrote, "basketball was no bigger than lacrosse or track or baseball or anything else. It was one of the other sports."

The Academy had a height limit of 6-6, which was a problem in basketball, as was the prevailing institutional disdain. The team played in the old fieldhouse and couldn't even practice there until after the Army-Navy football game. Until then, they wouldn't put the basketball court down, in case bad weather forced the football team to practice inside.

In George Hunter's two seasons, the Cadets had gone 10–11 and 8–11. Worse, they were 1–4 against Navy, which didn't go over well in any sport, including badminton.

In the fall of 1963, Locke and Knight coached their first game against Lehigh in the second-floor gym in the phys-ed building, where players going in for layups ran into the wall behind the basket, as if they were in high school.

The 26-year-old Locke was a font of emotion himself, who would one day be nicknamed "Tates as in hates." For the moment, Knight was only the junior maniac. When Locke was upset, he was inclined to kick whatever or whoever was in his way. When he and Knight played basketball, it was scarier than anything their teams ever did. Locke said they once came to blows in a one-on-one game. Another time, after their intramural team lost, Locke shoved his hand through a plate-glass window and needed 27 stitches. Yet another time, Locke said (and Knight denied), they were kicked out of intramurals "for beating the shit out of some guy."

"Tates was kind of a wild man," says Danny Schantz, a junior point guard in Locke's first season. "He'd go crazy in the locker room if we lost. One time we lost to Princeton and Bill Bradley, and Tates came into the locker room, and as far as everyone knew, he went into the bathroom and threw up. Then he came back out and kicked Bill Helkie, one of our younger players, in the leg."

"Knight and Locke had the same kind of intensity," says forward Joe Kosciusko. "And obviously, him and Locke, they were nuts about basketball. They'd stay up all night talking about strategy and stuff. But Bobby put more humor into things. One time I was practicing on the other end of the gym, a whole basketball court away from him, and he yelled, 'Joe, come over here.'

"I figured he had something really important to tell me, you know? He said 'Hi, Joe.' Then he said, 'Ha-ha.' He would do stuff like that, you know?"

In a program like Locke's, an occasional smile was like the sun breaking through, but competition made Knight grow fangs, too. Once, in a rough first half against Washington State in Portland, he and Locke drew technical fouls before halftime. Knight then vanished at the intermission while Locke talked to the team. Knight finally returned, looking sheepish.

"He had his head hanging down, the way he always does when he feels bad," Locke said, "and he said there was no need to worry about getting the tip at the start of the second half because he had followed the referees off the floor at halftime and gotten a technical. . . .

"He said he had something else to tell me. I said it could wait but he said he had to tell me right then. He said he was going to have to sit in the stands the second half 'cause he'd gotten booted. About that time, a Pinkerton guard showed up and escorted him into the stands."

They could have been twins separated at birth. Locke was a strong believer in man-to-man defense, like Knight's mentors, Taylor and Andreas. Knight was especially adept at figuring out a way to shut down the opponent's top scorer, one way or another. When they played highly rated NYU, led by Harold Hairston, a moody All-American forward known sarcastically as "Happy," Knight told Kosciusko to get in Hairston's face and stay there.

"Hairston was a hothead and we all knew it," says Kosciusko. "He's about 6-6, I'm about 6-1, 6-2, and I was guarding him. So right from the beginning of the game, I was about three inches from his face. Sure enough, six minutes into the game, he punches me in the nose, they kicked him out, and we won. That was the plan, the absolute plan, and it worked."

In the 1963–64 season, Locke's first, the Cadets went 19–7, the most games they had ever won, and received the second invitation to the NIT in the program's history. The NCAA Tournament then took only 22 teams, and the NIT was still prestigious. Army even got a trophy, edging NYU by one point in the consolation game to finish third. For Locke and Knight, it looked like the start of a beautiful friendship.

Knight's life was changing as fast as his career. On April 17, 1964, shortly after his first season at Army, he married Nancy Falk. They had been going out for five years, but Knight still approached the altar reluctantly.

"He came over to our house and we were in bed," says Pauline Boop. "We had a front bedroom and the window was open. He came around to the window and asked to come in and talk for a while, and I went to the door and got him and brought him in. And he sat and told us how much he didn't want to get married. He was, what, only 23?

". . . And I mean to tell you, I doubt if they ever had kind words for each other. They were the most mismatched couple I'd ever seen."

Nor was the wedding day conventional. Knight spent most of it with a high school guard from Schenectady named Paul Heiner, trying to persuade him to come to Army.

"I had to take a medical in the morning and then I had to take the physical in the afternoon," Heiner told Jack Isenhour for his book *Same Knight, Different Channel*. "And, during the interim, Tates Locke and Bobby Knight ran off and Bobby married Nancy. He recruited me on his wedding day! There was only an hour-and-a-half window when I wasn't with him."

In the fall of 1964, the Knights went back to West Point for Bob's second season under Locke, which turned out even better than their first. The Cadets finished 21–8, breaking the Academy record for wins they had just set, went back to the NIT, and finished third again. So Knight was stunned and upset when Locke suddenly resigned to become an assistant coach at Miami of Ohio, his alma mater.

Locke would become a cautionary tale. In five years, he would be in the ACC, coaching Clemson, taking the Tigers into the top 20 for the first time. Soon afterward, however, he became known as one of the most notorious cheaters in college basketball, swallowed by the dark side of his passion. As Locke would write in his book *Caught in the Net*, "I didn't cheat because the Jones did or because it made me a big man. I did it because I didn't want to get beat any more. That's all."

If they needed a replacement for the young phenom at West Point, how about an even younger potential phenom?

Knight was dismayed at Locke's resignation, which made his own future there a long shot. Hopefully, but without any confidence that he would get it, he applied for Locke's job and was pleasantly surprised to learn he had support within the Academy. Locke recommended him. Both Colonel Ray Murphy, the athletic director, and Brigadier General John Jannarone, the chairman of the athletic board, thought highly of him.

Knight was only 24, and Murphy said some of the brass thought he was "too young, too inexperienced, too volatile." However, the brass that mattered was willing to give him his chance. Knight counted Murphy as another of his mentors, later calling him "one of the five most influential men in my lifetime." Jannarone, who was also dean of the academic board and whose influence extended throughout the Academy, was no less supportive.

"John Jannarone really liked Bob," says Bob Kinney, the sports information director. "And at that time I believe Jannarone was the most powerful figure at West Point. Ray Murphy liked Bob, too, and they thought, 'Well, here's someone that we could take a chance on.' They had taken a chance on Tates Locke and Tates took us to two NITs with third place finishes both times, and Bob was part of that program."

With a wife, a son, and his enlistment almost up, Knight wanted to know where he stood, but Murphy told him to be patient. Two weeks after Locke's resignation, on a Friday, Murphy called him in and offered him the job, only to be told now that Knight would think about it.

Knight was still thinking about law school and had some offers to be an assistant coach. If he got the Army job, he had a list of things he wanted, starting with the use of the fieldhouse before the football season ended. But the main reason he held out, he said, was to assert his independence. Even before he got his first head coaching job, he didn't like the idea of being under anyone's thumb.

In this case he had overplayed his hand, since he didn't really have one, as Murphy's expression made clear. Knight scurried back in on Monday to take the job. He was still 24 when they began practicing on October 15, 1965, making him the youngest coach in Division One, and soon he would be known for more than that.

A head coach at 24, he looked even younger. His hair was bushy. His eyes blazed, so dark they almost looked black. He stalked the sideline, hurling his lightning bolts, wearing the same thing every game, a plaid jacket and a tie he always pulled loose, as though he were coming out of a bar fight.

Nancy would say her husband got his reputation because he became a coach so young. If anyone thought he was tempestuous later, she said, it was nothing compared to his early years at Army when he felt his coaching career was on the line.

"I had just finished a playing career during which I didn't do as well as I expected," Knight would write in the *New York Times*. "So at West Point, I made up my mind—*gotta win*. Not win at all costs. Never that. But winning was the hub of everything I was doing."

"At all costs" meant cheating, as in paying players under the table, which was the lingua franca of college basketball. No one could do that at Army and it would always be foreign to Knight, who didn't like making accommodations in general or pandering to teenagers in particular. Pandering wasn't an issue at West Point. Knight's players weren't the most sought after and, by statute, they couldn't be the tallest, but they were willing, he was tough, and they would do great things together.

"The place was insane," wrote Isenhour. "At the time Knight, uh, Coach Knight, was just another tough guy with a bad haircut. . . . At an institution dedicated to training leaders in the art of war, the ultimate competition, winning matters. It matters a lot. So while to outsiders Knight might have seem crazed, almost insane, to the insiders in charge of the Academy, he was a role model."

Knight's players were used to being treated like galley slaves. Their first year was an exercise in abuse in which the plebes were harassed and demeaned by upperclassmen. At any moment, they could have someone screaming in their faces, calling them "dumb smack" or "smack head" or "fuck face" or 1,000 variations thereof, ordering them to tuck their chins in until they butted up against their spines, or interrupting them as they sat at attention on the edge of their chairs at meals to make them recite doggerel about the food.

"How's the cow?" an upperclassman would ask, which meant, "Pass the milk."

"Sir," the plebe had to spit back, "it walks, it talks, it's full of chalk, the lacteal fluid extracted from the bovine species is highly prolific to the nth degree." To the end of his days, the plebe would remember it word for word, and the dozens of other speeches like it he had to memorize. In this martial environment, Knight, who was willing to work his players until they dropped and then go another hour, fit right in.

"Even people at West Point would say, 'He's too tough on the cadets.'" Knight told the *Indiana Daily Student*'s Bruce Newman. "Why shouldn't I be? I mean, you're watching Army play in Madison Square Garden, you ought to think these guys are going to get out and protect the country, too."

When Knight's first team began practicing in the fall of 1965, he started his players on his suicide drills, diving on top of each other for a loose ball. The Cadets called it the "animal drill." They weren't 15-year-old high school sophomores but young men training to be warriors, who regarded such tests as opportunities, so the collisions were all the more fearful.

"There was always a trainer assigned to the basketball team and there was also one assigned to the track team, which worked out of the field-house as well," says Kinney. "On those first days of practice, the track trainer helped the basketball trainer because there were lots of elbows and knees to bandage. But Bob's intent was to separate the men from the boys and find out who would sacrifice his body to get the loose ball."

Even in a place where aggression was a way of life, there were limits on Knight he would not have elsewhere. His bosses weren't athletic department bureaucrats or academics who'd become university presidents; they were military men, used to giving orders and having them obeyed. Ray Murphy was a colonel, John Jannarone a brigadier general. When Knight stepped over the line, they told him about it.

That fall, Boston College came over for a scrimmage. Bob Cousy, the former Celtic great who was coaching BC, thought it was more like a football scrimmage.

"We started scrimmaging," he wrote in his book *Cousy on the Celtic Mystique*, "and within ten minutes it was mayhem. We couldn't get anything done.

"'This isn't going to accomplish anything,' I said.

"'This is the way we do it,' was Knight's reply.

"We went back to the huddle. I remember saying to my guys. 'Scratch this one. Just protect yourself. Do whatever you have to do.'

"For the next hour-and-a-half, all we did was break up fights. It was completely useless. I remember saying, 'This is the last time you'll see us, pal.'

"Knight's philosophy had the perfect setting at West Point. He had all the structure and discipline he'd ever need. He could make killers out of those West Point cadets."

Knight, who didn't see it that way, vehemently disputed Cousy's account. However, Knight's players never forgot that football scrimmage either.

"The Boston College coach was Bob Cousy and I believe Bob Knight wanted to introduce him to Army basketball," says Dan Schrage, one of the best defensive players on Knight's first team. "I was particularly pumped up to play aggressive, and when a loose ball became available, I grabbed it along with a Boston College player and ended up body-slamming him to the floor. I remember Bob Cousy stopped the scrimmage and threatened to pull his team off the floor. . . .

"We were really pumped up—the players were, Bob Knight was—because Cousy was kind of a legend at that time. And I think Knight wanted to make the impression that we were a very aggressive team. They probably had more talent than we had, but we played a very aggressive man-to-man defense. We didn't switch on screens and it was very intense man-to-man."

"We did play physical and I do remember some words and I basically didn't like Cousy," says Bill Schutsky, then a 6-2 sophomore starting a stellar career in which he would average 18 points over three seasons. "I thought he was kind of temperamental and he thought he was a cool guy. And we were just out there working our butts off, trying real hard."

Cousy won't discuss Knight now. "My brief relationship with him was more of a negative one," he says. "And my feelings about him haven't changed."

Knight coached the way he lived and lived the way he coached, steamrolling anything in his path. Brooking no resistance but loving the spotlight, he had mixed feelings about the press, which, in turn, had mixed feelings about him. The press guys lived for shows and showmen, especially the writers from New York, where keen newsstand competition meant keeping an eye out for the sensational. They called him "Bobby T" for all the technicals he got, compared him to great generals when he won, and bashed him when he exploded.

"He was pretty much the darling bad boy of the press," says guard Jim Oxley, whom Knight would call the best player he ever recruited at West Point. "He was a fiery young coach who was winning at Army."

It was love at first sight when Knight splintered a chair in his Madison Square Garden debut as a head coach against BC in the 1965 Holiday Festival.

"There was a guy sitting behind the Army bench—not a bench, it was just a row of chairs—who'd had a little bit too much to drink," says Bob Kinney, the sports information director. "And the guy got up, I guess, to go to the bathroom or something. And there was a call that Bob didn't like, so he turned around and the only thing that he spotted was this empty chair now, and he kicked it more than once and broke the chair. The funniest thing was when this drunk came back to look for his chair and it was little more than a pile of kindling."

Knight was perfect for the Academy and it was perfect for him. At West Point, they were always talking about the Long Gray Line. Even if Knight sometimes bragged about serving out his hitch without putting on a uniform, he felt like he was in it.

"Knight was surrounded at West Point by the ghosts of Army past, those who went on to be generals and high-ranking officers," says Kinney. "He studied what they did in preparing their troops for battle and probably tried to pattern his practice routine after some of their philosophies. I think West Point was a big influence on him."

Knight, who embraced military history, went to work each day on hallowed ground. While he would always be compared to George Patton, the movie star of the generals, Knight had more sophisticated taste. He liked Patton's daring but not his naked ego and his strutting vanity. Knight preferred U. S. Grant, who did whatever was necessary, but wore a private's uniform. Knight saw himself that way, as the man in charge who cared nothing for attention. West Point was in the business of making leaders. Knight was a leader even among older, higher-ranking leaders.

"Here's a guy who was a PFC one day and the next day he's the head basketball coach," says Jimmy Oxley. "What was amazing to me is how he could deal with generals and others at West Point in a manner that would almost make you think that he was the general and they were the PFC. . . . Jannarone absolutely loved Knight. Jannarone used to come to practice with a referee shirt sometimes and be a smart-aleck. And Jannarone wasn't a kiss-ass kind of guy. If he thought Knight stepped over the line, I think he told him.

"But Jannarone was a guy Knight could sit down with and say, 'This guy's giving me a hard time, could you deal with it?' Or, 'What do I have to do to deal with it?'

"Because at West Point everyone thinks they know how to coach. All the officers think they know more than you do. So I think Knight was very smart in that he always surrounded himself with really good people who were also a bit older than him, like Jannarone."

Knight had adopted older mentors in Orrville and Cuyahoga Falls. Now that he was within hailing distance of New York City, he sought out two old greats of the coaching fraternity, Long Island University's Clair Bee and Joe Lapchick from St. John's. Knight was thrilled when they were receptive, basked in the warmth of their friendship, and sought their advice, even if he wound up ignoring the part about behaving. His autobiography, *Knight: My Story*, is full of long, reverent accounts of his interactions with his mentors. As far as he was concerned, the old masters were the real masters and he was the one who would make sure the modern world remembered it.

The coaches he revered, who would grow to include Pete Newell, Hank Iba, Everett Dean, and Frank McGuire, were surrogate fathers to him. When they looked in the paper and saw he had done something controversial, they would call each other to see which one of them would call Bob. One thing about having Knight for a surrogate son, it was a full-time job.

Knight's approach to basketball would always be old school, unimpressed by modern touches like gimmick defenses and jargon like "point guard" and "two-guard" and "wing man."

"I have always operated under the theory that basketball is not rocket science," he said. "It doesn't take Einstein to coach basketball."

The way he saw it, it was a simple game: get better shots than your opponent by working patiently for yours and putting so much pressure on him, he hurries his.

On offense, this meant passing the ball four or five times before a shot—like Gene Hackman coaching Hickory High in *Hoosiers* in a role that was modeled on Knight—in a motion offense with everyone cutting and setting screens, too. The rule was, if you weren't moving or setting a screen to free a teammate, you were wrong. It was fluid, obliging his players to be able to read and react, and would become the standard in college basketball. Knight, the boy wonder who was still in his 20s, was already packing in his peers when he did clinics. Kinney remembers having to make trip after trip to the deli for refreshments when the crowds turned out to be bigger than expected.

"The thing that blew me away, at Indiana we never ran a play," Isiah Thomas would say. "It was read and react and you really had to think your way through the game. The first time I ran a pick-and-roll was in the NBA."

On defense, Knight meant to deny opponents the space and time to work the ball around. His players were to keep their men from getting the ball, pressure them if they got it, and, if they passed it, try to keep them from getting it back. And, most important of all, when the game started, his teams would be as ready as ready could be.

"We read reams of copy about the will to win," Knight once said on *60 Minutes*. "We hear countless broadcasters talk about the will to win. I want to tell you something about the will to win. The will to win is the most overly exaggerated phenomenon that we have in society today. You have to have a will to prepare to win, not a will to win, because everybody's got that. It's the will to prepare to win."

In the beginning, Knight leaned on his assistant coach, Al LoBalbo, another of his older mentors, a tough little former high-school coach who preached a swaggering credo of defense in a thick Bronx accent. The Cadets were as rough as a team could be within the rules. Opposing coaches complained they effectively changed the rules because referees got tired of calling fouls and began letting everything go.

"Most players don't like to be pressed," Knight said in his profile in the Army media guide. "They like room—room to move, room to shoot. It's our aim to take that room away from them, to force them to change their style. Sometimes it works, other times it does not."

He was just being modest. What he meant was: *It works or someone is going to hear about it.*

Like any other coach, Knight was fired up for his debut, but no one got fired up quite the way he did. He not only preached patience and ball movement, he gave his players a pamphlet called *Let's Get a Good Shot.* On the cover was a drawing of a player standing on a ladder, holding the ball with two hands and carefully placing it into the basket.

Unfortunately, the 1964–65 season opener was at Princeton, a major power in the East that had just been to the Final Four before graduating Bill Bradley. The Tigers hadn't lost to Army in four years and ruined Knight's debut, hammering the Cadets, 70–49.

Knight's first victory came four days later, 71–62, over Division III Worcester Tech before a crowd of 400 in the fieldhouse. A week later the Cadets beat NYU, 76–68, as senior Mike Silliman, who had been suspended for the first two games for a drinking incident, returned. Knight called the 6-5, 230-pound Silliman one of the best players he ever coached and, with Navy's David Robinson, one of the two best service academy basketball players ever. Silliman was a former Kentucky Mr. Basketball who could have gone anywhere but, in Locke's greatest recruiting coup, came to Army. For all its limitations, Knight's first team represented the two years of gung-ho recruiting that he and Locke had done.

"People like to think that we played great defense and there was this great coaching, but during that period of time there were some really talented players," says Doug Clevenger, who would captain the 1970–71 team.

"Silliman was one of the best players in the country. They wanted him to play at Kentucky but Tates Locke brought him to Army. Oxley could have played at Villanova. Oxley was a really good player and Shutsky was a great player before that. So, we had a lot of talent, and people have never really recognized that. We had some real talent at Army in addition to Knight's ability to put it together."

They were 10–5 at midseason when Silliman suffered a knee injury that ended his career. While everyone waited for the Cadets to collapse, they won six of their last seven, including the all-important victory over Navy, finished 16–6, and got another coveted invitation to the NIT.

On March 12, 1965, at Madison Square Garden, Army defeated Manhattan, 71–66, in a first-round skirmish. The *New York Daily News* called it a "travesty . . . a rough-house game that at times resembled the Battle of the Bulge," pitting Manhattan against "the well-conditioned West Point muscle." Six players fouled out as the referees called 60 fouls.

Knight's infantry was expected to get its comeuppance in the second round against tournament favorite San Francisco, with future pros Erwin Mueller and Joe Ellis. Daring to go small, Knight put 6-1 Bill Helkie on the 6-8 Mueller and 6-1 Danny Shrage on the 6-6 Ellis.

With everyone collapsing on Mueller inside, Shrage pressuring Ellis outside and Helkie making 11 of his first 12 shots, Army won, 80–63. The *New York Post* called it "one of the greatest coaching jobs in Garden history."

"On paper, a lot of our opponents would be superior and the bookies would have Army as an underdog in double figures," says Bob Kinney. "Beating San Francisco in the NIT, we didn't have a player taller than 6-5 and they had some real tall guys, and we just kicked their butts."

Next up in the semifinals came Brigham Young, which was even bigger, with three 6-11 players, including future pros Jim Eakins and Craig Raymond. BYU was a western run-and-gun outfit, averaging 95 points to Army's 69. The problem was, when teams played Knight, he made sure they played at his pace, not theirs.

Army led, 58–56, in the closing minutes when BYU's star guard, Dick Nemelka, drove the lane and collided with Helkie, who was trying to take the charge. Referee Lou Eisenstein, a respected veteran, called it a block, sending Nemelka to the line and Knight into orbit.

Nemelka made two free throws, tying it, 60–60, and BYU went on to win, 66–60. Knight fumed afterward in his dressing room while his friends Locke and Lapchick tried to calm him down, or hold him down.

"There's me and Coach Lapchick trying to restrain Bobby in the locker room," Locke told Isenhour. "He wanted to kill Lou. We had everything under control and he bolted from us. Those little narrow halls in the old Garden? He went down that damn hall so fast. Criminy! He was in that locker room like a cat. Eisenstein looked like a deer in the headlights. . . . He was tryin' to grab him but Eisenstein was so fat, he couldn't lift him off the floor."

Knight then went to the postgame press conference, where he ripped the call. "Never have I ever said anything about officiating," Knight said. "But that was a gutless call tonight. Gutless."

It was like being in the middle of an electrical storm. The excitement never stopped. That evening, Kinney was in Knight's hotel room when Murphy called and Knight started yelling into the phone.

"Colonel Murphy thought it would be a good idea if Bob apologized to the official," says Kinney. "And he did not choose to do so and told Colonel Murphy in no uncertain terms that he would not. The head trainer, Ed Billings, and I were in the room with Bob at the time. We walked out, we said, 'Oh, boy, I wonder who's going to be coaching the team tomorrow.'"

Wrung out as they were, they lost to Villanova in the consolation bracket, but it was still an auspicious start for Knight. Murphy was thrilled to see the program continuing as it had under Locke, with the excitement the Corps of Cadets now showed for it. If Knight had been presumptuous enough to argue with him, it meant nothing to Murphy, who said later he didn't even remember it.

Of course, if these were the good times, what would the bad ones be like?

*　　*　　*

Knight was on the map now. He showed so much promise in his first season at Army, there almost was no second. He was offered the Florida job, just vacated by Norm Sloan, and told friends he would take it.

"Florida was interested in Bob and he was about ready to accept the position," says Kinney. "So, yes, there was always an interest in moving to another school. He was not going to be at West Point for his whole career."

Another young coach with his burning amibtion would have been out of there in a heartbeat, but Knight seemed to be looking for a reason to stay. Fred Taylor reminded him he owed the Academy something, and Knight was keenly loyal to Murphy and Jannarone. In the same way Knight was always consulting older coaches, it would always be critically important to him to know the older men he worked for would back him up.

In his autobiography, Knight wrote that he went in to see Murphy, who was signing some letters, and broke the good news that he would be staying. "I knew you would," Murphy said, without looking up.

When Knight thought about it later, he says, he figured it was actually a compliment. Murphy had been confident that he would do the right thing.

Knight's second season would be a transition, with Silliman and Helkie gone. The only consistent scorer returning was junior forward Bill Shutsky. The guards were unproven although there was a promising sophomore moving up from plebe ball named Mike Krzyzewski.

They started the 1966–67 season 2–5. Knight was especially hard on his captains under any circumstance, expecting them to act as coaches on the floor and to develop other leaders beneath them, holding them responsible for anything and everything that went wrong. Senior Danny Shrage, now the captain, says he found himself in "an extremely difficult and unpleasant position."

Shrage was the first to get the Full Treatment. As Knight told Joan Mellen for her book *Bob Knight: His Own Man:*

"*A player named Schrage, who was my best defensive player ever, gets a rebound twelve feet from the bucket right in front of the free*

*throw line. He goes up to shoot it. There isn't anybody within eight
feet of him. He shoots it and misses it, which is predictable.*

*"We get the rebound. I call time and I have him by the throat. I
can remember my fingers slipping off his Adam's apple or I would
have killed him.*

*"I had his shirt in my fist in the time-out and I said, 'I want to
tell you something. Someday do you want to be a goddamn general?'*

"'Yes sir.'

*"You've got no chance of being a goddamn second lieutenant if
you shoot that son of a bitch one more time."*

Schrage insists he can't remember the incident. However, it wasn't
at all uncommon for Knight to grab his players to make a point.

"I don't ever remember seeing him grab anybody by the throat," says
forward Paul Franke, a plebe that season. "The shirt was always the thing.
He would grab you by the shirt. He'd take that open claw, grab your shirt
just below your chin, just grab it straight down and twist it. He would get
himself so physically upset that he would be almost trembling."

There was no arguing that it worked. The Cadets responded, winning 11 of their last 14 to finish the 1966–67 season 13–8. They were
hoping it would be good enough for a fourth consecutive invitation to
the NIT but were snubbed by the selection committee. Knight wondered if he was being blackballed for going after Lou Eisenstein the year
before.

However, the following season, with Schutsky back and Oxley joining Krzyzewski in the backcourt, the Cadets led the nation in defense
and went 20–4. They pulled a major upset at St. John's, after which Lou
Carnesecca said of Schutsky: "If we're ever in a war, I'm glad this guy's
on our side."

This time Army got invitations from both the NCAA and the NIT.
Knight wanted to go back to the NIT, claiming it was because the Corps
of Cadets loved going to New York. Actually, Schutsky says Knight told
them, "'We've got a bid to the NIT and to the NCAA and we're gonna
vote. However, I want you guys to know this. . . . '

"He said the NIT teams weren't as good and we had a better shot at winning that and what do we want to do? And basically we were young kids and it was like, 'Wow, we got a shot at winning the NIT, rather than getting knocked out maybe in the first round of the NCAA and being embarrassed.'"

Unfortunately, the Cadets were matched against Notre Dame on St. Patrick's Day in the first round of the NIT. The inspired Irish, who liked being in New York, too, won, 62–58.

Nevertheless, it was a new era in Army basketball. The Cadets, who had been to one NIT when Locke and Knight arrived, had now gone to four in the last five seasons. The 20–5 record they had just posted was the best in Army history. Knight's legend had just begun.

THREE

A FAREWELL TO ARMS

ARMY, 1968–71

I think there was a certain realization for Coach that the Army was a good stepping stone, it was a good place to get started . . . but for him to take a program to the level that he wanted to take it, it would have to be at a different place.

So ultimately when the time comes—and he even made the same comment about Indiana . . . there was a point in there that he probably should have seen the signs and gone ahead and moved on. Because the tenor had changed, the politics changed, the philosophy changed.

—Army center Mike Gyovai

Everyone knew Army couldn't keep someone as good as Knight forever, or even for long, but few coaches were ever as well suited to their environment as he was at West Point.

Ambitious as he was, he wasn't in a hurry. For years, he seemed to look for reasons to stay rather than go, as when he turned down Florida after his first season. He was all set to go to Wisconsin after his third season in the spring of 1968, but backed out when athletic director Ivy Williamson announced it before Knight gave him a final commitment. Knight hadn't had time to tell Army officials before the story broke and he was embarrassed; Wisconsin officials, embarrassed in turn, threatened to produce a tape recording of the interview in which Knight verbally agreed to take the job.

Knight's insistence on being supported by his superiors, or working for good people, as he put it, was absolute. He turned down Wisconsin and signed his fourth one-year contract at West Point.

Nevertheless, it wasn't an easy time in the nation's history to be coaching the U.S. Military Academy's basketball team as it toured college campuses at the height of the Vietnam War. U.S. involvement had already begun under John Kennedy when Knight arrived at West Point in 1963, and had been expanded under Lyndon Johnson when Knight became head coach in 1965. By the fall of 1968, and the start of Knight's fourth season, the war had become a hot-button issue that transcended all else. Johnson had announced he wouldn't seek another term. The Democrats had just had their tumultuous convention in Chicago.

Kids wore American flags as patches on the seats of their jeans. Protesters chanted, "Hey, hey, LBJ, how many kids did you kill today?" Jefferson Airplane would soon release "Volunteers" and "Wooden Ships," and the Rolling Stones did "Street Fighting Man." Universities were wellsprings of resistance where students occupied campus buildings and "liberated" them.

Knight's teams went on the road to play basketball, not to sign up enlistees or speak in favor of the war. On the other hand, their rough, unapologetic style would have angered fans of any era, no matter where they were from. The Cadets found themselves obliged to fight their way through their schedule, although they didn't seem to mind.

If there was ever a basketball team you'd want to take into actual combat, this was it. In the fall of 1968, Knight had Mike Krzyzewski and Jim Oxley back at guard. Krzyzewski was as tough as a strand of barbed wire and Oxley was a gritty little sharpshooter who had chosen the Academy over good programs like Villanova.

There was also a rough-and-ready swingman coming up from the plebe team named Doug Clevenger, who would fit right in. Whenever there was a rumble at an Army game, Clevenger's picture would be in the next morning's paper in the middle of the melee.

The real menace was 6-5, 225-pound Mike Gyovai. Knight would call him his all-time favorite player, even if Gyovai wouldn't have made Knight's top 100 in ability. Knight had lots of physical, hard-nosed, devoted players but never one with the whole package like Gyovai, who had been raised for this. His father had survived the Bataan Death March, and Mike had attended a military academy in Illinois. Knight played Gyovai at center, where he was always going against a bigger player, which meant one thing: The bigger player was in trouble.

"We went to Wyoming where they had a 6-9 center," Knight said, "and going up for a rebound, Mike busted the guy in the mouth with his elbow. Blood spurted everywhere. I can see it now as plain as the day it happened.

"The 6-9 guy is standing there, holding his hand over his mouth, wondering if he has any teeth left. There's blood all over Mike, too. So, Mike wipes the blood off his shoulder and then wipes his hand off on the 6-9 guy's shirt and trots away, leaving the guy counting his teeth. That's my kind of player."

Gyovai wasn't showing off or volatile. He was just rough, every second of the day, as an underclassman named Ed Mueller found out one day in practice when he blocked too many of Gyovai's shots.

"They were running the offense and they were trying to get the ball into Mike," says Mueller. "And so they get it into him and Gyovai tries to shoot and I block the shot. Knight yells at Gyovai and says, 'Run it again.' So, they run it again. I block it again.

"So, then Knight yells at him some more, and Gyovai whispers to me, 'Block it again and I'll knock your fucking head off.'

"So, they run it again, throw it in to him, I block it again. Next thing I know, an elbow's hitting me right in the mouth. It cut my upper lip. I was bleeding all over the place. Had to get stitches in it."

For Knight, the hard part was keeping Gyovai eligible, since Gyovai didn't feel like being called "fuck face" by senior cadets.

"I was in a lot of trouble with respect to the West Point system," Gyovai says. "I didn't buy off on all that, you know, subservient behavior. My problem was that I tended to tell upperclassmen to take a flying fuck. As a result of that, it was 'belligerent behavior and abusive language toward a cadet superior while in the line of duty,' and, boom, I'm back in confinement. That's when you can't leave your room without signing a card because you're under an honor system. So, basically, I went to class, I went to meals, and then I went back to my room and that was the extent of my life at West Point."

The Academy didn't know how to deal with Gyovai, but Knight

never had a problem with him. Rules and regulations didn't impress Gyovai, but Knight did.

"Mike Gyovai was an absolute animal," Clevenger says. "That was why Knight loved him. Knight loved Mike because he was an animal but also because he would do anything Knight said."

The 1968–69 Cadets charged to a 5–0 start. They improved to 6–0 when two late free throws by Krzyzewski beat Bradley, 54–52, during a holiday tournament at Kentucky. The good times came to an abrupt end the next night in a 15-point loss to powerful Kentucky. According to the *Sports Illustrated* account, "Knight kicked in a locker and spat on the runner-up trophy after Army lost to the Wildcats and Dan Issel."

If Knight thought he had something special with this team, his hopes were soon dashed. The Cadets lost the next four games to fall to 6–5. His players remember it as his grimmest time at West Point, to that point. "Every loss would eat at Knight until he got the next win," says Franke. "So when we lost five in a row that year, it was just brutal."

Krzyzewski, the senior captain, later called it "the toughest period of my life as a player," saying, "I didn't understand what was happening and I felt responsible for what was happening." Knight bore down on his captains in the best of times and became a crushing weight in bad times. Knight made Krzyzewski understand he was personally responsible for everything that went wrong and had better do something about it fast. Krzyzewski, who was nothing if not dutiful, accepted the burden.

Compared to Gyovai, who looked like a longshoreman, Krzyzewski, slight and pale, looked like a waif who was in the wrong dressing room. A homebody who had led the Chicago Catholic League in scoring at Weber High School, he had been planning to go somewhere closer to his working-class Polish neighborhood until Knight came to visit and Krzyzewski's parents fell in love with him.

"My parents could not believe that West Point could come in and offer you this," said Krzyzewski. "They said it would change your life. I said, 'I don't want my life changed,' and I told Coach Knight I wasn't coming. Two weeks later, after, 'You're an idiot, you're stupid,' I finally just told my parents, 'Okay, I'll go because of you.'"

As soon as Krzyzewski got there, Knight moved him to point guard. Then he told him not to worry about shooting the ball any more, even if he had set scoring records in high school. Krzyzewski's wife, Mickie, would later say Mike was "scared" of Knight, using a word her husband never did, although all Knight's players felt the same way.

Nevertheless, Krzyzewski was as tough and committed as any player Knight ever had. Knight named him his captain in his senior year, which had now turned into a nightmare. Krzyzewski said he often went home after practice cursing Knight's name.

"We had some games in that five-game losing streak that we probably should not have lost," says Jimmy Oxley, Army's leading scorer that season and the main beneficiary of Krzyzewski's passes. "And so it became the gloomiest, darkest time. Bobby Knight was down and Mike Krzyzewski, the captain, he was down. There were more arguments during practice. There were actually a couple times when people got into fistfights with one another and Knight would just let it go rather than jump in and stop it."

Things got so tense that, one day, Krzyzewski took on the feisty Clevenger, who was up a couple of weight classes.

"We kept losing games and at one practice Knight decided to move me and Oxley to the second team during a scrimmage," Clevenger says. "So, we're playing and we're beating the first team and Knight gets all pissed and says, 'Clevenger, if you'd played like that during the goddamn games, we would have won these games, you insolent son of a bitch.'

"Then as I start walking off the court, I say, 'I ain't no goddamn insolent son of a bitch.' Then I start walking toward the locker room, which is unheard of. Krzyzewski, who's the captain of the team, so he's under tremendous pressure, he comes running up after me and throws a punch. He said he threw it right at me, face to face. But, no, it was one of the worst punches I ever saw. I was walking off and he hits me in the back of the goddamn head."

Then the fights became extramural. A win at Dartmouth ended the losing streak, but they were still struggling at 10–7 when they went to Rutgers. It was tense and physical until the end, when a brawl broke out.

"We were down by two points and we needed to get the ball back, so Clevenger grabbed this real big center they had," Gyovai says. "Then the kid turned around and took a swing at him. And I came from the other end of the floor, of course, because nobody was going to swing at one of our players unless they were going to answer to me. I mean, that was kind of where my head was at."

Before Gyovai could get there, Franke remembers, "Clevenger wheeled around and nailed the guy in the jaw and knocked him into the bleachers under the basket."

Gyovai says the Rutgers center was falling backwards when he arrived "full-blast from the other end of the court and basically did a gorilla stomp on the guy. Their fans in the bleachers came out, the benches emptied, fists were flying all over the place, the cops had to come out onto the floor."

After all the technical fouls were assessed and the free throws shot, Army lost, 49–47. This left one more challenge: getting off the floor. En route, Bill Parcells, then an Army football assistant and Knight's buddy, went after a fan.

"As we were leaving the floor, somebody made a gesture at Coach Knight and Bill Parcells grabbed the kid and threw him through a door," says Bob Kinney, the sports information director. "I could hear the wood splinter. Then we went downstairs to our locker room, and we needed police assistance to get off their campus that night."

In Knight's book, he describes the scene in the dressing room, where a sheepish Parcells told him he had "cold-cocked" the fan. Parcells was afraid that any police who showed up would be looking for him, so Knight had the players bunch up around Parcells, told him to duck down, and smuggled him to safety.

Parcells had become friendly with Knight when they lived next door to each other in the junior officers' quarters. They stayed up nights, discussing philosophy and X's and O's, and stayed close afterward, each recognizing a fierce, kindred passion in the other. Of course, even for Parcells, Knight was out there. "You know, I used to sit down with him," said Parcells later, "and several times I told him he was nuts."

The Rutgers loss dropped the Cadets to 10–8 but they won their next four. The last one was at Annapolis, making Knight 4–0 against Navy. Krzyzewski played his typical game, defending well, getting the ball to Oxley, who scored 18 points, and getting nine points himself. Knight had just given Krzyzewski the game ball when Krzyzewski received a phone call from Chicago. His father had died without warning of a cerebral hemorrhage.

Early the next morning, Knight drove Mike through a snowstorm to the airport, gave him some money, and said he would join him in Chicago. Knight caught another flight that night. For three days, he sat around the kitchen, eating Emily Krzyzewski's Polish food with his fingers. He didn't go back to West Point until Bill Krzyzewski was buried.

Mike got back just in time for Army's bus ride to Colgate. The Cadets won that game and the last one at Rochester to finish 16–8. For the second year in a row, they led the nation in defense, allowing 53 points a game. They were still so controversial, some members of the NIT Committee reportedly blanched at the thought of inviting them, but they got the last of the 16 berths.

Everyone knew by now never to write them off, but what ensued was still a surprise. They started by upsetting Wyoming, 51–49, moving them into the second round against tourney favorite South Carolina, a hulking team even the players didn't think they could handle.

"In those days the NIT played doubleheaders, and after we beat Wyoming, the second game that night was South Carolina," says Clevenger. "We're sitting up in the stands and watching their game with Knight and I'm thinking, 'Jeez, we're going to get our ass kicked.'"

The Gamecocks were coached by Frank McGuire, a Knight mentor, who had built a powerhouse at North Carolina. McGuire's move to one of the Tar Heels' hated rivals had made him a controversial figure in the ACC, and the season had been one brawl after another. McGuire now had three future pros, 6–10 Tom Owens, 6–10 Tom Riker, and 6–2 John Roche, a two-time ACC player of the year. Roche hadn't faced anyone like Clevenger, who shut him down. "Roche became so frustrated that I thought he was going to cry during the game," Oxley says.

Army slowed the game down and won, 59–45. The *New York Post* called it, "one of those beautiful Army jobs that have become a Bobby Knight specialty," noting, "Knight is the Army coach who could teach those government boys in Washington how to build an ABM defense system without spending six million bucks."

"Bobby Knight was always looking for the perfect game," Oxley says. "I think that was his goal as a basketball coach. When we played South Carolina and beat them by 14 points, that was as close to a perfect game as I can picture."

Even Bob Cousy, who didn't like Knight, called it "a masterpiece." But the masterpiece might have taken too much out of the Cadets, who fell to Cousy's Boston College team the next night in the semifinals, 71–63.

Army lost the consolation game, too, 74–62, to Tennessee and finished 18–10, exemplary by Academy standards; tolerable by Knight's.

By the start of the next season in the fall of 1969, Richard Nixon had taken office as president. The Vietnam War continued, the resistance grew, and the service academies remained convenient symbols. Army and Navy were obliged to withdraw from the annual Heptagonals track meet with the eight Ivy League schools when the Ivies refused to compete against them. At an Army baseball game at Dartmouth, fans knocked over the Cadets' dugout, and the Dartmouth players had to come to their rescue.

It took a special crew to handle everything that went on, but Knight had one, led by Oxley, their tough little captain, and Gyovai, their Incredible Hulk. They were 18–4 when they bussed to Syracuse to play the Orangemen and found the campus in turmoil. Two days before, students had taken over the ROTC building. The Army bus was greeted, not by mere catcalls, but by a large, unfriendly looking crowd. The students were the ones in the drab combat fatigues and the long hair. The Cadets were the ones in the crewcuts.

Usually the Army players shrugged this stuff off. "I mean, we didn't think of ourselves as baby-killers, know what I mean?" says Clevenger. "And we didn't even think of being in the Army. I was just going to college. I just happened to go to West Point."

The crowd looked so menacing, the Cadets were taken around to the back entrance of Manley Fieldhouse. The game was one-sided, Army winning, 79–54, but the crowd was unruly and getting more unruly by the minute.

"Mike Gyovai was playing," says Bob Kinney. "There was a point in the game where I think Mike might have been called for a foul . . . As he was walking off the court, going towards the bench, there were an awful lot of boos and they were actually unscrewing bolts out of the bleachers and throwing them. One came across the floor and hit me in the shin, enough to break the skin and draw a little blood. I kept it and used it for a number of years at West Point as a paperweight."

Gyovai walked slowly off the raised floor, through the boos, glaring at the crowd, daring someone or all of them to make a move in his direction.

Knight was so awed by the scene, he wrote in his book, that he did a radio play-by-play for Colonel Tom Rogers, sitting next to him on the bench: "Gyovai steps away from the foul line extended, he's moving toward our bench, but very slowly, Colonel, verrr-ry slowly. It may take five minutes for him to get here. . . .

"Ohhhh, the crowd is looking at him They're booing him."

Fortunately, the crowd kept its distance and everyone got home okay.

In the spring of 1970, the Cadets went back to the NIT. By then, Army was regarded as one of the Eastern powers. Everyone was used to the Cadets coming down and knocking off a kingpin or two before falling in some kind of heartbreaker that left everyone spent.

Nobody knew it would be Knight's last trip here with an Army team, and he went out in style in the biggest heartbreaker of all. The

Cadets beat their first-round opponent, highly regarded Cincinnati, 72–67, as the 6–5 Gyovai neutralized the Bearcats' 6–8, NBA-bound center, Jim Ard. Manhattan fell in the second round, sending Army into the semifinals against St. John's, the local darling.

St. John's would have fallen, too, but for a referee's call. Army led, 59–58, when Oxley hit a jump shot out of the corner with 1:32 left. With the clock running out and the Cadets still clinging to their lead, a St. John's guard named Richie Lyons took a desperate 30-footer, missed—but was bailed out when Oxley was called for fouling him. The call was so bad, the pro–St. John's crowd of 19,500 booed. Lyons made both free throws and Army lost, 60–59.

As Knight left the floor, he passed Marquette coach Al McGuire. McGuire knew all about the agony of close losses on bad calls but even he had never seen anything like the apparition that went past him.

"In a situation like that, maybe you shake a hand, offer a condolence," McGuire wrote later in his introduction to John Feinstein's *A Season on the Brink*. "I didn't say anything. The reason was because I'd never seen anyone look so drained, so *beaten* in my life. It was a look I'll never forget because I can't remember seeing another coach with that look. He had given the game everything he could and losing it just destroyed him. You could see it all over his face. Bob couldn't have been more than 30 back then [he was 29] but when he came off the floor, he looked like an old man. I've never forgotten that look."

Oxley says Knight threw up afterward and was crying too hard to talk to them. Knight almost broke up again in the postgame press conference. "It's kind of sad," he said, "we're not . . ." but got no further, choking back a sob. The hard-boiled Gotham press guys stood and applauded him.

Now, instead of going into the finals against Marquette, they were going into another consolation game, this time against LSU and Pete Maravich. Maravich had just set a new NCAA scoring record with an incredible 46.7 points a game. Mop-topped and highly publicized, Pistol Pete was a Cadet antithesis, and if that wasn't enough, his father, Press, the showboat LSU coach, had been openly rooting against Army. "They play good defense but they control the ball too much," said Press.

"I hate control ball and I wouldn't pay $7.50 to see a control-ball team play."

The sight of Clevenger's forearm in Pistol's rib cage would have been fun for the Cadets. To their dismay, Maravich sat out with what was announced as a sprained ankle and a touch of the flu, although the Cadets thought he looked healthy enough. They settled for beating LSU, 75–68, earning another third-place trophy.

At 22–6, the Cadets had broken the school record for wins and had gone to the NIT for the fourth time in five seasons under Knight. Going into his sixth season, there wasn't a cloud on the horizon.

Knight had a veteran team coming back for the 1970–71 season. However, it wouldn't be easy to replace players like Oxley and Gyovai under any circumstances, and with antimilitary feeling running high, Knight couldn't get the same kind of players he once had. It was a problem for the entire institution. Appointments to West Point, which required a recommendation from a U.S. Senator, had once been coveted; now the Academy couldn't find takers for all of them.

"When you're recruiting a young man, you're really also recruiting mom and dad," says Kinney. "Yeah, sure, come to West Point and your education is paid for and you're guaranteed a job for, at that time, four years. The job security is there and no other college or university could guarantee a job for four years but West Point could.

"However, where would that job site be? A foxhole in Vietnam, in a tank, wherever. And mom and dad were very concerned about where their son would wind up following graduation and advanced training. So recruiting was very, very difficult."

Knight's teams hadn't been loaded with superstars before, so if they had slipped dangerously close to the minimums in firepower, no one sensed it beforehand. The Cadets began the season 3–1 and cracked the top 20 rankings, seemingly on track for another good season.

Then the track ended, abruptly. They went down to Madison Square Garden to play St. Bonaventure, the little upstate New York school that was now a power in its own right, and lost by 15. They came home to play Seton Hall and lost by two. They went to the Quaker City Tournament in Philadelphia and lost by 11 to Utah and by three in overtime to Syracuse. They were 3–5 and what remained of their coach's composure disappeared.

"We lose at the Quaker City Tournament in Philadelphia to Syracuse, a good team," says Clevenger, the team captain. "We only have one or two days off because, you know, we have to practice and do all this stuff. So, I'm home. I happened to live in Philadelphia so I was able to go home. I get a telephone call from the assistant coach who says, 'Coach wants you up here right now.'

"Well, I had been home for just a matter of—well, I might have spent one night at home. I don't even know if I did that. He called me and he called the other senior up there, Max Miller, and he wanted us down in his office. So, we go see him down in the office. He calls us in and he says, 'You're both kicked off the team.'

"I said, 'Bob, what the fuck are you doing? You could have told me that on the phone so at least I could have been home with my girlfriend and my parents for a couple of days.'

"And he's screaming and yelling and screaming and yelling. And he goes, 'I'll tell you what, you can be on the second team if you apologize.'

"So, then we both walked up to our rooms and we're talking. And the assistant coach—because he always does this—says, 'Hey, look, if you guys come down and apologize to Coach, he'll let you be on the second team.'

"And I said, 'For what? I busted my ass, I didn't try to lose the goddamn game and I'm not going to do it.'

"And Max says, after we talked about it, 'Look, we'll go down together. I'll apologize, you don't say anything and maybe he'll let us back on the team to play second team.'

"Which he did. You know, Max apologized, we go back, we're on the second team for a couple of practices and then we're back on the first team. I mean, that kind of pressure—he can play head games with people, there's no doubt about it."

Bad times were nothing new and Knight often bounced off the walls, telling players they were off the team, taking them back, and so on. Somehow, they always emerged from it better for the experience, but not this time. The Cadets won three in a row at home, then went back out for a real test at Penn State and were hammered, 65–48.

The hard part was the ride home, all four hours of it, on the same bus with Knight, who wouldn't let them drink their Cokes, or turn the lights out, or sleep.

"He gets in the locker room and yells, 'You've got five minutes to take a shower and get on the bus!'" says Clevenger. "Then he continues to rant and rave for five minutes. He gets done and he says, 'You've got 30 seconds to get on the bus.'

"So, we've got no time to shower. We just throw our uniforms on because we wore uniforms at that time when we traveled, and got on the bus. Now, Knight always sat up at the front of the bus, right in the very front, and everyone else gets on the bus. So, we get on the bus and, you know, we'd always have a Coke when we'd drive back . . . We all get our Cokes and we're sitting there. Knight comes on the bus and goes, 'Give me those Cokes! Give me those Cokes!'

"He runs up and down the aisle, grabbing the Cokes. He says, 'You're not allowed to drink a goddamn Coke.'

"He says, 'I'm keeping the lights on in this bus for the whole goddamn time we're going back here and if I find anybody that falls asleep, I'm going to kick you off the goddamn team!'

"We're all, 'Holy shit!' He sits up front and he has a [partition] right where he's sitting . . . Every stinking five minutes—I think five minutes but it was probably 15 minutes—you'd hear his leg go, Bam!

"He'd get up and walk back and get in somebody's face, either mine or somebody else—Goddamn, if you did this! He was screaming and yelling and then he'd go back and sit down. Fifteen minutes later, he'd get up and do the same thing."

Says Ed Mueller: "Wally Wojdakowski had a broken hand at the time and he couldn't even dress. And Wally and I were sitting there together and Wally leans over to me and says, 'I wonder what he's going to say to me.'

"And I think he yelled at Wally more than he yelled at anybody else, that if he wouldn't have been such a wimp and hadn't broken his hand, he could have been out there and helped us. And he went on and on. And he just yelled and yelled at Wally for 15 minutes, probably, and he didn't even play. Wasn't even dressed. . . .

"I mean, we got back probably two-thirty, three in the morning, something like that. You know, we had to be at class. We had to be at breakfast formation at six o'clock, just like everybody else."

Unlike the rest of Knight's explosions, this one had consequences. The story quickly got back to the Academy brass, which was becoming more and more concerned.

Knight's pressure had always worked. His teams had always exceeded expectations, but this one was going downhill and picking up speed. Knight was so angry, his players were no longer coming out of his ferocious practices feeling empowered in games. Now, they were afraid to make mistakes.

"He put me in but I could never do anything right," says Ed Mueller. "And every time I would try to do something—I remember one game, I think it was the Seton Hall game, we're working for the last shot [of the half]. They get the ball in to me, down on the block, right side, and I faked baseline and came back across the middle with a left-hand hook. . . . The ball kind of slipped off my hand and I shot an air ball. I missed everything. And the guy from Seton Hall gets the rebound, throws it the length of the court at the buzzer and hits the rim.

"And the entire [second] half, Coach Knight was yelling and screaming and yelling at me because I can't even hit the fucking rim from five feet and the guy can hit the rim, you know, the length of the court. I'll never forget that."

As usual, the heat fell on the captain. However, Clevenger wasn't like the dutiful Krzyzewski, who felt Knight's pain and tried to take it upon himself. Clevenger talked back. Somewhere in the six-game losing streak that started at Penn State, he can't remember where, Clevenger was suspended for arguing with Knight during a timeout.

Clevenger had been yelling at a teammate. Knight thought he was yelling at a referee and snarled at him to stop.

"We sat back down on the bench," says Clevenger, "and, I don't know if you've noticed what Knight does, I think he still does it today, he gets down in a catcher's squat in front of the players and talks to them. So, we sit down and he yells, 'Don't yell at the goddamn refs,' he says to me.

"I said, 'I wasn't yelling at the goddamn refs, I was telling Eddie to get back here.'

"He says, 'Don't you tell me what I heard, you don't yell at the refs!'

"Well, I had this damn bottle, a water bottle, and I threw it down on the ground in disgust and the water just sprays out all over Knight. Well, you gotta know what our facility was like. All the officers—we had great teams, so all the officers, everyone loved to go to those games. So we played in the fieldhouse, in this real big open area, and he goes to me, 'Get out! Get out!'

"And the place was just silent and, you know, we've got the generals and the majors there, and I get up and I just walk all the way across the floor, all the way up the outside staircase and I just go in and go up into the damn locker room. And everyone is just like, 'I can't believe that this just occurred, that he's throwing the captain of the team out of this whole thing.' It was unbelievable. . . .

"Then the assistant coach comes up and he says, 'Get down there.'

"And I'm in the shower and I said, 'I'm not going down there, he threw me out.'

"And he says, 'No, you better go.'

"And I said, 'I'm not going down there, he threw me the hell out, the hell with him.'"

Clevenger rejoined the team but the trouble continued. They scored 38 points—total—in a loss at Manhattan. They lost at home to Fairleigh Dickinson, coached by Knight's old assistant, Al LoBalbo, who'd left the season before amid bad feelings.

"He was a wonderful man," says Clevenger. "He was offered the job at Fairleigh Dickinson, a little school in New Jersey. Bob was off on one of those fishing trips. Al was unable to get hold of Bob. He was trying to get hold of him to inform him that he was offered this job. Bob wasn't around, so after some time, Al had to give the guys an answer and he told them he'd take the job.

"Knight comes back, Al tells him. Knight was livid. He cut him off, and they were best of friends. He didn't talk to Al LoBalbo for seven years. . . . Well, in 1971, which really makes the story good, Fairleigh Dickinson went and beat us at Army my senior year. That probably pissed Knight off unbelievably and Al calls it the greatest winning day of his life."

At their low point, the Cadets were 7–13 and the reverberations could be felt throughout the Academy. Now, however, Colonel Murphy and General Jannarone, Knight's two most powerful supporters within the Academy, were gone. The new athletic director was Gus Dielins, whose relationship with Knight had been strained since Knight left a meeting in his office, punched a door, and broke one of his knuckles.

"Apparently things got heated in the AD's office," says Kinney, whose office was nearby. "And Bob came out—and they had Plexiglas dividers then—Bob hit that and startled the secretaries, there were two ladies there, then punched the door and broke a knuckle in his right hand. He then proceeded to leave that office and outside of it, there were a lot of framed pictures. . . . And Bob kind of slammed one of those framed pictures that hit others and broke a number of them. But what he hurt his hand on was the door. And he came into my office and asked me if I'd drive him over to the hospital so he could have an X-ray taken."

Nancy Knight told the *Louisville Courier-Journal's* John Flynn that when she subsequently drove her husband to see a doctor, Knight told him to tape it rather than make him wear a cast.

"The doctor looked at him and said, 'You must be one of the tough son of a bitches,'" Nancy said. "Bob replied, 'The toughest.'"

"And I added, 'The dumbest, too.'"

They won their last four games but finished the 1970–71 season 11–13. Before Knight, this would have been routine for Army. With Knight, it was a disaster.

One losing season after five great ones doesn't normally get a coach in trouble, but this wasn't just any school or just any coach. Knight's behavior had raised eyebrows before, but now the brass was taking action.

"I had to go into the commandant's office as the captain of the team," Clevenger said, "and they wanted me to just rag on Bob and say he's out of control and this and that. Which I did not do, but as far as I'm concerned, they were out to get him."

The commandant was General Sam Walker, one of the most respected men in the military and a close friend of William Westmoreland. And Walker was losing patience with Knight.

"I started out very friendly with Bob," Walker says, "but I didn't approve of some of the things he got in trouble at Indiana for. You know, punching out lockers and stuff like that after the game, when the dean and I walked into a locker room and he was in there, punching out lockers and the Cadets all had their heads down between their knees . . .

"As commandant of cadets, I absolutely didn't like the fact that he manhandled, shook, or grabbed my soldiers. And so while I played golf and went fishing with him and so forth when he first came, I had to tell Bobby that that was not acceptable. And that I would not tolerate that any more."

With all the offers Knight got, it was remarkable that he had stayed six seasons. Now with his old sponsors gone and new bosses who were bearing down on him, he knew it was time to go.

"I left West Point a few months before he did," says General Walker. "I went on a trip with General Westmoreland, around the world to pay his respects before he retired as chief of staff of the army. And the story that I was told when I got back is that the five-man athletic board got tired of some of his antics and the way he operated very visibly in public with the Cadets. And the word I got was that Knight said he would stay at West Point but only if he got a raise. And they said no, we're not giving you a raise.

"That's when he went to work at Indiana. But the guy you should really hear this from is Gus Dielens. Dielens without a doubt would be the guy."

Dielins won't discuss Knight in any detail, saying only, "I don't want to get into a pissing match with Bobby Knight. But we didn't renew his contract after that season. What does that tell you?"

*   *   *

In 1991, Knight's Army players invited him back for a two-night tribute in the West Point Officers Club. Jimmy Oxley, who was by then Dr. James Oxley, says former players showed up who hadn't been back to West Point since they left. So did Knight, who had only been to town a few times in 20 years and hadn't stopped over.

Dick Schaap was the emcee. A lot of Academy brass pointedly skipped it. Kinney wrote a salute in the program, noting Knight had left "with some heavy mixed emotions, with no fanfare and no farewell dinners. He had put Army back on the national basketball map and it was almost like no one really cared."

"Since Bob left" says Kinney, "and I believe that's been 31 seasons, West Point basketball teams have had winning seasons only four times, and three of those were when Mike Krzyzewski was coaching. I would have to say, what Bob did in basketball hasn't been equaled by any coach in any sport at West Point."

Knight was 102–50 in six seasons, by far the best winning percentage in Army history. He was 22 when he arrived, 24 when he became coach, and 30 in the spring of 1971 when he left. If in retrospect it seemed like the Hundred Years' War, he was only warming up.

FOUR

SHERIFF BOB

INDIANA, 1971–72

He didn't win all those games and those championships because of the way that he treated alumni or the way that he treated the press or the way he treated women or even the way he treated his players. . . .

I've never been around anybody that knew the game like him. Now, I was recruited by UCLA and Coach Wooden . . . but I had never been around anybody that knew the game, had studied the game like Coach Knight did, and I never knew anybody that worked that hard.

—John Ritter, IU forward, 1970–73

He looked like he was about 22 years old. He was tall, in good shape. He looked like he came out of some physical training program and very, very young. . . .

They wanted someone to come in and not only clean things up, but also to put down the hammer. And when Knight came in, it was somewhat like one of those Westerns where you hire hire a bad guy to clean up the other outlaws. But then when he cleans it up, you've got to live with him. Knight was a military guy and a hardass and he brought law and order but at what consequence did Indiana get that? The consequence, for years, was constant and total abuse of college kids.

—James Anderson, IU professor of history

And so, Caesar came to Rome.

Later it would be hard to remember there was a time before "Bob Knight" and "Indiana" went together. There was, before he was hired in the spring of 1971, and it wasn't a happy one at IU.

The great Branch McCracken was six seasons gone and the once-great program was in shambles. The preceding season had not only been disappointing, the team had split on racial lines, some players had threatened to reveal the payoffs they were getting unless Coach Lou Watson was fired, and Watson had resigned while this disaster could still be contained.

Any change could only help, but Knight brought a whole new lifestyle. He was well known to college basketball insiders but only slightly recognizable to Indiana fans from his days at Ohio State. While his Army résumé was impressive, there weren't that many Hoosiers fans who followed Eastern ball.

In the Midwest, the East was barely on the map. Eastern ball was a gimmicky, slow-down coach's game, as opposed to Big Ten ball. If Fred Taylor had introduced a defensive ethic to the Big Ten, it hadn't taken over. The conference still loved its old barnburning style, and nowhere more than in Indiana, the hottest hotbed of them all, the home of Mc-Cracken's Hurryin' Hoosiers, who won NCAA titles in 1940 and 1953.

Basketball was an unofficial religion, known as Hoosier Hysteria. Dr. James Naismith himself said he had invented the game in Massachusetts but it had grown up in Indiana.

The biggest building in an Indiana hamlet was often the high-school gym. In Kent Benson and Steve Alford's New Castle, a town of 18,000, the gym held 9,325, making it the largest in any high school in the nation. The next four, according to a 2004 *USA Today* survey, were in the Indiana towns of Anderson, East Chicago, Seymour, and Richmond. The state tournament was so big, John Wooden, the star of Martinsville's 1927 champions, later said, "For a high-school player, winning the Indiana state championship was far more meaningful than winning the NCAA is today or has ever been."

IU's Assembly Hall, seating 16,666, was about to open when Knight arrived, replacing the old fieldhouse, which seated 10,000 and hadn't been filled in recent seasons. With all those extra seats, the fact that they were getting a new coach who kept scores in the 50s was, as IU athletic director Bill Orwig noted, "a concern." Local fans were used to scores in the 50s by halftime.

The good old days of Branch McCracken were over. If anyone needed new blood, IU did. Luckily, there was some available.

* * *

The IU selection committee, chaired by Orwig, fastened quickly on Knight, who was hired in April 1971. Knight was not only well suited to deal with their situation, he wasn't hitting them with a bunch of demands. He accepted Orwig's first offer, $20,000 a year, and started working without a contract or any agreement as to how many years he would get.

So, Knight got the job, which would become a throne. It was not only a Big Ten job but recruiting heaven. That first season, Knight wrote, he watched two of his holdovers, 6-8, 250-pound Steve Downing and 6-8, 225-pound Joby Wright, climbing all over the backboards and told assistant coach Dave Bliss, "This is the first time I ever had two like that on *my* side."

Nevertheless, many of Knight's friends worried. He had enough problems at Army, where press coverage was light, and expectations minimal. Here, the entire state would hang on his every move, and expectations were out of sight.

"I told him the situation at Indiana would be different from his experience at West Point," said Dick Otte, his old confidant from the *Columbus Dispatch*. "Things that would go unnoticed at the Academy would be controversial in a small basketball town like Bloomington. I told him that because he was controversial, not everybody would be with him. I warned him that people were going to take sides."

As Knight wrote in a story for the *New York Times*: "My move from West Point to Indiana was not particularly endorsed by most people from whom I sought advice. Only Clair Bee was excited about the change. . . . Many people envisioned all kinds of problems in adjusting from the regimented life style of the cadets to the free-spirit approach to life on a campus such as Indiana."

One day, Knight asked sophomore guard Dave Shepherd which barracks he lived in before he caught himself. Nevertheless, IU would have to adjust to Knight more than Knight was going to adjust to IU.

"So, you know, he just had that military mentality because that's where he'd come from," says Shepherd. "And that was back in the early seventies and, I mean, Indiana was a liberal school. I mean, there were a lot of kids, lots of hippies, lots of long hair. . . .

"I mean, that was the one thing that kind of irritated him. You know, guys had longer hair, you know, you dressed a little different. It was different. And, it was the first time he'd really been exposed to it, I'm sure, since he'd been at Ohio State, because he'd been at West Point for so long."

The dress codes were never an issue. Knight didn't have issues. It was a simple world now.

"I love long hair and beards and mustaches," said Knight. "Yes, sir, if you want to look like you want to look, dress like you want to dress, act like you want to act, play like you want to play, shoot like you want to shoot, do your own thing, I say, great. But you're sure as hell not coming to Indiana to play basketball. At Indiana, we're going to do my thing."

In his autobiography, Knight says Orwig told him that they had "a little problem." Actually, it was a little worse than that. The Hoosiers, a preseason Big Ten favorite the year before with stars like George McGinnis and Downing, had gone 17–7, missed the NCAA Tournament, and had turned down an NIT bid, rather than prolong what had become a nightmare.

College teams all over the nation were facing the stirrings and implications of the rising black consciousness in the wake of the civil rights movement. Near the end of the 1970–71 season, the Hoosiers' black players enlisted the counsel of a faculty adviser named John Brown and threatened to boycott the second-to-last game at Ohio State. The team, 17–5 to that point, lost at Columbus.

John Ritter, a white guard, supported his coach, Watson, angering the black players, but race was only one of the team's problems. When they were freshmen, Downing and McGinnis hadn't been eligible, so they spent the year playing intramural ball. Even without them, the freshman team beat the varsity and the joke was that the varsity was the third-best team on campus behind the freshmen and McGinnis and Downing's intramural team. When Downing and McGinnis moved up, holdovers like Joby Wright and Ed Daniels had to move over and they didn't like it. Still, when Wright, Daniels, and more unhappy black teammates then decided to base their protest on racial grounds, claiming they were being discriminated against by Watson, their white coach, Downing and McGinnis went along with them in the name of solidarity.

"Well, the bad thing was that [a corporation] had Joby Wright and Daniels on their payroll and they really weren't working there," says Dave Shepherd. "So these guys saved their pay stubs and went to the coach and said, 'Hey, listen, if you don't resign, we're turning you in.'"

The players were then granted an audience with the IU president, Dr. John Ryan, to demand Watson be fired. Watson resigned that night, leaving behind an out-of-control program. Prominent players had gotten cars as well as no-work jobs. Shepherd says McGinnis had a Cadillac, that Downing and Bootsie White had cars, and so did he.

"I had a Camaro," says Shepherd. "My dad was a coach, a high-school basketball coach. [It was from] you know, just a couple of doctors from Bloomington, that was just part of the deal."

The doctors were Bill and Jim Howard, two brothers widely known as the program's biggest boosters, who befriended the players and hung out at the practices with other assorted friends of the program. That was about to change. As soon as Knight arrived, he announced that all practices would be closed to outsiders. As Frank Wilson, then a senior guard, noted, there were "major hurt feelings" around town.

Knight had been brought up in a more innocent time. Fred Taylor had been a straight-up guy who hadn't cheated to get Jerry Lucas and John Havlicek. Knight had been a good student, as were many of his teammates, notably Lucas. The last thing in the world he needed was a bunch of townspeople hanging out in his gym, spoiling his players, patting him on the back, and telling him what they thought.

Knight spent several months figuring out who was taking care of whom. Then he went to see Orwig with a list of people who would no longer be granted access to the Indiana basketball program, starting with the Howard brothers. "I know you hired me as the sheriff to kinda come in and clean up the town," Knight told Orwig. "Have I missed anybody?"

In his book, Knight wrote that everyone in the room "kinda chuck-led, looked at each other and said, 'No, you've made a pretty good sweep.'"

The arrival of a man on a white horse was welcomed throughout the state, which was more rural in outlook than its neighbors, Illinois and Ohio, and wouldn't stand for a racially torn, out-of-control pro-gram at IU.

The southern half of Indiana, which included Bloomington, was similar in outlook to the border states of the Confederacy. Racial poli-tics were an ongoing subplot in Hoosier Hysteria, which romanticized the exploits of all-white, small-town high school teams, the most fa-mous being Milan, which captured the 1954 state title, and inspired the movie *Hoosiers*. Bruce Newman, then at *Sports Illustrated*, later noted there had been no blacks on the team or even in the stands in Milan, quoting a local resident who said, "They don't come and they wouldn't be welcome if they did."

The big, predominantly black inner-city schools didn't dominate Indiana high school basketball as they did in other states, and the sys-tem was set up to keep it that way. No Indianapolis school ever won the state title until Oscar Robertson's Crispus Attucks in 1955 and 1956. In his 1985 article, Newman noted that the last four state-championship teams hadn't had a single black starter. In the first 58 years that the *Indianapolis Star* selected Mr. Basketball, through 1998, only nine were from Indianapolis. The smaller districts frequently con-solidated so that their high schools were just as big as those in the cities.

"I'll put it this way," says Gene Cato, once commissioner of the In-diana High School Athletic Association, "Kokomo had two high schools, which weren't very successful. Now they're back to one."

Knight had barely arrived when George McGinnis announced he would turn pro, signing with the Indiana Pacers. The hard-driving Knight wasn't the easygoing McGinnis' kind of coach, but McGinnis had a more compelling reason: The Pacers offered him a big contract, his father had just died in a construction accident, and his family needed the money.

The cast grew even thinner that summer when Shepherd, a sharp-shooting little Mr. Basketball, was injured in a car accident outside Bloomington. Shepherd, a sophomore, had been the first holdover Knight had called because he said they would be together the longest. Now Shepherd was surprised to see Knight at his bedside.

"What was amazing," says Shepherd, "he had left that night to go down to recruit Robert Parish in Louisiana, and he was in Louisiana and got the phone call that I was in a real bad car accident. I had several broken ribs, a broken jaw in three places, had over a hundred stitches in my head, broken ankle. . . . And the next morning, he was there by noon. . . . He left Louisiana to come back. So, you know the guy's got feelings, you know. I mean, it's amazing. But then he just does things that, you know, it's just—nobody can figure the guy out."

In preseason drills, Knight put his new players through his survival course, which had fit with the program at West Point but was an eye-opener in Bloomington. When practice started, the players were introduced to Knight's suicide drills, diving on each other for loose balls, then getting up and trying to score before their teammates could tackle them. They learned to take charges in another drill in which, as Ritter noted, there could be "some pretty serious collisions," with 250 pounds of Steve Downing bearing down on a teammate. Until then, they had played for coaches who were delighted to see them dive on the floor. Knight not only expected it, he made them practice it, as if it was a skill they had to acquire. What other coaches hoped for, Knight demanded as a condition of participation.

The Hoosiers were no longer playing basketball, they were working at it. It was like a college course; they were required to take notes on what he told them, in special notebooks.

"We used to kind of jack around a lot, shoot hook shots, just joke around a lot, BSing," says guard Frank Wilson. "And I remember one time very early, he walked across the out-of-bounds line and he said, 'Come here.'

"He brought us over. He said, 'You see what it says on this line?'

"I go, 'No.'

"He goes, 'Thou shalt not shoot any shot that you wouldn't shoot in a game.'

"It was like he was mad at us because we were out there jacking around, shooting half-court shots, stuff like that. The big impression I got was this intense seriousness about basketball and about himself. There was not any joking around. Most of us just kind of looked at each other and just tried not to laugh."

They learned that Knight often got mad—at players, press people, boosters, anyone who crossed his path. One day as they practiced in the soon-to-open Assembly Hall, the construction crew working on the ceiling dropped a nut, which fell onto the floor below.

"Knight yelled at the guy and told him to come down, and he was really popping his cork," says Wilson. "This foreman comes up and he's this big construction guy with a hard hat on. Knight's screaming at the guy, cussing him out, and one of the assistant coaches had to come and break them up and I'd swear in another 30 seconds there would have been an all-out brawl on that floor. And that was like the second week of practice or something like that. . . .

"The thing with throwing the chair across the floor? He threw some chairs in the locker room that were just over our heads or smashed them up against the wall. He'd throw chairs."

Then, there was the press. At Army, coverage had been sporadic, but now that he would have press people coming around every day, Knight wanted to make sure everyone knew his place. Knight insisted he didn't care what people wrote, but he cared a lot, whether it was in a national magazine or the local sheet with a circulation of 15,000. At his first IU game, John Flynn of the *Louisville Courier-Journal*, who went way back with Knight, described a scene in which he jumped J. D. Lewis of the *Bloomington Courier-Tribune*. Lewis had written a column, joking about Knight's temper ("Warning to those attending the Ball State–Indiana basketball game tonight in Assembly Hall. Beware of coach. May be dangerous. Has been known to erupt on moment's notice. If so, every man for himself.") It seemed harmless but not to Knight.

"J. D. Lewis proved to be every man that night," wrote Flynn.

"Bobby Knight tongue-lashed him for several minutes after the game while Lewis sat in silence. It was vintage Knight from the old days at West Point and there was no apology forthcoming.

"Knight in fact still has the column stuffed away in his desk. 'It was filled with untruths. . . . I don't need a pseudo–Jim Murray writing about me,' snapped Knight. 'And Howard Cosell's a friend of mine but one of him is enough. No writer is going to make me look like an ass before 60,000 or three million readers and then expect me to take him over in the corner somewhere and say, 'Uh, gee, I wish you hadn't written that.'"

Nor would a respectful posture keep a reporter out of trouble. Knight considered even their questions an affront. Russ Brown, a former IU grad who covered the Hoosiers for the *Louisville Courier-Journal*, got the bad news in their first conversation, after his colleague, Flynn, got Knight on the phone for him, thinking he was doing Brown a favor.

"The first question I asked him was about McGinnis," says Brown, "because it was a legitimate question, there were a lot of rumbling or rumors that he was going to turn pro. I just said, 'What about George McGinnis? You plan to talk to him or what do you think about this?'

"He said, 'That's the dumbest fucking question I've ever heard. I'm not going to answer that.' . . . So I knew right then it wasn't going to be a lot of fun dealing with this guy."

With McGinnis gone and Shepherd out, expectations were modest in the 1971–72 season. So it was a pleasant surprise when they started 8–1, including a double-overtime win at Kentucky with Downing getting 47 points and 25 rebounds.

Knight's style was jarring, though. The team that had averaged 89 points the season before was down to 77. The Hoosiers were no longer hurryin' and the fans weren't fallin' over themselves to go see them. The crowds for the first three games in the new building were 14,853, 13,897, and, even after they started 2–0, just 11,736 for the game against No. 14–ranked Kansas.

This wasn't the game Hoosier fans knew and loved. This was Eastern coaches' ball. One night when the Hoosiers were running their delay game with a 50–48 lead, a fan yelled, "We want 100!" Even Knight enjoyed that.

"Delay game" was a euphemism for what Hoosiers fans called "stalling," and it wasn't something that had ever occurred to Branch McCracken. Nevertheless, as at Army, Knight's team was winning games it wasn't supposed to have a chance in, like the one against Kansas. IU won that one, 59–56, as Ritter kept drawing charging fouls on All-American Bud Stallworth, who fouled out.

"They had a player named Stallworth that I think was averaging about 30," says Ritter. "I wasn't guarding him. I couldn't guard anybody. Despite his [Knight's] best efforts, I couldn't guard anybody but I was a pretty smart player, so I'm not going to guard Stallworth but I knew where he was supposed to be, because we had better scouting. . . . So, I knew that Joby Wright was guarding Stallworth and I knew Joby was going to overplay him, and I knew Stallworth was going to back-cut to the basket, and I knew the Kansas guard was going to pass it to Stallworth and he was going to shoot a layup—except that because I knew all that, I just got over in his lane and he charged me four times. . . .

"Our scouting reports were so good—and this was a tribute not only to him [Knight] but to the assistant coaches—there were times in the second half of games and my opponent was getting tired that I almost wanted to grab him by the jersey [and say], 'Wait, you're supposed to be cutting this way, buddy.' . . . He [Knight] knew the game better than anybody and he worked harder at it than anybody. Now, he expected us to work very hard, too. And I always felt like in practices, the games were so much easier than practices, and that was never the case before I played for him. But there was so much intensity and so much structure to the practices that it was a relief to be able to go out there and play against an opponent and play in a game."

At 4–0, they flew to Athens to play Ohio University and lost. Ritter found out there were myriad things that could upset Knight, including some he wouldn't have expected.

"We went over there and got beat and I didn't take very many shots," Ritter says. "When we get back to Assembly Hall, he tells everybody to go home and says he wants to see me up in his office. We go up in his office, and he closes the door, and he opens the mail, and I'm waiting to see what he's going to do. And he eventually says, 'John, do you think they hired me to win basketball games here? Is that why they hired me?'

"I said, 'Yes, sir.'"

"And he said, 'Well, tell me this'—and in his language, you know, not, 'How am I going to win basketball games if my best shooter won't shoot the ball?' It was, 'How am I going to win any goddamn fucking basketball games, my best goddamn fucker won't shoot the goddamn fucking ball?'

"I say, 'Actually, Coach, I don't know.'

"He's pretty good on theatrics. Before he had done all this, now, he'd sent everybody else home. It's maybe 12:30 or one o'clock in the morning. So, there's nobody in Assembly Hall except him and me, and yet he closes the door. There's nobody in there, so he had my full attention.

"And, anyway, he said, 'Well, I'll tell you this, we play Notre Dame in a couple days and if you don't take at least 15 shots, and I don't care if they're from half court or if they're hook shots or whatever, if you don't take at least 15 shots, you'll never play another minute here as long as I'm coaching, and I'll guarantee you I'm going to be coaching longer than you're going to be playing.'

"He says, 'Do you understand?'

"I said, 'Yes, sir.'

The next game was a 94–29 massacre of Notre Dame in Digger Phelps' first game against IU. Ritter had 31 points, outscoring the entire Irish team.

"I didn't play the last 11 minutes," he says. "But when I came out of the game with 11 minutes to go . . . I went down to the end of the bench to the statistician.

"I said, 'How many shots did I take?'

"And he said, 'Seventeen,' and I said, okay.'

"Because if he had told me 14, I was going to ask Knight to put me back in. That's how much I believed Knight when he told me I had to take 15 shots. I actually went down and checked on it."

*   *   *

Not all the holdovers were thriving in the new program. Shepherd, recovering from his accident, wasn't ready when the season opened. He was a deadeye shooter and Knight had high hopes for him, but when he returned to practice in December, he was frail and tentative.

On Christmas day, it all came to a head.

"I weighed about 130," Shepherd says. "I'm 155–160 normally, so I had lost all this weight because I couldn't eat any solid foods and my mouth was still wired shut. I'd gotten the hell beaten out of me at practice, you know. My mouth was bleeding, I was playing bad, he was all over me. We were shooting free throws at the side basket and John Ritter, who was my roommate at the time, I was throwing a ball back to him and I was all pissed off. He led the Big Ten in free-throw shooting so all I had to do was just stand there and grab them out of the net and just send them back to him.

"After about the third shot, it came through the basket and I threw it behind the back to him and he was spotting up again, looking down at the ground. . . . He wasn't expecting the ball to come back. So, I threw the ball back behind my back and it flew over his head and it went right to Knight.

"Knight stood on the ball, you know. He just says, 'Get the hell out of here, Shepherd.'

"I decided I was leaving school. I said, 'I'm out of here.' So, I got all my stuff packed in my gym bag and, you know, I got my coat on and I'm ready to walk out and [assistant coach] Dave Bliss is waiting on me, right outside the locker-room door.

"And he said, 'What are you doing?'

"And I said, 'I'm out of here.' I said, 'I'm going 'cause I can't take this stuff.' I said, you know, 'The guy's crazy. . . .'

"So, the next thing, Bliss has got me in the locker room, throwing me around. He just grabbed me. He wasn't hitting me or anything. He just grabbed me because, like I said, I only weighed about 130. I mean, I was like a woman. I wasn't going to do anything. I couldn't go anywhere. What he was doing was just trying to get control of me. . . . It was like good cop, bad cop.

"You know Knight. I knew it was a setup. I didn't know it at the time, but, you know, that's the deal. Knight throws you out of practice and then the assistants go down and wind you back in."

Bliss made Shepherd promise he would go to Knight's home that night with the rest of the team for the annual get-together at which Nancy made her famous Sloppy Joes. Instead, Shepherd went to the home of Bill Howard, his old benefactor, and told him he was leaving. Howard called Knight, who told him in no uncertain terms to make sure Shepherd came over.

"So, I go over to his house," says Shepherd, "and when I got over there, everybody else was leaving. He's got like a trilevel and his mother answers the door. I go in and all the lights are off in the midlevel, where you walk in. . . . I'm sitting in there for like a half hour by myself and I'm thinking, 'What the hell is going on?' And I turn, I can look and I can see Knight in the reflection. He's down there just watching television. And I'm starting to wonder if he even knows I'm here. . . .

"So, he comes up in the living room and he just goes off. I mean, he's going nuts. Telling me, 'You're not worth a shit,' and, 'You're not playing against'—his favorite story was, 'You're not playing against Herbie Smutz from Elwood City.' He said, 'You're playing against guys like Allen Hornyak from Ohio State and they're going to kick your ass.' He's going on and on. And, 'How can you do this to the program?' This sort of thing. Well, what was amazing is, I'm talking to him for about a half hour and within 40 minutes, he's got me pumped up so high about playing. 'Okay, buddy, now we need you. We're getting ready to play Brigham Young and they play a zone and you're our best outside shooter.'

"And, I mean, it was unbelievable. And I was on the airplane the next day going down to Norfolk, Virginia, to the Old Dominion Classic, and I did play and I played okay. But he just has that knack, you know. When you're 18, you're not 50 or you're not 40."

On December 29, Shepherd made his debut, coming off the bench to score eight points against an Old Dominion zone, helping the Hoosiers to an 88–86 victory and the Classic title.

IU was 8–1, ranked No. 5 in the nation and about to fall off its merry-go-round. The Hoosiers lost the Big Ten opener at Minnesota, coached by Bill Musselman, an old Knight rival from their Ohio school-boy days. Knight didn't shake Musselman's hand, chased the referees to their dressing room, then went after his own players.

"Jerry Memering's in the locker room getting undressed," Shepherd says. "He doesn't play, and Knight comes in throwing shit and going crazy, just going crazy. And he kicks this bench. And all these Cokes start falling off the bench. There must have been 25 Cokes. You know, they got ice in them. He [Memering] starts picking them up and putting the lids back on them, like a good guy, see. And Knight looks over at him and sees he's picking these Cokes up and he runs over to him and he grabs him by his warmups and throws him up against a locker and he goes, 'Memering, you can't be a pussy, you've got to be a wild man!'

"And I mean to tell you, there wasn't a word said the whole way home. We get on the bus after the game. You know, the bus driver, hell, he doesn't know anything, he's talking to everybody. . . . We've got nine guys and they're all in the back of this big, long bus and Knight sits right behind the bus driver, right behind him. And we look up and we know what's going to happen because Knight's going to go crazy. And about every 30 seconds all the way out to the airport, 'God damn it! Mother-fucking sonofa . . . '

"And the bus driver would jump. I mean, he couldn't hardly drive the bus because he thought Knight was going crazy. He did it all the way home in the airplane. We had our own Learjet. I couldn't believe him."

They lost their next three, running the losing streak to five games and dropping them into the Big Ten cellar at 0–4. After practice one day, Knight confided to Bob Hammel, the sports editor of the *Blooming-ton Herald-Telephone*, that he didn't know if he was good enough to coach in this conference.

However, as Knight's Army teams had, his first IU squad closed fast as it got his system down, winning nine of its last 10 to finish 17–7, 9–5 in the conference. The Hoosiers accepted an NIT invitation, their first postseason appearance in six seasons. They didn't stay long, though, los-ing in the first round to a loaded Princeton team led by NBA-bound guard Brian Taylor, which pressed them full court.

"After we lose to Princeton, in the dressing room, there's no ranting and raving, there's no kicking things or anything else along those lines," says Ritter. "Coach Knight comes in, he says, 'Guys,' he says, 'it's been a good season. The trainer will give you money to get something to eat tonight and the bus leaves for the airport tomorrow morning at eight-thirty.' And that was it.

"On the plane on the way back, he called me up to the front of the plane. He said, 'We really had trouble getting the ball up the floor . . . but right now we're talking to two guards from Illinois and if we can get them to come, I promise you, we'll be able to get the ball up the floor next year.'

"And I didn't even know who it was. It turned out to be Jimmy Crews and Quinn Buckner."

Knight's run had just begun, but Shepherd wouldn't be around for it. The little Mr. Basketball, whom Knight had called first because they would be together the longest, whose bedside he had rushed to, had decided to transfer. Shepherd then made the mistake of telling a Bloomington writer during the NIT, who wrote it before Shepherd could tell Knight. After they got home, Shepherd called Knight, who no longer felt like talking about it, or anything.

"I said, 'Hey, Coach,'" says Shepherd. "I said, 'This is Dave Shepherd.'

"And he goes, 'Yeah.'

"'No,' I said, 'This is Dave.' And he goes, 'Yeah.' Like that. He goes, 'Yeah.'

"He'd already obviously seen the newspaper, okay? And so I said, 'I need to come by and talk to you.'

"He said, 'Shepherd, I'm leaving in 15 minutes.' And hung the phone up.

"So, I'm going, 'Oh, fuck.' So, I get in the car, go over to his office and I walk in his office and he's got his feet up on the desk, with his legs crossed, okay? I walk in, sit down in front of him, say, 'Listen, I'm transferring.' I said, 'I know you know about it.' I said, 'I'm sorry that it happened the way it did, because I didn't know they were going to write an article.'

"He didn't say kiss my ass. He didn't say screw you. He didn't say good luck. He didn't say squat. He just sat there and I got up and left. He never got up, didn't say a word. And I was there for about five minutes and I was gone."

Shepherd was Knight's first transfer at IU, but the drill would always be the same. You were either with Knight, which meant he'd be all over you for four years and then would keep you in his heart forever. Or you were nothing.

FIVE

GLORY DAYS

*"Take a good look at these kids because you're never going to
see the likes of them again."*

—Bob Knight on Senior Day, 1976,
Knight: My Story

At 32, Knight was on the threshold, a highly regarded young coach
at a major program who was known for exceeding expectations.
Nevertheless, the only thing he had ever actually won was the
Old Dominion Classic the season before. He hadn't even been to the
NCAA Tournament.

Arriving at IU in the spring of 1971, he had barely had a chance to
recruit before his first season. He and assistants Dave Bliss and Bob
Weltlich had made a desperate sweep of the state but everyone was spoken for. Pete Trgovich of East Chicago Washington was going to
UCLA, and his teammate, Junior Bridgeman, was headed for Louisville.
Mike Flynn of Jeffersonville, who was Mr. Basketball, was going to Kentucky. The IU coaches couldn't even get them to visit.

Now, however, in the fall of 1972, they were bringing in a highly
rated class, with Quinn Buckner, Scott May, Bobby Wilkerson, Tom
Abernethy, John Laskowski, and Jimmy Crews. They weren't the
hottest prospects in the nation; UCLA landed Richard Washington
that year, and Notre Dame got Adrian Dantley. Robert Parish, whom
Knight had recruited, stayed at home in Louisiana at little Centenary.
However, the IU recruits were Knight's kind of players.

Knight once said, "I never got over Army." Now he had players who were just as tough and dedicated as his Cadets, but bigger and more talented.

Even with Steve Downing and John Ritter back in the fall of 1972, little was expected of Knight's second IU team, which would include freshmen for the first time under new NCAA eligibility rules. May and Wilkerson hadn't made a qualifying test score and were sitting out the season. Buckner was playing football and would need time to make the transition. IU wasn't even ranked in the preseason AP poll.

This was college basketball's age of giants, and IU wasn't one of them. UCLA was in mid-dynasty, with Wooden having just won the eighth of his 10 titles, going 30–0 while starting three sophomores, Bill Walton, Keith Wilkes, and Greg Lee. David Thompson was at North Carolina State alongside 7-4 Tom Burleson. In the Midwest, Al McGuire had a powerhouse at Marquette with Maurice Lucas and Bo Ellis. The Big Ten favorite was Minnesota, coached by Knight's archrival, Bill Musselman, with Jim Brewer, Ron Behagen, and Dave Winfield.

Nevertheless, with Knight's precocious new group, nothing went quite the way he thought it would; it always went better. Buckner started every game that season, which was a distinct surprise to Knight. The opener was only a week away when the football season ended, and Buckner hadn't even practiced with the basketball team. For his part, Buckner intended to ease into it, too. He was all set to go home after his last football game against Purdue before Downing and Ritter, Knight's co-captains, came to see him.

"Steve Downing and I are waiting for him when he comes out of the dressing room to tell him that basketball practice is at two o'clock the next day and he's got to get rid of that mustache first," says Ritter. " I mean, that was part of our job. That was fine for football, but, okay, Quinn, basketball starts now."

The Hoosiers held their public scrimmage the next night. Knight had Buckner sit on the bench next to one of his assistants to point out what they were running. Then Knight let Quinn play with the second unit. When that went all right, Knight let him play with the first unit.

Not long after that, Buckner put the ball under his arm and began telling everyone where they were supposed to be.

Knight was so thrown, he called his guru, Clair Bee, in upstate New York to ask about starting a player who hadn't been with them ahead of the others who'd been working for six weeks. Bee told him his first obligation was to field his best team. Buckner then started the opener against Harvard, and two seconds into it, he stole the ball.

A remarkable young man, Buckner had been Knight's first national recruit but it wasn't easy. Buckner's father had been an IU football player and wanted him to go to Bloomington, but Quinn wanted to go to UCLA, "so bad he could taste it," says his brother, Loren. On the last day, July 31, Quinn had chosen IU.

Indiana guard Billy Cunningham would call Buckner "the Bo Jackson of my era," but Quinn's athleticism was merely the start. "He was the closest thing to Coach Knight on the floor," says another teammate, Mark Haymore. "If you were out past curfew, you'd rather have Coach catch you than Quinn."

Knight appreciated nothing more than a player who kicked everyone's asses the way he would have if he'd been there. He doted on Buckner so openly, the other players joked Quinn was his illegitimate son.

Buckner was the embodiment of Knight's peculiar vision of a player, an ass-kicker who exuded leadership. At 6-2, 205, Buckner was a barrel-chested point guard who played safety on the football team and had been All–Big Ten as a freshman. He had been a big scorer at Thornridge High School, leading his team to two state titles by overpowering opponents and shooting turnaround jump shots over them. However, Knight's players didn't take turnaround jump shots and Buckner wasn't going to be allowed to take many shots of any kind.

Buckner's admiration for Knight would border on worship, but for the four years he was at IU, their relationship wasn't as easy as people thought.

"He was never content with that role of not shooting the basketball," says Loren Buckner. "Any time you deal with Bobby Knight, it's like riding a roller coaster. It's just up and down. And they had their, and I'm not trying to be politically correct, but they just had their times when Quinn didn't care for him very much. . . . My dad didn't like it. He didn't sugarcoat it. He didn't like it [Knight's treatment of his son] at all. Many times Dad wanted to get in his car and go out and punch his lights out."

The Hoosiers went 19–5 and 11–3 in the Big Ten in Buckner's freshman year and were ranked No. 6 in the nation. Going into the last game, they were tied for first place with Minnesota, which then fell to 1–12 Northwestern, making the Hoosiers Big Ten champions.

In those days, only the conference champion was invited to the NCAA tournament. On March 15, 1973, Knight and his players made their tournament debut, upsetting favored Marquette as Downing outscored Maurice Lucas, 29–12.

Two days later, the Hoosiers beat Kentucky to advance to the Final Four to meet UCLA—unbeaten, ranked No. 1, and trying to win its seventh title in a row—in the Checkerdome in St. Louis.

"I was first man off the bench," says John Laskowski, "and here I am two years from being a thin little kid. And, back then, watching UCLA come in and wax Notre Dame and win 88 straight games. . . .

"So, we're playing UCLA in St. Louis, and I'm thinking, 'Whoa, what are you doing? I mean, sheesh, why are you in this game?' Because there's Walton and Keith Wilkes and David Meyers and John Wooden and all those guys. At least, I didn't picture us as being able to get there that quickly. Because just two years ago I'm in my home, in high school, watching them win it all."

UCLA was the giant Knight most wanted to slay. It was only nine years since he had been thinking of working as a graduate assistant under John Wooden, but a lot had happened since. When Knight was up for the IU job, a friend had asked Wooden to put in a good word. Wooden was a native Hoosier, and even though he had attended Purdue, his word carried weight back home. When Wooden took the call, the *Long Beach Press-Telegraph*'s Loel Schrader was in his office. Wooden told Knight's friend, "No, I said I can't do that and I won't. Besides, I've already recommended someone else for the job—Jerry Tarkanian of Long Beach State."

Knight regarded Wooden as a hypocrite who turned his head and let the notorious Bruin booster Sam Gilbert shower his players with gifts. Privately, Knight called Wooden "Johnny boy." The relationship would only get worse when Wooden made an allusion to Knight's temper, saying he was "a wonderful coach but I wouldn't want my son playing for him." One of Knight's closest friends says Knight "went right up through the ceiling" when he heard that. In all Knight's years at IU, neither he nor any of his players would ever attend the Wooden Award banquet, including 1993, when IU's Calbert Cheaney won.

Knight had no use for Walton, either, saying his refusal to play in the '72 Olympics "left a sour taste in my mouth." Walton disliked Knight back, calling him "the death of hope."

Now, however, Knight maintained a discreet silence, going into the Final Four against a UCLA team that was on a 73-game winning streak dating back to January of 1971, when Knight was still at Army.

The Hoosiers went right after the Bruins, taking an early 18–13 lead. However, Knight liked to sag off one player, challenging him to make shots, and the Bruin he selected, point guard Tommy Curtis, caught fire. UCLA went on one of its patented runs, and the next thing the Hoosiers knew they were behind by 22. Few opponents withstood those rampages, but Knight's teams were nothing if not tough-minded. The Hoosiers roared back in the second half, drawing within 54–51 when Walton, whom Wooden had hurried back into the game with four fouls, drove to the basket and crashed into Downing.

Walton got the call. Downing got his fourth foul and his fifth followed moments later. UCLA escaped with a 70–59 win and went on to steamroll Memphis State for the title, as Walton made 21 of 22 shots.

Knight fumed it was "one of the two worst big calls my teams have ever had," along with the one against Jimmy Oxley in the last second of the St. John's game in the 1970 NIT.

"I'm prejudiced," says John Ritter. "I was on the floor when the play happened, I was sure that it was going to be called on Walton and then I couldn't believe it when it happened the other way. But there were times when I was in high school that there were some calls that probably went my way. I was kind of a star back in high school. I think you see that in basketball at every level, and Bill was certainly a star."

Nevertheless, there was no doubt the Hoosiers were on their way. As Knight told two Orrville friends on the way out of the Checkerdome, "We weren't good enough to win it, but we'll be back with a team that *will* win it, soon."

They were a recognized power now. In the fall of 1973, the Hoosiers went into the season ranked No. 3, behind UCLA with Walton and North Carolina State with David Thompson.

This was a compliment indeed, because Downing and Ritter were gone and Knight would have three new starters. Downing's place was taken by freshman Kent Benson, a 6-10 high school All-American from New Castle. May, who was now eligible, was the scorer the group needed. Wilkerson was the defender Knight had waited all his life for, a 6-7 superathlete who jumped center and guarded anyone from a 6-10 center like Minnesota's Mychal Thompson to a greyhound guard like Michigan's Ricky Green.

"If you go back to look at the years when Indiana really turned it around, Wilkerson was the starter," says teammate Wayne Radford, who would arrive a year later. "I mean, people can say all they want about Quinn, they can say all they want about Scott May, Kent Benson, but until we put Bobby Wilkerson into the starting lineup . . .

"Now we had the presence of a 6-7 guard who was terrific defensively, a heck of a passer. And when you talk about fast break, if you go back and look at some of our teams, when we got a rebound, Bobby would take that ball up that middle and just blow by anybody, and he could lay it in or dish it off. And teams didn't know how to defend that."

Knight's teams always acted as units, but even for a Knight team, this group had remarkable cohesion. They bought into Knight's program but they were strong-willed and not afraid to improvise.

"I'll never forget the story about them running a play against Michigan," says Loren Buckner. "Bob Knight ran the play with Benny—Benson was supposed to go over and pick for Scott and Scott was supposed to come off the pick. So then they walked out onto the court and Quinn huddled them together and said, 'Benny, forget that play, here's what we're going to do. I'm going to set the pick. You go over there and do something else.'

"And so Quinn comes across and sets a pick, I think it was on Wayman Britt. Wayman was guarding Scott and Quinn almost threw a crossbody block on him and just nailed him. Scott gets open and hits the shot.

"And as they're going off the court, you know, Coach Knight is trying to catch up to him to yell at him. . . . And they just ran into the locker room. And he comes in there and picks up a garbage can and throws it all over the place. And he's ranting and raving, as usual, and they're just looking at him like, we got it done."

The IU starters differed in their attitudes toward Knight. Buckner and May were archloyalists. Benson was fearful. Wilkerson was the one who glared back.

"Bobby did things very defiant in his own way," says Loren Buckner. "Like Bobby had this big Afro that he always wanted to wear. So, Coach Knight was always on him about how you should be, what your appearance should be. And Bobby would put a bunch of water on his hair and then pat it down real tight, to make it look smaller.

"And I mean, Bobby was never one to outwardly or openly just defy you. He just would look at you and did what he wanted to do, or did what he thought he had to do. He just wouldn't say anything back, and that would just infuriate Bobby Knight.

"Scott and Bobby and Quinn, they all dealt with him different. Scott would just tune him out and go do what he was doing. When he made a mistake . . . he [May] would run down the other side of the court from where Coach Knight was. He didn't listen to all that stuff. They all did it. You know, they all said, 'Man, we make a mistake, I'm just going to the other side of the court.' He'd be yelling all the way across the court."

Nevertheless, they were a marvel to Knight. "It's a very interesting group to watch, even to me," he said. "Our whole operation is totally collective. There's no fiery individual getting the rest of the guys fired up. It's more like a board with everyone having an equal say. It's the closest I've come to a collective team in my coaching career."

The Hoosiers went 23–5 in the 1973–74 season and tied for the Big 10 title with Michigan, but lost a playoff with the Wolverines, who got the NCAA tournament berth. Knight was obliged by his IU bosses to play in a made-for-television postseason tournament called the Collegiate Commissioners Association tournament, instead of his beloved NIT. The Hoosiers won it, drubbing No. 15–ranked USC by 25 points in the finale in St. Louis. Knight was out for bigger game, though, and his time was coming.

With all five starters back in the fall of 1974, the Hoosiers were again rated No. 3 in the preseason Associated Press Poll. Benson, their plodding, religious hulk, was coming fast. He would never be tough enough for Knight but his progress would be impressive, going from 9.3 points a game as a freshman to 15 this season as a sophomore.

They were 2–0 on December 8, a cold Saturday afternoon in Bloomington, when a crowd of 17,148 jammed into Assembly Hall for the annual border war against Kentucky, an eagerly awaited early-season diversion in both states.

Both programs were state religions, although they had dissimilar approaches, at least since Knight's arrival. The UK program was out of control, and had been since the days of Adolph Rupp, with heavy participation by wealthy boosters, including some of the owners of the famous thoroughbred stables in Lexington. The NCAA even closed down the Kentucky program for one season when Rupp was there. It wasn't hard for Hoosiers to look down their noses at the Wildcats, or for Wildcats to dislike the thorny Knight.

"It was already in the air that we ran a squeaky-clean program," says Steve Green, who hailed from Milan, 10 miles from the Kentucky line. "And there were jokes about the Kentucky players taking pay cuts to go to play in the NBA. There were whispers about the horse farms and debatable summer employment and speaking engagements where players made a thousand bucks."

Knight was 4–0 against UK, but this wasn't one of the rivalries he took personally. He and Kentucky coach Joe B. Hall were good friends; they had even gone on a three-week fishing trip together.

UK started a young team with two freshmen, 6-10 Rick Robey and 6-10 Mike Phillips, and a third, Jack Givens, coming off the bench. They were 2–0, too, but they weren't ready for the Hoosiers, who ran up a 34-point lead. IU won by 24 points with Benson going for 26 and Wilkerson keeping Kentucky star Kevin Grevey from touching the ball for the first four minutes. However, with less than a minute left, Knight was still fully engaged, going all the way down to the Wildcats' bench to rail at the referees for a call against IU.

"The situation was, he was yelling at the officials from in front of my bench, in front of me," Hall says. "And as he turned to go back to the bench, I said, 'Way to go, Bob, give 'em hell.' Good-naturedly, because this was a friend of mine.

"And he turned and broke down, almost like an attack position, and he screamed at me, 'Don't ever talk to me during a game! Why don't you coach your own motherfucking team?'

"And his facial expression was—what do I want to say?—distorted in anger so that I felt moved to do something. So, I followed him up and I said, 'Hey, Bob, I didn't mean anything by that. You know I hope you're not upset by what I said because I didn't mean anything personal to you. You've kicked our butts soundly, you've got a great team.'

"And I turned to walk away and he popped me with an open hand at the back of the neck. Pretty strongly. And I turned in response and he again broke down in attack mode and he said, 'I didn't mean anything by that, either.'"

Knight insisted he meant it as an affectionate pat, like the ones he gave his players as they came off the floor. Of course, with Knight, it could be hard to tell affection from aggression. It didn't look friendly to Hall's assistant, Lynn Nance, a just-retired FBI agent whom Knight later described as "some son-of-a-bitch jerk . . . I don't even know his name."

Nance bounded off the bench and jumped into Knight's face. They stood there snarling at each other until referees and players pulled them away. "I told him, 'Hey, try that shit with me, pal! Try that on me, you son of a bitch,'" says Nance. "There was always an intimidation factor with Knight. Knight picked that up at West Point. And I think what he discovered is what the military teaches—that you can intimidate and control a lot of people by overreacting to a situation and just being very raucous. And Bobby Knight has become pretty good at it."

Hall refused to shake Knight's hand after the game or to walk off the floor with him. "All I want is another chance to play them," Hall said. "Knight personally humiliated me and I'll never forget it."

Later that night, Knight plopped himself down next to the Louisville *Courier-Journal*'s Dave Kindred, who would become one of his confidants. "We won a big game today and I feel like we lost," said Knight. "How do I get myself into these things?"

It wasn't just a rivalry now, but a blood feud. When the Wildcats got back to Lexington, Nance was summoned to the office of the athletic director, Harry Lancaster.

"I get in there and he says, 'Sit down!'" Nance says. "I think, 'Oh crap, I'm going to get fired before I even get started.'

"He says, 'I want to tell you something. I reviewed that incident at Indiana. You had a chance to hit that son of a bitch. If you ever get a chance like that again and you don't hit him, I'm firing your ass.'"

Knight blamed the furor on Hall, noting in his inimitable style, "If it was meant to be malicious, I'd have blasted the fucker into the seats."

The incident generated big headlines in both states—"Hoosiers and Knight Cuff Wildcats and Hall, 98–74" in the *Lexington Herald-Leader*; "Verbal Dispute a Tie But IU Routs Kentucky" in the *Indiana Daily Student*—but the story didn't go national. "That was because he wasn't quite Bobby Knight yet," says IU guard Jim Wisman. "He didn't have his total reputation."

The Hoosiers didn't look back. They were rarely even challenged. On February 22nd, they were 26–0 with an incredible average victory margin of 26.9 points in Big Ten games, when May broke a bone in his left forearm in an 83–82 win at Purdue.

IU finished 29–0, but Knight was shaken. Knowing he would still need May, Knight put him in at the end of their first two wins in the NCAA Tournament over Texas–El Paso and Oregon State.

The 31–0 Hoosiers advanced to the regional finals in Dayton against who else but Kentucky. The Wildcats had been living for another shot at them since the slap heard 'round the commonwealth. In an unusual move after UK won its semifinal game, Hall let his players watch Indiana play Oregon State. IU was up by 21 at halftime when Hall decided to call it a night.

"Indiana is great," said guard Jimmy Dan Conner. "Too bad their coach is a damn kid."

The Kentucky coaches had never let their players forget that day in Bloomington in December. In the ensuing three months, the players heard about it over and over. It wasn't just a ploy; they genuinely hated the Hoosiers.

"We used that game for fuel all season," says Lynn Nance, "but we really worked it before we played them again. . . . The night before when we were practicing, I ran Jerry Lucas out of the practice and yelled at him, told him to get out. We knew that he had been teammates with Knight. We didn't want him in the practice. And the players liked that."

Hall was determined to play this game Kentucky racehorse style rather than grinding it out again, Knight style. Hall junked his standard 1-3-1 zone, which the Hoosiers had bombed, and played man-to-man, hoping to speed up the game. Hall also told his guards, Conner and Mike Flynn, to take any open shot, knowing Knight's defense would sag on their big men, and if they missed, to keep shooting.

Most of all, the Wildcats were determined to be the aggressors this time. In Bloomington, Hall says Benson hit his freshman center, Rick Robey, so hard, Robey almost bit his tongue in half. Knight's motion offense depended on setting tough screens, which the UK coaches claimed were more like football blocks. This time, whether the referees called fouls or not, the Kentucky coaches ordered their players to run the Hoosiers over. Nance says he told 6-9, 240-pound Bob Guyette, "When Steve Green sets that first screen, if you don't run over his ass, if you don't knock him flat on his ass, we're taking you out of the game."

"And, if you look at the game film," says Nance, "that's the first thing that happens. Guyette knocked Green on his butt and he's sitting on his butt on the floor, looking at the officials with his hands spread, asking, What the heck? That set the tone."

Hall's new tactics caught the Hoosiers off guard. Knight, expecting Kentucky's usual zone, put May, his best shooter, back in the starting lineup four weeks after getting hurt. Since then May had only played three minutes.

"Scott had a pin in his wrist and a five- or six-week time frame for his bone to heal," says Wayne Radford, then a sophomore guard, "but here was Knight thinking that we couldn't win this game without Scott May. But we had already won three Big Ten games without Scott, and then two tournament games convincingly. Then all of a sudden, before we play Kentucky, now we're practicing with Scott May. He's on the starting unit. He has a cast on his wrist. So, no one is going to play aggressive against him because you're thinking if you hurt Scott, Knight is going to be very upset. So you could just see our intensity changing at practice. Everybody was playing not to hurt Scott."

With a cast on his left wrist and the Wildcats playing man-to-man, not zone, May missed his first four shots, turned the ball over three times, and watched Kentucky's star Kevin Grevey zip past him for seven minutes until Knight pulled him. The Wildcats jumped into an early 13-point lead, giving them the confidence they could play against this team, but IU tied it by halftime, 44–44.

Midway through the second half, the Hoosiers went ahead, 68–67, on a Benson hook. The Wildcats then went on an 18–7 run to go up, 85–75, led by Flynn, the former Mr. Basketball from Indiana Knight had tried to recruit, who scored 15 points in the second half. As Knight raged on the sidelines, the Wildcats also got several calls against the Hoosiers for moving on screens.

IU cut it to 90–88 with :20 left, but Buckner, trying to steal the ball from Grevey in the backcourt, fouled him. Grevey coolly made two free throws to make it 92–88. John Laskowski's jumper cut it to 92–90 with :14 left but that was as close as the Hoosiers got.

"To this day, it was the one locker room that I was in that I didn't feel like I belonged in there," says Rick Bozich of the Louisville *Courier-Journal*, who was then on the *Indiana Daily Student*. "Nobody was talking. All the players were like scrunched up in a semifetal position and they had all been crying, especially Steve Green and Laskowski and those guys who were seniors, because they knew it was over.

"They just had a look on their face of utter disbelief that they had lost that game. I think they were disbelieving that they weren't going to the Final Four, they were disbelieving that their perfect season had been ruined because they just rolled over everybody. I can't remember when the last time was before that they had a close game."

Knight was never more gracious than after this game, calling Kentucky "the better team," sticking his head into Hall's press conference to congratulate him and even thanking the press. When a crowd of 1,000 greeted the Hoosiers at the Bloomington airport that night, a deflated Knight told them in a hoarse voice, "You fans have followed us through our ups and downs and if there had been any way we could have given you this ballgame, we would have done it."

Replied a campus policeman through his bullhorn: "Don't worry, Bob, you've given us much more!"

For Knight, it would be the most crushing defeat of his career but he would never show his grief. In his autobiography, he deals with it matter-of-factly, saying only, "Our defense just wasn't good enough in the regional finals and the best team I've ever had was eliminated by Kentucky, 92–90."

Nevertheless, Knight was devastated. After the game, after his players and assistants had left the dressing room and boarded their bus, freshman forward Mark Haymore, who had forgotten his gym bag, came back.

"So, I ran back in there to get it," Haymore says, "and I heard this guy inside the toilet stall. This guy was crying his eyes out, really painfully, and I could tell by the shoes, you could look underneath the door, it was Coach Knight. He wore those Army shoes.

"It was him. He was bawling. And I got this sick feeling in my gut and it brought tears to my own eyes. I thought, 'This guy really cares about us. This guy really cares.' And that was really the most human side I saw of him."

*   *   *

The Hoosiers returned in the fall of 1975 to find the sign that Knight had put up in their dressing room:

KENTUCKY 92 INDIANA 90
OUR DEFENSE WAS RESPONSIBLE
FOR THIS

It was going to be hard playing all season with broken hearts, so it was like a gift from the TV gods that they got to start the season with an extravaganza, matching the Hoosiers, who saw themselves as the uncrowned champion, against UCLA, the crowned one, which had beaten Kentucky in Wooden's farewell.

The game was at the Checkerdome in St. Louis, where Wooden, Knight, Walton, and Downing had met in the 1973 Final Four. Wooden wouldn't be there, but his successor, Gene Bartow, had most of the '75 champions back, including All-Americans Marques Johnson and Richard Washington. To Knight, it was perfect, a way of getting his players' attention in the preseason and making a statement about who was who.

Sure enough, things had changed. This supposed matchup of the No. 1 and 2 teams became an 84–64 IU rout. The Bruins no longer owned college basketball. There was a new sheriff in town, and his name was Bobby Knight.

The night was warm and the hockey ice under the floor melted, making the court slick. The Bruins, who had enough trouble negotiating all the IU screens, were just happy to get out of it in one piece.

"You know, traction was not good for either team," says Wayne Radford, then a sophomore, "but I remember UCLA had trouble dealing with our motion offense. I mean, they were actually arguing amongst themselves because they didn't know who was guarding whom every time there was a screen. And, when someone popped open, it was always the other guy's fault. So, they actually kind of broke down from the cohesiveness that you normally think of with a UCLA John Wooden team."

Knight raged up and down the sideline anyway, arguing with the scorekeeper about the number of timeouts he had. He kicked a chair and played his starters until the last minute. He got letters afterward from UCLA fans complaining about running up the score, which, he said, was funny, coming "from a place where it had seasons where its average winning margin was 30."

Knight drove his players as only he could that season. On their trip to Hawaii for a tournament over Christmas break, he kept them prisoner inside their hotel when they weren't playing or practicing.

"We were coming from practice," says Haymore, then a sophomore forward. "Oh, let me tell you, you know, Hawaii's beautiful. And somehow Scott Eells [a freshman forward] says from the back of the bus, 'Excuse me, Coach Knight? Coach Knight?'

"Like that. And everybody's like, 'Oh, man, what could he want?' Coach Knight stood up and he says—and the bus is still moving—he says, 'Yes, yes, Scott?'

"Scott says, 'Is there any way we're going to get back and get some time to spend on the beach?'

"That was a serious question that he had. You know he was a freshman. I'm talking *green*. Coach Knight said, 'Stop the goddamned bus.' So, the bus driver—we're in three lanes, you know—pulls over and he stops the bus and he opens the door.

"Coach Knight says, 'If you want to see a goddamned beach, there it is, right there. Take your shit and your scholarship and hit the beach.'

"And Scott just sat there. And we were all like, wow. So, when Scott didn't get up, Coach Knight just started cursing us all out. 'Are there any other of you sons of bitches want to get to the beach with Scott, now is your chance. There are 40,000 people at Indiana, I will find ten people that will do what the hell I want here, not hit the goddamned beach. . . .

"I mean, we didn't eat lunch after that. 'No lunch, just go to your room, see you at dinner.' I mean, he would punish us like that. He gets the [telephone] bill, you know, showing where you call. I mean, the phones would be shut off in our rooms. We're not here to be on the phone.

"When we were in Hawaii, we went from airport to gym to hotel to gym to airport, back to Indiana. Not one second of listening to some puka shell or whatever people do in Hawaii. There was nothing. 'If you want to enjoy Hawaii, one day you come again and you bring your ungrateful kids and your overweight wife and you bring them all back here. It'll still be here. We're not here for that.'"

It was dangerous to run as hot as Knight did. The 1975–76 season was the one in which he became notorious as well as famous.

On February 7, the Hoosiers went to 19–0 with a 72–67 overtime win over Michigan. Junior guard Jim Wisman, who wasn't supposed to inbound the ball against the Wolverine press, did it anyway, and threw away two passes in a row. Knight called time out and, as Wisman returned to the bench, grabbed him by the jersey—or, as then–IU sports information director Tom Miller says, "almost ripped it off of him"—with his face mottled with rage.

Knight later insisted he had never done such a thing before, and said he apologized to Wisman. Actually, it had been standard practice for years. One of Knight's Army players, Paul Franke, said grabbing them by the shirt "was always the thing" and described Knight's standard "claw" technique. However, this was the first time Knight had been caught on camera, and the picture taken by *Indianapolis Star* photographer Jerry Clark ran on the front page the next morning, and in newspapers all over the country.

Among them was the *Bloomington Herald-Telephone*. The next morning, an irate Knight called SID Tom Miller, fuming about sports editor Bob Hammel, who had run the picture off the Associated Press wire.

"So, his wife, Nancy, called me at the office one day," Miller says, "and said, 'Hey, can you get things patched up between Hammel and Bob?'

"I said, 'I don't know, I doubt it.'

"She said, 'He canceled our paper and I don't know what's going on in town.'"

Knight told Hoosier fans to call the *Star* to protest. In response, Bob Collins, the paper's feisty sports editor, published Knight's unlisted

phone number and urged Hoosier fans to call *him* to protest his treatment of his players.

To that point, everyone knew Knight had a temper, but so did lots of
coaches. His run-in with Joe B. Hall had started a firestorm in Kentucky
and Indiana but hadn't moved on the wire services. The Wisman photo
would brand him forever as the bad boy of college basketball.

To the players, who were around Knight all the time, it was just business as usual. Nevertheless, says Radford, "It turned into such a big story
that every guy who was being recruited by IU, their parents and high-
school coaches were getting sent these clippings from other teams saying, 'Do you want your son to play for this guy?'"

In a pattern of damage control that would also become standard
practice, several players, of whom Radford was one, were told to call the
recruits and assure them the Wisman thing was no big deal.

Then there was that old bane of coaches, sex. Knight didn't like the fact
that several of his seniors had moved out of the dorms and into apart-
ments, especially May and Buckner. The players were young and single,
not to mention gods on campus, but Knight regarded girlfriends as dis-
tractions. The Hoosiers were 22–0 on February 21st, when Knight
benched Buckner against Minnesota and kept him on the bench for the
Iowa game two days later. The public explanation was that Buckner was
"dehydrated."

Buckner and May moved back into the dorms and the Hoosiers won
their last three handily to finish the regular season 27–0. They beat St.
John's in the first round of the NCAA Tournament by 20 points and eased
past No. 6–ranked Alabama to reach the Midwest regional finals in Baton
Rouge, Lousiana, where No. 1–ranked IU would meet No. 2 Marquette.

The rosters were so loaded that all 10 starters would play in the pros.
McGuire, the fast-talking Marquette coach and a friend of Knight, had
said before the season IU had "the best team, the best players and the
best coach." IU won, 65–56, after McGuire said one thing too many and
drew his second technical foul with :25 left and his team within three
points.

It's a good season when fate brings your favorite adversary back around so you can run him over again. The Hoosiers moved on to the Final Four in the Spectrum in Philadelphia against none other than UCLA.

After losing to IU in the opener, the Bruins had lost just once more all season to finish 28–2 and were ranked No. 5. They still thought of themselves as royalty, sneering at the Hoosiers before the game. Richard Washington, UCLA's 6-11 center, said Oregon State's Lonnie Shelton, not Benson, was the best center he had played against. Marques Johnson said the Hoosiers were "mechanical," adding diplomatically, "I'm not saying that in a derogatory sense. It's a compliment but they're almost mechanical."

The IU players didn't comment, as usual. Normally, they weren't available to the press at all. In this NCAA-controlled setting they had to attend press conferences, but Knight was monitoring every word out of their mouths. Nevertheless, they bristled at the UCLA players' comments.

"All UCLA was about was finesse," says Wayne Radford. "I mean, UCLA reminded me of what I used to think of the North Carolina Tar Heels in the early days. Or what I used to think of the ACC years ago, just a finesse conference. And UCLA and the ACC would have just suited each other well.

"And then we were a very aggressive, physical team. This time there was no excuse of playing on a slippery floor. They were still getting in trouble with our screens, they still were not able to read a switch and just pick up where the offensive guards are going."

This time, the Bruins gave a better effort but still lost, 75–61.

"All I remember is [UCLA reserve] Gavin Smith and Knight," says Marques Johnson. "We were making a run and Gavin was playing well. So Bobby Knight called a time out. So Gavin's walking by Bobby Knight, going, 'Yeah! Yeah!'

"So Bobby says, 'Fuck you, Smith!'

"So Gavin goes, 'Fuck you, Knight!'

"So they go back and forth, 'Fuck you, Smith!' 'Fuck you, Knight!' It was a pretty wild scene."

A year after taking their heart-breaking loss to Kentucky, the Hoosiers were 31–0 and in the NCAA finals at last. For the third time that season, their opponent would be Michigan, the nation's No. 9–ranked team. IU had won both prior meetings, but both had been close. The game in Bloomington had been an outright escape, with Benson rebounding a Jimmy Crews airball and scoring to tie the game at the end of regulation.

This game started on an ominous note for the Hoosiers, too. Jumping into the path of Michigan forward Wayman Britt, Bobby Wilkerson was hit in the temple by Britt's elbow and knocked cold. Wilkerson lay on the floor for 10 minutes, was wheeled off on a stretcher, and taken to a nearby hospital as a precautionary measure. With Wisman trying to guard Wilkerson's man, Ricky Green, the human blur, the Wolverines led, 35–29, at halftime.

At intermission, Knight, the man of a thousand surprises, gave the IU players a two-sentence speech and walked out.

"He comes in the locker room," said May, "and he says, 'There's nothing I can say. If you want to be champions, if you want to accomplish something special, you have 20 minutes to prove it.'

"And then he walked out. It was like total shock. Somebody told me later that Coach Knight had been waiting two years to deliver that speech."

The Hoosiers were known as a second-half team that wore their opponents down, but they simply crushed this one. They outscored Michigan, 57–33, in the second half, riddling its zone defense, with May shooting over it for 26 points and Benson overmatching the smaller Wolverines inside for 25. The game turned into a rout.

At that night's Academy Award presentations in Los Angeles, actress Isabelle Adjani, about to name the best editing, announced, "And the winner is . . . "

"Indiana, 86–68," said her copresenter, Elliott Gould.

At 35, Knight had his first national title. "As I look at this," he said afterward, gazing at the championship trophy, "I think of an 80-year-old man in the mountains who watched the game on television. Clair Bee would have been here today but for an eye problem. He called me every day we were in Philadelphia and there is nobody in my life who has been more instrumental than him." He went on to express his pride in his players and to thank Pete Newell, John Havlicek, and Fred Taylor.

Knight's Hoosiers had just gone 32–0. They were 63–1 over two seasons, and 108–12 over four with Buckner's class. Nevertheless, Knight seemed more subdued than ecstatic. Years later, he wrote in his autobiography it was "more of a relief than anything else." While the Hoosiers celebrated around him, Knight said his thoughts turned to the losing coach, his friend Johnny Orr. The next day when the Hoosiers returned to Bloomington and fans lined the road from the airport, Knight wasn't with them. He had gone to watch a high school tournament.

He left the Spectrum that night with Hammel, the Bloomington sports editor, who congratulated him.

"Thanks," said Knight, "but it should have been two."

SIX

OUR MAN IN SAN JUAN

INDIANA AND PUERTO RICO, 1976–79

> The VIII Pan-American Games were of unprecedented size
> and splendor—and for the United States, humiliation. Oh, we
> won the most medals; we always do. . . . But the triumphs
> were stained by the gross incivility of the basketball coach, a re-
> minder that the American the hemisphere despises—arrogant
> and insensitive—is by no means extinct.
>
> —*Sports Illustrated*, July 14, 1980

No one could ever say that success spoiled Bob Knight, who remained what he was, or more so. With an NCAA title at age 35,
the youngest coach in NCAA history to reach the 100- and 200-
win level, he was a certified boy wonder. With his new cachet, players
would line up to play for him, so the best seemed to lie ahead.

However, Knight wasn't like anyone else and his program wouldn't
be like anyone else's. For Knight, success didn't breed more success, at
least immediately. At IU, the seasons after titles turned hellish. The
more the other great coaches won, the better players they got. The more
Knight won, the less he thought he needed the best players.

John Wooden won his first two titles at UCLA with 6-5 Fred
Slaughter at center, but his next center was Lew Alcindor (later Kareem
Abdul-Jabbar) from New York City, and two years after Alcindor came
Bill Walton of San Diego. Of Wooden's 10 championship teams, all had
at least one player who would be an NBA All-Star and some had three.
Knight was content to confine his recruiting to his three-state area—
Indiana, Illinois and Ohio—looking for tough, smart players who fit

into his system, and became more than they were. In 29 years at IU, he would have one NBA All-Star, Isiah Thomas.

More triumphs seemed at hand for Knight in the fall of 1976. He was coming off two seasons in which IU had lost one game and he had pre-season All-American Kent Benson back, with a hot freshman class that included Mike Woodson, who was Mr. Basketball in Indiana; Butch Carter, who was Mr. Ohio; and Glen Grunwald, who was Mr. Illinois.

However, while no one knew it, the age of giants had just ended. Programs all over the country had geared up to challenge UCLA, and none would ever be as dominant again. It would be 27 years before any-one won two titles in a row. Still, everyone in Indiana would always wonder what might have been if Knight had just kept all his players on the lot, particularly a scrawny freshman who had showed up two years before, in the fall of 1974, named Larry Joe Bird.

It was an item of faith in Indiana that any Hoosier player who trans-ferred under Knight wasn't tough enough or good enough. The one they could never explain was Bird, the greatest player the state would ever produce, who enrolled at IU, but never played a game there.

Bird was a late bloomer, and no one suspected what he had in him when he arrived on the mammoth IU campus from tiny French Lick, as wide-eyed as if it were New York City. He wasn't a blue-chip recruit; he had been a 6-7, 160-pound center who had sprung up three inches in his senior year at Spring Valley High School. His team hadn't gone any-where in the state tournament. He not only hadn't been Mr. Basketball, he wasn't even first or second team all-state. Knight didn't even offer him a scholarship until Steve Collier of Hanover Southwestern, who was the co–Mr. Basketball, turned the Hoosiers down.

Except for the honor, Bird might have passed on the invitation. He was from a wide spot in the two-lane blacktop with a population of 2,100 in the southern part of the state. Knight had never recruited any-one from French Lick and the townspeople did everything but hold prayer vigils, hoping Larry would accept.

"My first high school coach went to IU," Bird says. "My second one went to Louisville. Purdue, Louisville, all them schools around there were after me. I liked Indiana State probably the best when I first went out and visited because it was smaller and I sort of felt it would be good for me. But playing for IU is playing for IU. I did feel obligated to go there, but I made the decision."

He was lost from the start. In Knight's program, no one held a freshman's hand or showed him how to sign up for classes. No one cared if, like Bird, he had no money and few clothes and felt out of place rooming with a handsome young BMOC like Jim Wisman, one of the coolest Hoosiers ever, and a future vice president of the big Leo Burnett ad agency in Chicago.

Nor did Bird's new teammates go out of their way to make him feel at home. Freshmen counted for nothing until they showed they could pull their weight and since Knight didn't customarily play them much, they were usually sophomores by the time it happened. However, country bumpkin that he was, Bird already had the beginning of a great player's attitude, and there was only so much he would take.

"He knows he's the guy from French Lick," says John Laskowski, a senior guard in the fall of 1974, who had met Bird on a recruiting visit, "and all these guys are from a bigger city and they're smarter and they're dressed better and they may have better grades, and you're catching hell from the basketball team.

"You know, I went over to his room that first week and he and Wisman were there and I said, 'Hey, guys, it's great to have you here. We're going to be playing at the gym about three o'clock, come on by and if there's anything I can do to help . . . ' Which is probably the way all the guys should have done it, but I don't think that happened. And you know, he's saying, 'Man, there's no way I'm going to hang out here, I'm outta here.'

"I mean, the one thing that Larry had was this sense that he could just stop anybody. He had this run-in at the Indiana All-Star game the summer before because the coach took him out of the game and put another guy in, when he knew he was better than that guy. So, now the coach tries to put him back in and Larry says, forget it, I'm not playing. I mean, I'm Larry Bird.

"I heard that Benson picked on him a lot. Benson got picked on when he was a freshman. The mentality back then was, if you're a freshman, you're not going to be able to help our team because you can't play and until you guys show us you can do something, just be quiet and do what we tell you to do.

"And so, I think, Benson got on Bird and it was like, 'What are you guys doing? I'm a really good player.' I mean, we could sense he was a good player.

"And just think of what would have happened if Scott May breaks his arm and we bring Larry Bird in. Oh my gosh."

By then Bird was long gone. It wasn't one thing that chased him home. It was everything. A few days before he left, Bird called Cooper Speaks, an English professor who tutored several players. "When he called me on that Friday before he did not return, he said, 'Do you know what a theme is?'" says Speaks.

"And I said, "Yes, of course, I've been teaching freshman English for 30 years.'

"And he said, 'Well, I'm supposed to write a theme on Monday and I don't even know what a theme is.'"

Bird would later complain about Benson in his autobiography but never about Knight, whom he barely even glimpsed in his brief stay. There was a story claiming Knight had snubbed him in a restaurant but Bird says it never happened. Years later, Bird kept a photo of himself with Knight, taken when he signed with IU, on a wall in his home.

"When I got there it wasn't for me," says Bird. "I was homesick and broke. What I did was best for me. It's turned out pretty good. I got to go to Indiana State and score my points and do my thing.

"I really knew if I didn't get out of there and get a job, I would have never finished my education. I just didn't have anything. I mean, people don't believe that, but I had a couple pairs of pants, a few shorts, some tennis shoes and no money. It was tough."

Knight didn't give Bird's departure a second thought at the time. If he hadn't had to babysit his stars like Quinn Buckner or Scott May, he wasn't going to disturb himself over a homesick freshman. However, it was only a couple of seasons before Knight began to rethink his position as Bird began to show what a treasure had slipped through his hands.

After 24 days on the IU campus, Bird left in the fall of 1974, hitch-hiking home and, getting a job on a garbage truck. He enrolled at Indiana State the next fall, sat out a year to become eligible and became a consensus All-American by his junior year. As a senior, he took Indiana State to the 1979 NCAA finals and its celebrated match-up with Magic Johnson and Michigan State. Within two more years, Bird had won an NBA title with the Celtics and he and Johnson were already considered the league's saviors.

Bird says that even if Knight had come after him, he wouldn't have gone back, but no one will ever know. What Knight wanted, he usually got. Knight later called the entire episode "one of my great mistakes."

"Bobby told me once, 'I should have spent more time with that kid,'" says Tom Miller, then the sports information director. "I think Bobby realized later this was a special case and he should have picked this kid up and talked to him a little bit. Because we'd have had a team they'd still be talking about if we had him."

In the fall of 1976, the Hoosiers came off their NCAA title with great expectations that were quickly dashed. Their 57-game regular-season winning streak was shattered in the second game with Toledo. They were 4–5 after losing both of their games in the Sugar Bowl Classic in New Orleans, where Knight was heard during a timeout yelling at Benson, "Your play is a disgrace! We may lose tonight but not with you! You're done! If we're going to go down, we're going to go down with guys who are busting their ass!" When Benson was named to the all-tournament team, which Knight said "amazed" him, he wouldn't let him go back onto the floor to get his trophy, sending his son, Tim, out for it instead.

Earnest and bulky, Benson had been skilled enough to fill a role on a talented team that knew how to protect him. However, he wasn't strong or athletic, and when someone his own size began taking it to him, as Alabama's Leon Douglas had in the NCAA tournament the preceding spring, everyone had to dig back to rescue Benny. It became a running joke with Bobby Wilkerson, who covered the most ground and often wound up guarding two men, his own and Benson's.

"Bobby Wilkerson would be in the living room of his apartment," says Loren Buckner, "and he'd play like Benny's man was the refrigerator and his man was the table in the living room, and he would pretend he was running back between the two of them and he'd say, 'Hey, this is how I play the game.'"

Now Wilkerson was in the NBA and Benson wasn't getting enough help. Knight wanted him to be a leader, but even as a senior, Benson was no Quinn Buckner. Soft-spoken and devoutly religious, Benson had come in as a Mr. Basketball who had overwhelmed prep opponents with his sheer size. He was a starter at IU from day one but Knight was all over him, to the point that Benson considered transferring his freshman year.

"Almost immediately, they clashed," says Cooper Speaks, who tutored Benson. "And there was one famous incident that Benson told me about and referred to on several occasions, in which Knight really pushed him. . . . Knight's way of pushing was usually revilement and cursing and so on, and on one occasion he said to him something like, 'Okay, you'd better depend on your God now to do something for you.'

"And that hurt Benny, I think, a great deal, and he often referred to it."

Benson improved annually, but never enough for Knight. In Benson's sophomore year, Rick Bozich, then writing for the *Indiana Daily Student*, saw Knight jump all over him for missing a hook shot, which Knight considered a sissy shot for a 6-11, 265-pounder.

"He was standing 30 feet away and took the basketball and threw it and hit Benson," Bozich says. "He said, 'Benny, that's what I think of your goddamned hook shot! You should take that hook shot and cram it up your ass. I don't want to see you take another hook shot until you're in the NBA, do you understand that?'"

In times of stress, everyone had to partake of Knight's temper. After a 15-point loss at home to Kentucky, he shoved Wayne Radford in the back on the way to the dressing room at halftime.

"Right before halftime, Kentucky's Jay Shidler—I still remember the play—has the ball at our place," says Radford, "and he's coming up court, and I'm trying to stay three feet off him because I didn't want him to blow by me. And as time was running down, I'm watching him and he pulls up and takes, like, a 35–40 footer. I didn't jump out at him and try to block it because the last thing you want to do from a shot like that is foul the guy. Well, he hit the shot. So, you know, we're going into the locker room, and I didn't know he [Knight] was behind me, he just gave me a shove going into the locker room."

Knight would later claim it was the only mean thing he had ever done to a player at IU. His players thought the actual number was higher than that. That was the season they started going over the wall.

In five years at IU, Knight had only had two players—Dave Shepherd and Don Noort—transfer. Now, in 18 months, he would lose six.

Knight had driven the Hoosiers hard on the way to their 1976 title, and as soon as the season was over, the talent drain had started. In the summer, within months of winning the championship, sophomore forward Mark Haymore transferred to Massachusetts. Sophomore guard Bob Bender, a coach's son from Quincy, Illinois, and his roommate, sophomore forward Rich Valavicius, a tough rebounder from Hammond, Indiana, thought about leaving that summer, though they both returned for their sophomore year.

"Next thing you know, Knight calls us down to the locker room, both of us," Valavicius said later. "We came in there, scared to death. [He said] 'Listen, you two shitheads, I heard you're leaving. What's this all about?' I'd never been called a shithead before."

Bender left a few weeks later, before the 1976–77 season started. Valavicius departed during the season, as did Mike Miday, another sophomore forward.

"Miday quit after a handful of games," says Mark Montieth of the *Indianapolis Star*, who was then with the *Indiana Daily Student*. "Miday in high school had longer hair and I think a beard or a mustache, and Knight, when he signed him, said, 'You'll have to shave your face if you're going to play for me.' And Miday said, 'Oh, I'll shave my head if you want me to.'

"Knight used to tell that story on the banquet circuit. 'Here's a kid who I think is going to be a great player,' he said. So, then, Miday quits after a handful of games and winds up going to Bowling Green."

Until then, none of the departing Hoosiers had publicly criticized Knight, but Miday and Valavicius complained about him in the *Daily Student*. Miday said he "couldn't stand the way he treated me as a human being." Valavicius said, "It got to the point I actually hated playing."

None of the departing players was a full-time starter so the mainstream press took scant notice—and after that, they became un-Hoosiers. In the IU media guide, there's no mention of Miday and Valavicius in the 1976–77 team statistics; their numbers were lumped together under "others." As far as the fans were concerned, they were quitters or worse.

"Well, let me tell you, " says Cooper Speaks, who tutored Valivicius. "when Val announced that he was leaving, I would say that I saw at least 20 letters written to him by alumni and fans telling him what a no-good-punk pussy he was for quitting the team. I mean he got phone calls which he would tell me about: 'I got another phone call from a nut last night.'"

Bender transferred to Duke, where he started on the 1978 team that made the NCAA finals. He ultimately became the coach at the University of Washington and an NBA assistant with the 76ers and Hawks. Valavicius transferred to Auburn, where he started, and became a high-school coach in Alabama.

"There were times when one of the guys I played with, Jim Wisman, I mean, Jim couldn't take it either," says Wayne Radford. "None of us could. But because you always saw the other guys a year or two before being able to survive it, you always thought and you always imagined you would, too. After a while it just got to the point where some kids just felt like, 'I can't play for the guy, I'm not relaxed, I don't enjoy it.'"

The defending NCAA champion Hoosiers went into the last game of the 1976–77 season against Ohio State with a 13–13 record, needing a victory to avoid Knight's first losing season at IU. They won, 75–69, led by 6-11 freshman Derek Holcomb, touted as Benson's replacement, who got 23 points and 15 rebounds. That summer, Holcomb transferred to Illinois.

IU finished 14–13. When Minnesota, which had beaten them twice, was hit by NCAA sanctions and forced to forfeit all its games, the Hoosiers were awarded two more wins and wound up 16–11, but no happier.

If winning was problematic to Knight, losing seemed to clarify everything for him, restoring his equilibrium and his ambition. In the fall of 1977, he went back to work, trying to rebuild his program. This wasn't square one. Returning were Woodson, who had been the Big Ten's freshman of the year, and Radford. Coming in was a 6-10 freshman, Ray Tolbert. The Hoosiers went 21–8 and finished second in the Big Ten at 12–6.

One more player, sophomore guard Billy Cunningham, quit. A Buckner prototype, Cunningham was a 6-4, 200-pound former high-school football safety who was so gung-ho, he stayed around in the summer to work out with the strength trainer while taking a psychology course because, "I wanted to try to better understand Coach Knight and some of his philosophies and that kind of thing. Sort of like [reading] *The Art of War*. I was going to figure him out."

Cunningham was as stubborn as he was eager. He heard the coaches didn't like black players dating white girls, but he didn't care. "You know, that's a thing about athletes in college," Cunningham says. "When you're in college and you're having a good time, you don't want anybody telling you who you can date or who you can't date. I mean, when I was at IU, I had girls that wanted to meet me. Was I going to turn them down because they were maybe not the same nationality as me? No, I wasn't going to do that. I mean, there were a lot of beautiful girls at Indiana University.

"I'd gotten wind—I don't know if this was like Knight's thing—but I'd gotten wind that a couple of the coaches didn't like the fact that some of the black athletes were dating white girls or whatever. But, hey, you know what? If a beautiful girl comes up to you or if she wants to meet you, I think the manly thing to do is to just go with it, right?"

One day, Knight threw Cunningham out of practice, which was routine at IU, but Cunningham never came back. Nevertheless, the Hoosiers won their last eight games to finish the 1977–78 season 21–7 before losing to Villanova in the second round of the NCAA Tournament. Better times beckoned, or seemed to.

With another promising freshman, 6-10 Landon Turner, and a tough shooting guard, Randy Wittman, arriving in the fall of 1978, hopes were high. Unfortunately, so was most of the team.

The season started with upset losses to Pepperdine and Texas A&M at the Seawolf Classic in Anchorage, Alaska. Back in Bloomington a few days later, Butch Carter, a sophomore guard, told the coaches his teammates had been smoking marijuana.

"I'm going to lunch with the coach," says Roy Bates, the old Ohio prep coaching great whom Knight had hired as an assistant, "and Carter comes by. And I said, 'How you doing?' And he kept right on going.

"I said, 'Bob, excuse me.' And I grabbed him [Carter] by the ass and said, 'What the hell's going on with you, man? Got a problem or something?'

"And he starts to cry. So he unloads all this stuff. Now, to this day, those people [teammates] will tell you Carter was trying to help himself but I'm not in on that scene because, honest to God, I don't think the kid ever felt that. Because at that time he was bleeding Indiana."

In the psychedelic '70s, campuses fairly reeked of marijuana and coaches customarily handled problems internally. "If every kid who smoked marijuana was kicked off a college basketball team at that time," says Bates, "they'd be playing with the cheerleaders." However, Knight didn't even drink beer and had no use for illegal recreational substances.

An investigation ensued. Three players, sophomore point guard Tommy Baker, sophomore shooting guard Don Cox, and senior shooting guard Jim Roberson, were thrown off the team, according to Knight, by a vote of their teammates. The others who were implicated were given probation. They included Woodson, Tolbert, and Turner, the three most important players.

Baker, the starting point guard, was alleged to have brought the stuff to a party. Cox says he refused to tell Knight anything, and Roberson denied he had done anything, contrary to what Carter had told the coaches.

"I'll tell you what I think and I think this is egotistical but I'm the only guy coaching today who will stand up and do something," Knight proclaimed. "If I had to, I'd kick three off the next year and three the next year and three the next, if it was a matter of principle."

Nevertheless, with his stars managing to stay on the team without missing any games, there was speculation about Knight's selectivity.

"A lot of the guys I can remember, I hate to mention names, but Ray Tolbert, Landon Turner, those guys broke down crying and I believe it saved their careers there," says Cox. "I mean, Ray didn't do anything. He was pure and clean. Ray's one of the best people you ever want to know, comes from a Christian background.

"Landon, on the other hand, he was no different than I, but those guys broke down crying and begging for their careers and da da da da. I did not do that. I did not cry and beg for forgiveness. I don't know if anything could have saved me. I was a struggling student there and he already had Randy Wittman in the wings to come in that following year to replace me, so I don't know if he had plans for me anyway."

There was no staying out of this one. It was a nightmare for all involved.

"We get called into the locker room one night by the team and Butch gets up and announces that he's going to Coach Knight that these guys brought pot back," says Steve Risley, then a sophomore forward. "And we're like, 'Well, fuck, wait a minute, we'll deal with this internally. We don't need to take this shit to Coach.'

"But Butch went and took it to Coach and then, of course, all hell breaks lose. Well, then it becomes a witch hunt. Knight's pissed off at a couple of these guys anyway and kind of wants to get rid of them . . . and there's five guys that are just gonna be slapped on the wrist.

"I was one of the five players that weren't implicated in the whole thing. There were like five of us that weren't, you know—Wittman and [Ted] Kitchel, I think, and Scotty Eells and me and one other guy [Carter]—I guess we were the squeaky clean idiots. So, essentially, what happened is, all the kids that are implicated are asked to leave, and then we're supposed to make the decisions. And it was voted upon by the players of the team that the three would be dismissed. . . . It was probably the toughest thing I did at IU. I was young and I look at it now, and if I had to do it all over again, I probably would ask a lot more questions. But, you know, you're there, you're a sophomore or freshman in the program and, you know, this is all happening and you don't really have a clue as to what's going on. I felt at that point in time that I voted the way I was expected to vote."

In their next game, the 3–3 Hoosiers upset sixth-ranked Kentucky in the Assembly Hall, starting a six-game winning streak, as congratulations tumbled in from around the the nation for Knight's stand. In the end, however, there was no pulling this team together. The Hoosiers finished the 1978–79 season 22–12 but just 10–8 in the Big Ten. They didn't get an NCAA bid and had to settle for winning the NIT.

"It was a very difficult year," says Risley. "We struggle, you know, we don't make the NCAA. I don't think we ever get over it. We really never get over what happened. There's a lot of distrust on the team with Butch and things like that. And then a lot of our guys that were our leaders like Woody and a lot of the great players we had, they were beaten down.

"Knight brought it up whenever the hell he felt like bringing it up. 'Goddamn it, Woodson, if you fucking weren't out smoking fucking pot instead of fucking playing basketball, we fucking wouldn't be in this mess.'

"You know, shit like that, that stuff came up all the time."

This Sturm und Drang—Knight raging, Knight running off players, players fleeing Knight—was played out in public and tacitly endorsed by the IU administration, which expressed no concern, internally or publicly. It was accepted by the press and fans as the way Knight did things. Knight insisted he was always in control and was justified in going to such lengths to motivate his players, who were not, as he put it, at a church tea, a PTA meeting, or playing canasta.

In fact, everyone around the program was at the mercy of Knight's moods. He could lose it completely, as he did the day he attacked the slight, young assistant sports information director, Kit Klingelhoffer.

This had nothing to do with the heat of competition in big-time college basketball, having occurred in the sports publicity office. There were two witnesses, sports information director Tom Miller and secretary Terry Cagle. Miller reported it to IU president John Ryan, who investigated casually, but took no official action. It happened in the late 1970s, but nobody has ever been able to pinpoint exactly when. It was covered up and didn't surface until Cagle acknowledged it to an Indianapolis TV station two decades later.

"I had turned over the active part of basketball to my assistant [Klingelhoffer] and the assistant had failed to censor one of Knight's after-game comments and left it in IU's postgame notes," says Miller. "It was rather innocuous. It wasn't that great a deal but it ticked Bobby off and he came up and was ranting about it. He came inside my office and there was talk there. All of a sudden . . . he just swung on Kit and knocked him to the floor. . . .

"I told Bobby, I said, 'Get out of here. . . .' And he stood around and jawed for a while and then he left. And the university wanted me to sweep it under the rug, but I said, 'I want to talk to the president about this.' Well, underlings came over [from IU President John Ryan's office] and talked about it. And Bobby was very contrite about it, afterwards.

"The underling was a very good friend of Bobby's and he wanted to sweep it all under the rug. I kind of dug my heels in on that one, because I thought we had to have something come out of it. . . .

"I'm sure that somewhere along the line they told him [Knight] to take it easy, but I don't know. Nothing official ever appeared in the papers about it."

Miller's account is corroborated by Cagle.

"I was sitting there," says Cagle. "And Tom, the SID, and Kit were in the same office, and he [Knight] just came bursting into the room like he sometimes did when he was angry, and went over and started shouting at Kit, incredible profanity that he—he's so creative, anyway. He picked him up, sort of by, I think, by the shirt and threw him on the floor and then he stormed out. And Kit sat there for a few seconds and then he got back up and we all went back to work.

"And then the next day he [Knight] came in . . . and he had some kind of a lacrosse—I think it was a lacrosse shirt—and gave it to him. And I don't know that he apologized but that was obviously meant as a peace offering. Kit basically worked for Bob Knight and he wanted to keep his job, I suspect. And I just was a loyal secretary and I wouldn't have rocked the boat."

On the surface, however, things seemed to be settling down in the spring of 1979. Knight had an interesting summer lined up, coaching the U.S. team in the Pan-Am games in Puerto Rico.

International competition thrilled Knight, who took it as an honor to represent his country. He had a team loaded with talented young players including Minnesota's Kevin McHale, Kentucky's Kyle Macy, North Carolina's Mike O'Koren, Iowa's Ronnie Lester, and Georgetown's John Duren. There were also two high-school players, a spindly 7-4 yearling named Ralph Sampson, and Knight's own prize recruit, Isiah Thomas.

Knight set about getting them ready his way, scrimmaging them against his IU players.

"He'd look at me and just say, 'Just go in there and just knock the fuck out of Sampson,'" says Steve Risley. "He thought Sampson was the biggest pussy he'd ever seen. I mean, he couldn't stand the son of a bitch. What Knight hated about him—and he thought Ralph was a good kid—but, you know, the guy's got more talent than any human being who's ever played on the team before and just could do so little with it.

"And that's what infuriates Knight. That is just what makes him get on you, the fact that you have a tremendous amount of talent and you don't even come close to using it. You know, he can't tolerate that to any degree. He had us do all we could to rough up Sampson. And not kill him, but just try and make him mean. I mean, try to develop Ralph.

"You know, all of these guys came out of there saying there's no way they could play for Knight and this and that. You know, if Sampson had spent four years with Knight, Sampson might just be now finishing up his NBA career, instead of coaching some junior-high basketball team somewhere, or whatever he's doing."

In Lexington, they scrimmaged against former Kentucky players and won but not impressively enough for Knight. After they landed in Bloomington, he called a practice and introduced his players to the suicide drill, which was standard for his IU teams.

"I remember we did this drill," says O'Koren, "and I've never done it since. He would literally roll the ball out and one guy would come from one end and one guy would come from the other end and whoever got to the ball, you dove on the floor, however you wanted to get it. And that got our attention and from then on, you know, we were very serious about winning the gold medal."

In case they weren't as serious as he was, Knight had them all carrying little pictures of a gold medal around. By July 2, when the competition started, they were as ready as they could be.

They opened with a 136–88 blowout of the Virgin Islands and their first international incident. They were up by 35 in the second half, but Knight was still fully engaged, protesting a call, drawing a technical foul, arguing the point, and getting ejected. He had to make a command appearance the next day before the International Amateur Basketball Federation, where he was warned he'd be sent home if he did it again.

Said Knight, unimpressed: "I didn't really apologize. I just said I wouldn't want to go through it all again."

If he couldn't harangue the refs, he still had his players. Their third game was an 82–78 squeaker over Brazil. Thomas missed a dunk with the United States 14 points ahead, and Knight jumped in his face, shouting loud enough to be heard on press row. "What the hell's the matter with you?" Knight yelled, according to the *Washington Post*'s Tom Boswell. "Do you think I'm going to put up with this bullshit?"

Wrote Boswell: "To call Knight a Jekyll-and-Hyde personality would be understatement. It took Jekyll several seconds of gasping and fang-growing to become Hyde. Knight can do it in a flash."

A few days of relative peace followed, until the fateful Sunday morning of July 8, at Espiritu Santo High School, where all the teams practiced.

"When we got there it was raining," says John Duren, "and the bus left, and we couldn't get in the gym. So, we were kind of standing in the rain waiting for the other team to finish practicing and they went over their practice time. Finally they come out and we go in.

"So, we're practicing. The next scheduled team, the Brazilian team, the females, they get there a little earlier than they're supposed to, and naturally our time is going to run a little later. When they knock on the door to come in, Coach Knight says, 'Well, let them in.' We're not going to leave them in the rain like the previous team had left us in the rain, so they could sit down and, you know, watch the rest of the practice.

"At this time we were just sitting in the gym on the stage taking notes. He always wanted you to take notes at the practice and his lectures. Meanwhile, we had an incident with Isiah, some kind of disagreement, he had thrown a bad pass or something. So, Coach Knight had kicked him out of practice and made him go sit on the bus. . . .

"What happened was, next thing we know, the girls started talking loud. So, Coach Knight asked Mike Krzyzewski [now coaching Army and assisting Knight at the time], 'Can you go down and tell them to keep the noise down?' Fine, so the noise dies down a little bit. Then the noise started rising up some more, so Knight said, 'Look, you tell them to keep the noise down.'

"Meanwhile, there's a police officer sitting down there too, watching everything. So Mike Krzyzewski goes down and says, 'Look, you all have to be quiet or we're going to have to have you go outside.'

"So, the police officer says, 'Who are you telling to go outside?'

"So, he [Krzyzewski] says, 'Well, tell them to keep the noise down because we're holding practice or they're going to have to leave the gym.'

"And the police officer says, 'Well, they aren't going to have to leave the gym.' Like that.

"Meanwhile, Coach Knight is watching what's going on between Coach Krzyzewski, the Brazilian women, and the man. So, as he's walking down—he's a little upset now—he's walking down and saying, 'Hey, hey, you're going to have to keep the noise down or get out.'

"The police officer comes and says, 'Hey, you don't talk to them, this is Puerto Rico. This is Puerto Rico.' Like that.

"And Knight says, 'Well, look, we came up here, they made us wait in the rain, I was nice,' on and on. They have some words and he catches Coach Knight in the eye . . . And at that point Coach Knight pushed him, right?

"You know Coach Knight is a bigger fellow than this guy. So, he kind of moves back a bit and grabs his handcuffs and then said, 'You're under arrest.'

"And then they had a little scuffle. Nobody threw a punch, he was just trying to put the handcuffs on Coach Knight but he really couldn't because Knight was too strong. So, Coach Krzyzewski says, 'Just let them put the handcuffs on you and we'll get this over with.'

"Meanwhile we went out to the bus and Isiah was sitting on the bus, saying, 'What happened?' Because he sees them bring Coach Knight out in handcuffs."

Knight claimed the policeman, 33-year-old José de Silva, had poked him in the eye and, indeed, Knight's eye was red. After that, Knight said, he put his hand up "in a purely reflexive action to push him away with the heel of my hand under his chin." Knight also claimed that in the process of being put into de Silva's car, the policeman brandished a nightstick, touched his nose with it several times and told him, "Goddamn you, brother, this is what I'd like to use on you."

De Silva denied poking Knight and claimed Knight had called the Brazilian players "whores," and had called him a "nigger."

Knight was taken to a nearby police station, locked up for about 10 minutes and freed after a delegation of USOC officials led by executive director F. Don Miller hurried down. No charges were filed, but the next day de Silva filed an assault charge of his own. Practices were called off while Knight huddled daily with legal advisers. The Americans kept winning but the atmosphere was becoming more charged by the day. In their 18-point romp over against Cuba, guard Tomás Herrera punched Kyle Macy and broke his jaw.

"We'd beaten them by 40 [22, actually] in the qualifying rounds," says Macy, "and we were up 20 at halftime and probably on our way to another 40-point victory and it was just the start of the second half. I mean, it was like at halftime they decided they were going to take out one of our players and, unfortunately, I got to be the lucky one, I guess."

With his million-dollar wound, Macy was sent back to the States. Knight told the rest of his players he didn't want them in jeopardy because of him, and if they voted to go home, he would honor it. They voted unanimously to stay.

"We were young," says O'Koren. "I don't know what we were but we were there and we wanted to win."

"We were told don't walk around by yourself," says Duren. "If you're going to go to the cafeteria, at least go in threes or fours. The Puerto Rican guys [basketball players], all of a sudden, man, they're looking at us a little funny, and all this type of stuff, as far as we're in the village and everything. Now, it's a heated game. They want us and we want them, you understand what I'm saying?"

On July 11, three days after the incident with de Silva, Judge Rafael Riefkhol ruled Knight had to stand trial for aggravated assault and threw out his countersuit against de Silva. Knight was ordered to appear in court two days later, the day of the championship game in which the Americans would face the host Puerto Ricans.

Two days later, on Friday, July 13, Knight sat stonily in court with his two attorneys, Clarence Doninger, a former IU basketball player who had hurriedly flown to San Juan, and a Puerto Rican lawyer, Luis F. González Correa. González Correa asked for a postponement, joking lamely, "It is the responsibility of all of us to be prepared for tonight's game, which Puerto Rico is going to win."

Like the U.S. team, Puerto Rico came into the finals with an 8–0 record. A crowd estimated at 13,000 jammed into 9,600 seat Roberto

Clemente Coliseum, hoping against hope for the upset, but the United States won, 113–94.

"I mean, they had the whole place packed," says Duren. "It was a real concern because we had heard some gunshots. Some of the track team told us that they had a couple of incidents while they were walking around with their USA stuff on, with Puerto Ricans saying Americans think you're all this and all that. And it was known that there had been some gunfire near the village. It was fenced in, but you had had gunfire and stuff like that. They would come and give us a report every day, just telling us to be careful.

"We were blowing them [Puerto Rico] out, then it got real close, and that's when Isiah just totally took over the game."

No U.S. high school basketball player had ever had such an impact in international competition. Thomas scored 21 points, including a four-minute burst in which he hit three shots, assisted on two baskets, and blocked a shot as the Americans pulled away.

"I remember, we all picked Coach Knight up because we really rallied behind him," says O'Koren. "And I remember, we picked him up and he was yelling at the crowd. . . . They were throwing stuff at him.

"I remember the cops. They had cops out there, but they had the military type policemen, you know, with the military gear on and the green beret hats on, you know what I mean? And they had like submachine guns and ammo all over the place. It got a little hairy, but it was fun the way it turned out. We got our gold medals, man, and we had a ball. They were trying to get us on the bus. They were throwing things at us and all that, but, you know, we couldn't care. We had a ball."

With his prize in hand, Knight celebrated on the floor with his players, spewing defiance, dismaying even his admirers. Taunted by the crowd while his players were given their gold medals, Knight told several U.S. reporters, "Fuck 'em! Fuck 'em all! I'll tell you what, their basketball is a hell of a lot easier to beat than their court system. The only fucking thing they know how to do is grow bananas."

Knight told the USOC's Mike Moran to gather the U.S. press, "just the Americans, don't let any Puerto Ricans in." When a reporter began writing it down, Knight snarled, "You'd better not write that. That was a private conversation. I have some rights. Somewhere in this world, I have some rights."

When the United Press's Jenny Kellner tried to ask Knight a question, he blew up, calling the island "a hellhole." Kellner had been there for two weeks, and had gotten a dark tan. She said later she thought Knight had taken her for a Puerto Rican.

As recounted by *Sports Illustrated*'s John Papanek, Knight got into an argument with Genaro Marchand, who was the Puerto Rican representative to the IABF.

"You were supposed to help us," said Knight.

"We tried, but you have no respect for anybody," said Marchand.

"I have respect for people who respect me," said Knight.

"You do not deserve respect," said Marchand. "You treat us like dirt. You have said nothing but bad things since you got here. You are an embarrassment to America, our country."

Then, as Knight stalked off, Marchand added, "You are an ugly American!"

Knight flew out the next morning at daybreak, ignoring his obligation to appear in court.

"I think when we woke up that morning, it had to be five-thirty or six, Coach Knight was rolling out," Duren says. "We didn't leave until four P.M. that day. I think Indiana University had already sent their plane down there to get him."

The aftermath would become familiar: Knight was widely condemned in all but one of the 50 states of the union. The basketball competition, which usually drew little attention, had become the story of the Pan-Am Games, with the U.S. press denouncing Knight, too.

Wrote *Newsweek*'s Pete Axthelm, who was close to Knight: "I should begin by admitting some prejudice. . . . Knight happens to be a friend of mine. And I think that he is a little crazy."

"The news here is that his friends are worried for Knight," wrote Dave Kindred, the Knight insider who was now at the *Washington Post*. "They are worried that his genius is fatally flawed. At 65, Woody Hayes punched a kid from another team and was fired. Bobby Knight is 38 and growing old in a hurry. His old Ohio State coach, Fred Taylor, his closest adviser and friend now, said, 'Bobby is driven by a force greater than any coach I've ever known. Nobody could keep up that pace without it reflecting in his face and emotions.'

"Only three years ago, Knight's hair was mostly black.

"Today it is mostly gray."

Knight never returned to Puerto Rico. He was tried in absentia, found guilty, sentenced to six months in jail and fined $500. A spokesman said Indiana Governor Otis Bowen "would not be willing to allow Bobby Knight to be extradited." Knight offered to resign but IU President John Ryan wouldn't accept it.

Even in retrospect, Knight didn't think he had done anything wrong. As he told Kindred, "If I walk away, where do I draw the line next time?"

The U.S. border looked like a good place to draw the line. The act they loved in Indiana set off a bonfire in the tinderbox that was San Juan.

SEVEN

THE BOOK OF ISIAH
INDIANA, 1979–82

Isiah came in in the second half and when it got close again, Knight just turned him loose. [Laughing] There ain't no other way to put it.

I mean, it was like almost a one-man show at that point. They took it out, gave it to him, he was going from end line to end line, just making layups. And every time they would help out, he would kick it to Kevin McHale or Mike Woodson for dunks. . . .

Me and Sam Clancy and Ralph Sampson sitting on the bench were like, "Whoa, you see that?" I mean, it was something to watch.

—John Duren, on the Pan-Am finale
against Puerto Pico

So began the relationship between Knight and the best player he ever coached, which was as much a duel of titans as a partnership.

Despite Isiah Thomas' tender age and dewy appearance, their war of wills had already begun in Puerto Rico, where Knight raged at him on the floor during the game against Brazil and threw him out of a practice; that was the day when Isiah was sitting on the team bus and he saw the San Juan police bring Knight out in handcuffs.

During the Brazil game, Knight wrote, he yelled at Thomas, "You'd better go to DePaul, Isiah, because you sure as hell aren't going to be an Indiana player playing like that!" Afterward, Knight pounced on Thomas so furiously, Pan-Am teammate Mike O'Koren asked Isiah if he was still going to IU.

"He had no hesitation about saying, 'No, of course I'm going. Nothing's going to stop me from going there,'" says O'Koren. "He was a tough guy. Boy, I'll tell you, he's a tough son of a gun."

Thomas' angelic, wide-eyed countenance notwithstanding, he was a hard case, too. Knight's players couldn't help but be intimidated but Thomas wasn't like the others; he was more like Knight. Like Knight, he was charismatic, strong-willed and driven. Like Knight, he had personas so discrete, he was almost two different people. If Knight was a tyrant with a warm side, Thomas was a choirboy with a street tough inside.

Thomas wasn't the usual Knight player waiting to be melded into a system. Knight wasn't into playground legends with their macho and scar tissue and had never tried to harness a spirit like this. He relied on the kind of character that didn't typically come out of abject poverty in a single-parent family with nine kids on Chicago's West Side.

Thomas had a burning desire to make it, but would never forget where he came from. He was rhapsodic in recounting the adventures of his youth, like the famous one when his mother, Mary, stood in the doorway with a sawed-off shotgun to chase off the Vice Lords, when they came to sign her boys up. Thomas later added in his book, *Fundamentals*, that the Vice Lords were really there because his oldest brother, Lord Henry, had stolen eight ounces of heroin from them and they wanted their product back.

Isiah's brothers had nosedived into street culture. Lord Henry and Gregory, known as Gay-Gay, were already out of the house and well into the drug lifestyle. Isiah's role model was his next oldest brother, Larry, who, he wrote, pimped for three women and dressed the part. Isiah was so taken that he dressed up in Larry's Superfly stuff one day and went outside.

"My brother was not amused," Thomas wrote. "He was cruising by in his powder-blue Cadillac. He recognized the clothes before he recognized me, then he dragged my bell-bottomed butt back home."

Isiah, the youngest of the seven boys and two girls, was the one they placed their hopes on. His brothers had been high-school stars but Isiah, who was playing on the eighth-grade team when he was in fourth grade, was a prodigy. He got a scholarship to St. Joseph's, a nice Catholic high school in the suburbs, and rode a bus an hour each way every day. He was such a quick study, he says, his friends in the neighborhood told him to stop "walking white."

Meanwhile, 200 miles away in Bloomington, Knight was still looking for the path back to the heights he had reached three years before. In the three seasons after winning their 1976 title, the Hoosiers would only get into the NCAA Tournament once. Knowing he was missing an important piece, Knight sent his crusty assistant, Roy Bates, to see Thomas. Bates, who was 62, wasn't enchanted about going out in the middle of winter, but this wouldn't be like any other scouting trip he ever made.

"I'm cold and I'm hungry," says Bates. "And I walked in this gym. I've seen so many basketball games, they're coming out my butt. Well, if you count my reserve varsity games, that's over 2,000, so that's a lot of basketball, you know. And I've seen all I want to see. And I get in this place and I see this kid. I'll tell you this, when I saw that kid, if you didn't like him, you had to be sick."

That was the thing about Thomas. With his dazzling game and his ready smile, people didn't just like him, they fell in love with him. He was everybody's type.

Knight was as enthralled by talent as anyone else, he just didn't want to have to make the usual accommodations to get it. However, Thomas played for a tough coach at St. Joseph's, Gene Pingatore, who sang his praises. Knight knew Thomas could name his price at any number of schools but Isiah was still open to coming to Indiana. This was important to Knight, whose standard pitch to a recruit who hadn't made up his mind between Indiana and somewhere else was a dismissive, you'll be better off somewhere else.

Landing Thomas would still be hard. People in Chicago wanted him to stay home and attend DePaul, where Mark Aguirre, his friend, was playing. Isiah's personal favorite was Notre Dame. The only ones who liked the idea of going to Indiana were his mother, Mary, and his sister, Rudy, but that meant a lot. Mary wanted someone with a stern hand to watch over her baby if she couldn't, and liked the fact that Knight was brutally honest and promised nothing.

"Let me put it square so everybody knows it," says Bates. "Bob Knight recruited Isiah Thomas and I'll tell you what did it. His mother was a tough and fine woman, as far as I'm concerned. She's a tough old lady but I liked her. I got to see a lot of her and his home, you know, but she told her son, never take money from anybody because you'll always regret it.

"And the brothers just went nuts. He likes his family, so you got to be careful about how you talk about them because he's a family kid, he loves his brothers and so forth. But those kids were mad because they wanted some money.

"Bob Knight took a lot of shit to get that kid."

In one of the all-time scenes in the history of recruiting, Knight came up to the Thomas home to make his final pitch with a delegation that included Pingatore, Bates, Quinn Buckner, and Milwaukee Bucks GM Wayne Embry.

Thomas wrote in *Fundamentals*:

> They all jammed into our living room with Knight's gang on one side and the Thomas gang on the other. From the start it looked like a rumble more than a recruiting visit. My brothers were all over Knight and he didn't back down. They fired question after question at him, demanding to know what my role was going to be, how much playing time I'd get and where their seats would be at home games. Gay-Gay was in typical form that evening. He had particularly strong feelings about Knight's coaching methods and he let him have it with both barrels.
>
> Bobby did not back down. It got very hostile between the two of them and finally, both were up out of their chairs, standing nose to nose, screaming at each other in the middle of the room.
>
> Knight's team and my other brothers jumped in to break it up but there was no salvaging the purpose of the visit, at least in that environment. Coach Knight and his entourage walked out. My

brothers got into an argument among themselves as the Knight team
left and ended up brawling in the front yard.

Knight's team retreated to Pingatore's office at St. Joseph's. They
called Thomas and asked if he would come over with his mother and sister but no brothers. He did, and Isiah committed to IU that night.

That turned out to be the easy part.

At IU, freshmen had to prove they could keep up. With Thomas, arriving in the fall of 1979, things were different. Everyone had to prove they
could keep up with him.

If he was small, more like 5-11 than his listed 6-1, Thomas was explosive, with a flashy style and an arrogance that let him take the ball to
the basket over bigger players. He wasn't a sharpshooter but he got on
amazing rolls. On a basketball floor, he was a little force of nature.

"I believe God has taken seven, eight, nine, ten people, and tapped
them on the head and said, 'Your purpose in life is to be great at basketball,'" says Steve Risley, a junior forward that season. "I mean you look
at Chamberlain, you look at Russell, you look at Bird, Johnson—you
know—Shaquille, Jerry West, these guys, their sole purpose was to be
great basketball players. That's what God created them for and Isiah is
in that category.

"He was that good. From the minute he walked onto the court his
freshman year, he became our heart, our soul, our leader. I mean, here's
a 19-year-old kid right out of high school and he became the dominant
player on a dominant program. You know, it was unbelievable."

The IU program was actually in transition, as was Knight, going
back to work after his Pan-American misadventure. *Sports Illustrated,*
which had presented him as an ugly American four months before, now
made IU its preseason No. 1 pick. The Hoosiers had Mike Woodson,
Randy Wittman, Ray Tolbert, and Landon Turner coming back but the
selection was a tribute to Thomas, whose fame was already spreading.

The magazine asked Knight to pose for a cover shot. "What I had in
mind," editor Walter Bingham told the *Indianapolis Star,* "was to get

Knight out to any stop light in Bloomington and catch him in some pose symbolizing how his defense stops opponents."

What Knight had in mind was a different kind of symbolism. He was incredulous that someone could "tear you to pieces . . . like *Sports Illustrated* did to me after the Pan-American Games and turn around and expect me to pose for their cover. I told them to walk outside the Time-Life Building in New York, reach up and stick the whole building up their ass."

Knight's regard for the press had been low enough before it blasted him for his conduct at the Pan-Am Games. He had a particular distaste for *Sports Illustrated,* starting with the irreverent college basketball writer Curry Kirkpatrick. Kirkpatrick was a sportswriter version of Tom Wolfe, cutting a dandy figure in his mod clothes and tinted glasses. Like Wolfe, Kirkpatrick wrote for maximum effect with a keen eye for foibles—and no one had more than Knight.

Knight, who demanded respect, didn't appreciate Kirkpatrick's sense of humor, as in a 1975 story that began: "Just because Indiana University Coach Bobby Knight, that mellowing maniac, has not punched a player, strangled a referee, pistol-whipped a writer or howled at the moon in the last few minutes is no reason to ignore his team."

Kirkpatrick also recounted a scene in which Knight apprehended an unidentified writer—Kirkpatrick—talking to a player without permission, whereupon Knight "screamed, stomped and physically threatened the man, then stormed off, reviewing every bleep his military upbringing could dredge up. Later he apologized and shared a relaxing dinner with the culprit."

All coaches had complaints about the press, but none were prepared to go to the lengths Knight did. In 1980, he ordered Kirkpatrick to leave a postgame press conference, threatening to end the session on the spot if he didn't go. Kirkpatrick replied, "In deference to my colleagues, I'll leave. I'm leaving but I'm leaving for these people's sakes."

"You're leaving because I told you so, asshole," said Knight.

However, if Knight was an ogre to the press, he loved to perform and, despite his protestations, loved the attention. As the hard-boiled

New York guys had loved him at Army because he gave them so much to write, the national press followed his every move.

Everyone was mesmerized. *60 Minutes*, the hard-nosed scourge of presidents and kings, had a camera crew filming away in Assembly Hall for a feature on Knight in the spring of 1980 when he fired a starter's pistol at Russ Brown of the Louisville *Courier-Journal* just outside the press room. The *60 Minutes* crew had just shot the postgame press conference but, in a striking omission, didn't even mention the macabre prank in its story.

"The paper wanted to know if I wanted to sue for wanton endangerment and all that," says Russ Brown. "People always said to me, 'Well, that was a mean thing to do, no normal person would have done it.' But, I guarantee you, it was Knight's idea of a joke. . . .

"I was going to the locker room to interview players. And I got maybe, it's hard to know, but maybe 10 to 15 yards down the hall. And he yelled, 'Hey, Russ!' And I turned around and he had a gun and he shot it. . . . He didn't really give me time to be scared. I mean, it was like before I knew it, the gun had gone off. I knew either it wasn't real or I wasn't shot.

"I said, 'You missed.'

"And he said, 'Wait until you shake your head.'

"The worst part of it was the sound. I mean, it was in a concrete hallway in Assembly Hall. And that sound of the gunshot just ricocheted off those concrete walls. And it was really loud. And you know, really, to this day, neither one of us has mentioned it. Except that he has told people, it got back to me, that he appreciated the way I reacted to it because I took it as a joke."

When Knight fired the pistol, Bob Pille of the *Chicago Sun-Times*, who was standing next to him, told him, "Bob, you're crazy."

Replied Knight, paraphrasing a line from a Willie Nelson song: "I've got to be crazy, it keeps me from going insane."

Thomas' freshman season didn't turn out to be the triumph *Sports Illustrated* predicted. The Hoosiers went 21–8 and won their first Big Ten title since 1976, going 13–5 in the conference. Then, however, they lost in the second round of the NCAA tournament to, indignity of indignities, Purdue.

With Thomas, Mike Woodson, and Ray Tolbert, they were one of the most talented teams Knight would ever have, but they weren't close to being the most cohesive. Everyone had always known who was in charge before, but now, Knight said to do it one way and Isiah went onto the floor and did it another. The other Hoosiers were like spectators at a tennis match.

"Well, what you end up having is, now you've got a control freak and a regimented coach," says Steve Risley, "and now you've got one of the most free-wheeling, free-spirited, talented kids to come into college basketball since Magic or Bird, and probably more talented than either one of those.

"And now you've got Isiah wants to run the team one way and Knight wants to run the team the other way. So, that season, I believe, looking back, we really struggled trying to figure out who the hell was going to run this team. I mean, we loved playing with Isiah but we loved Coach. . . .

"It wasn't like there was a huge yelling and screaming match all the time, but there was just this constant friction of Knight trying to tone Isiah down and Isiah trying to turn the program up. And it just went on and on and on and we couldn't get an identity. . . . We didn't know who we were."

In Knight's motion offense, no one was supposed to dribble much. Everyone moved the ball, cut, and set screens for teammates until they got a good shot. Thomas could blow by anyone on the dribble and didn't see why he should make the game any more complicated than that.

"Here's Isiah," says Phil Isenbarger, a junior that season, "and he's a true playmaker and somebody who doesn't need the motion offense to create a shot for him. Doesn't need the motion offense to create a shot for somebody else because he can do it with one-on-one basketball. And so there was always this struggle to sort of meld the motion offense with Isiah's talents."

Knight bore down on Thomas as only he could. Every IU player had his moments when he didn't know if he could handle it and, says Thomas, "I was no exception."

Nevertheless, in the world Thomas had grown up in, there were scarier things than being yelled at. He didn't mount an overt challenge to Knight, but he didn't tremble before him as everyone else did.

"Isiah was perhaps the only player that I've seen play for Knight who wasn't intimidated by him," says Russ Brown, who covered the IU beat for 14 seasons. "I remember I was talking to him one night after a game in the locker room. And I don't even remember what he said to me but one of the other players said, 'You'd better watch what you say, Coach Knight isn't going to like that.'

"And Isiah said, right in front of me, 'I don't give a shit what that son of a bitch says.'

"All the other players, you could tell, were scared to death of Knight. And Isiah wasn't. He just wasn't."

Knight was up to his neck in Thomases. At home games, he often had Isiah's brothers yelling at him, notably Gay-Gay, who wore outfits Bloomington folks otherwise had to go to the movies to see. Once, Mary Thomas even barged past the guard at the dressing room door to unload on Knight for yelling at her baby.

Isiah would later help his brothers get sober, and described the circus around him in *Fundamentals*:

> *Some of my brothers behaved pretty badly when they came to campus. A couple of them were still into drugs in those days and the prospect of coming to see me play in Bloomington, Indiana often put them on edge. The campus in the cornfields seemed like hostile territory to my brothers. . . .*
>
> *On more than a few occasions, my brothers came to my games and got a little out of control, yelling things at our opponents and at Coach Knight if he got on my case. . . .*
>
> *Coach Knight never had security guards clear them out and he was respectful to my mom, even when she bulled her way into the locker room and gave him a piece of her mind in front of the whole team.*

Knight had never brooked the slightest resistance from a player, to say nothing of having to sit still for input from the player's family, too, and the strain showed. Finally, Knight went off in a dressing-room eruption in which he was said to have railed at one of his players that he would turn out "like all the rest of the niggers in Chicago, including your brothers."

The story would be first disclosed by Butch Carter in *Born to Believe*, a book he and his brother, Cris, an NFL star, co-wrote in 2000, when Butch was coaching the NBA's Toronto Raptors. Butch didn't name the player Knight yelled at but the reference to Chicago made it clear it was Thomas. Thomas would promptly deny it, as would several of his teammates. Carter was roundly bashed and the furor was quickly contained.

However, Steve Risley, who played four years for Knight and still counts himself as an admirer, says the story is true.

"Carter said it did happen, right," says Risley. "And all the players came out and denied it. And I think maybe even Isiah denied it, but it happened.

"It was a very, very unfortunate thing and it's probably the only time I've ever seen Knight with tears in his eyes. It was just one of those deals where you know, they were wrestling for control of the team, Isiah and Knight. And really they had so much respect for each other's ability, but yet just such different approaches for what needed to be done.

"And they were just in the locker room arguing one time and they go at it and at it and at it. . . . And Knight just got frustrated and said, 'Goddamn it, I've put up with your damn family, I've put up with you. You're nothing but a goddamn ghetto nigger.'

"And the minute he said it, the room went dead fucking silent. He ran out of the room. I mean, he ran out of the room. Isiah's locker was right next to mine and I looked at him and Isiah was in tears. I mean, Isiah was crying. We didn't know what to do, we all had our heads down.

"Coach had never, ever—this was not a racial thing, it was just a frustration thing. And Knight, when you've got that kind of a vernacular, you're going to say stupid things occasionally. And I don't think to this day anybody felt worse than Knight.

"We sat there, probably for two minutes, it seemed like two days, you could hear a pin drop anywhere in the building. I mean, nobody said a word. Isiah was sobbing and this was something we had never seen. . . . And two minutes probably went by and he [Knight] came back in the locker room and basically made everybody get out, except Isiah. . . .

"I wasn't as close to Isiah as some of the other guys were, so I never really pursued too much what was said, but I think it was pretty well patched up and I think that part was pretty well forgotten. But it did happen. I mean, it happened in [front of] my eyes. I mean, I remember the incident and I just explained to you in front of my eyes what happened.

"So, when Butch came out—and I don't have a lot of respect for Butch because of what went on with stuff—but I was kind of surprised that people vehemently denied it. When I was asked by the media about it, I just said, 'Look, there are a lot of things that happened back then and I can't recollect them all.'

"Because I didn't want to get in the middle of it and that was when Coach was being fired and I wanted to be able to show support. But I was really surprised at the people that came out and said that the incident did not happen. . . .

"It's one of those things that I don't really know what value it does to bring it out in public and that's what was kind of surprising to me about Butch but when it's out in public, it's out. I mean, I squelched that thing for 20 years."

Somehow, Thomas, Knight, and everyone else got past it. Thomas never complained about it and, indeed, kept the secret as faithfully as Knight and the other players.

If Thomas' freshman season was a disappointment, his sophomore season looked like a disaster. After 12 games, they were 7–5 and going backward, having just been beaten in the Rainbow Classic in Honolulu by Clemson and little Pan-American.

Knight had a new problem with Thomas: just keeping him around.

Until the preceding spring when Magic Johnson left Michigan State as a sophomore after leading the Spartans to an NCAA title, few undergraduates had turned pro. Now, suddenly, the gates seemed wide open. Magic, Isiah, and Mark Aguirre, who was now a junior at DePaul, were friends and there was speculation Isiah and Aguirre would follow Magic into the NBA.

Knight had never tiptoed around a player but he was afraid to confront Thomas, for fear of chasing him off. However, not knowing made Knight crazy, too.

"This is a point in time when he's calling me in and other seniors in," says Phil Isenbarger, "and saying he's going to quit, it doesn't make any sense to coach anymore, he could be a broadcaster, he's got other things he can do, this team doesn't want to win. You start to believe it. . . . He got to the point that he was convinced, or tried to convince himself, I guess, that Isiah had decided already that he was going to go pro.

"And to tell you how bad it was, we were such good friends with Isiah—and I regret this to this day—we went back as a group and said, 'Isiah, you gotta make up your mind. What are you going to do? Come on, you're screwing things up. Just say you're going to stay or you're going to go. If you're going to go, go.'

"Because that's what he [Knight] wanted us to do and that was wrong. Because Isiah wasn't going to go. He might go at the end of the year or might not, but for now he was doing what the rest of us were doing, just trying to get through it, playing ball. . . .

"I can remember standing in Coach's office and him saying something like, 'You guys are just going to have to get Isiah to decide. Is he going to play or not play? Just decide. I'd rather have him leave now if that's what he's going to do so get a commitment or something.'

At that point, Thomas says he had no idea what he would do. He didn't even know if there was a real possibility of going to the NBA.

"Believe it or not, I didn't even know," says Thomas. "Because when you're in Bloomington, Indiana, you're so isolated. Like, Mark

Aguirre was really leading the charge, he was the one telling me, 'Well, you know, we can go pro and I talked to Magic and we can do this.'

"And I was getting off the phone and telling my girlfriend, who's my wife now, 'Mark says we can go hardship and go to the pros and all that.'

"And she's like, 'What are you talking about?'"

With so many undercurrents swirling, the season got crazier by the day. In a win at home over Purdue on January 31, Thomas tangled with the Boilermakers' Roosevelt Barnes. In a February 19 loss at Iowa, Isiah was ejected for hitting Steve Krafcisin.

With charges going back and forth before the rematch with Purdue, Knight announced on his TV show that he had invited Boilermaker athletic director George King to come on but he had declined. Knight said he had a stand-in who was just as qualified to discuss basketball. "His name is Jack," said Knight, as the camera swung to a donkey wearing a Purdue hat. King was so upset, he filed a protest to Big Ten Commissioner Wayne Duke. Meanwhile, T-shirts showing a donkey in a Purdue uniform went on sale in Bloomington.

Without fanfare, Roy Bates dropped out of the picture in the second half of the season and went home to Ohio. Knight was always calling Clair Bee and Pete Newell for advice, but he also liked having someone senior on his staff. At Army, it had been Al LoBalbo and, at IU before Bates, it had been Andy Andreas, his old boss at Cuyahoga Falls High School.

Nevertheless, the mentors who were there every day could be terminated on a moment's notice. Knight had renounced LoBalbo for years for taking the Fairleigh Dickinson job, although they later made up. At IU, Andreas had dropped out of sight one day, without explanation.

Bates had been a major figure in Ohio prep circles, coaching Dean Chance in baseball at Northwestern High when Knight was at Orrville. Bates was a Knight type, hard-driving, salty, and imaginative. Once when one of his high-school players was giving a teacher a hard time, Bates made him wear lace panties to practice.

Bates even lived with the Knights in Bloomington when he joined the coaching staff. At 65, he was a crusty guy who said what was on his mind. He still had his own radio show on a 50,000-watt station in Wooster, Ohio, where Joe Tait, the Cleveland Cavaliers' broadcaster, once described him as "Rush Limbaugh on speed."

Bates had become especially close to Thomas. In later years, after Bates moved back to Ohio, Isiah would send a limo to bring him to games when the Pistons were in Cleveland. Thomas once said, "I never made a major life decision without talking to Roy first."

Bates, who died in 2004, never said publicly why he left IU. However, he was one of the few assistants who dared to talk back to Knight.

"The first question I ever asked the man when I got the job was, 'Do I have to kiss your butt or can I tell you the truth?'" Bates said. "Well, he was a little speechless. So that's the way it was. The man never heard the truth. I told him the truth. I bet you when I was out there, I was asked over 100 times, 'Would you please tell this to Bob, he ought to know about it.' And the coaches wouldn't do it. And everybody, the hangers-on, kissed his ass all the time. . . .

"I'm a friend of his. I've got to tell you a couple of things I think you ought to know. Number one is, the guy does not cheat. I think he made very few adjustments, though, to the change in the culture and I think that got to be a problem. You understand what I'm saying?

"I don't think there's any question about it. And he's a great basketball coach but he doesn't know crap about dealing with kids. . . . When you deal with Knight, if you disagree with him, you're being disloyal, if it gets down to the nitty gritty."

On February 19, they lost, 78–65, at Iowa, to drop to 16–9. With five games left in the season, the players weren't thinking miracle finish, but please, can we get this over with?

In the biggest surprise of all, Knight then gave up his iron-handed control and turned Thomas loose. To Knight, it was like being physically assaulted.

"Okay, we go to Iowa and we get pounded," says Risley. "And we come back the next day and I remember it so vividly. And we're thinking, 'Shit this is going to be another horrible week of practice and we're going to get reamed again.'

"I'm dreading this like there's no tomorrow. And he comes out, you know, and calls everyone in the locker room. And this is where I recall the famous line being said. He grabs us all aside, and he says, 'Listen, goddamn it, let me tell you all something about this.' He said, 'If rape is inevitable, just sit back and relax and fucking enjoy it.'

"And Isiah Thomas took over that basketball team and you know what happened from that point on. We never got close to anybody again. I think until this day, we still hold one of the highest average winning margins in the tournament.

"I mean, the greatest coaching move he ever made was to realize if this team was going to win, that he would have to either get rid of Isiah or give in to Isiah."

Just when it looked as if nothing was going to go right, everything did. Knight had been raging all season, and for two seasons before that, at forward Landon Turner. At midseason, Knight told him he might as well enter the NBA draft, too, because he wasn't going to play at IU any more.

Turner was big (6-10, 240), talented, and aimless. He had been a star at Indianapolis Tech but he had other things going on in his life, or as he later put it, "I wanted to chase women and have women chase me." He would play well, then disappear in the next game, or miss class or mope through practice. Whoever else was in the doghouse could always curl up next to Turner. Now Landon was a junior and Knight still hadn't gotten to him, although he wasn't through trying.

"I remember one time we were about to begin a team meeting," says Turner, "and I was just sitting there, waiting for the coaches to come in and talk about the next game. And so the coaches came in and Coach Knight had a bag. I'm looking at him thinking, 'What the heck is in that bag?'

"And Coach Knight said, 'Landon, the coaches and I pitched in to buy you a present. We want you to have it.'

"So he handed me the bag and I reached in the bag and pulled out a box of tampons. He looked at me with this little grin and said, 'You're playing like a pussy.'

"And everybody started laughing and everything. I didn't think it was so funny. But I guess it was his way of telling me to play more aggressively and to motivate me to be a meaner player. It didn't really motivate me or demotivate me. I just had the same attitude. But when you really don't want to play for somebody, it does make it harder to respond to his coaching. . . .

"He wanted me to quit. He didn't want me to play any more for Indiana University. He wanted me off his team and he told me I should turn pro because I wasn't going to play for Indiana. He wouldn't talk to me. The assistant coaches wouldn't talk to me. My teammates wouldn't talk to me.

"Then we played Northwestern [February 12] and he put me in the game and I made some mistakes. He pulled me out of the game and then he put me back in because he wanted all the fans to see the reason why he was going to kick me off the team. But I did some good things out there and he began to change his thinking."

Turner, who had been averaging 3 points a game to that point, averaged 15 after that. Another piece of the puzzle fell improbably into place.

Knight's teams were known to finish strong, but none of them turned around like this one did. With everyone waiting for the Hoosiers to blow up, they turned into a juggernaut.

After the loss at Iowa, when Knight loosened the reins, they won their next three at home, beating Minnesota, Ohio State, and Michigan by an average of 14 points. They beat No. 16–ranked Illinois, 69–66, in Champaign, and closed the season with a 69–48 win at Michigan State to take the Big Ten title.

Their five-game winning streak boosted them to 21–9, No. 7 in the nation. In the first round of the NCAA in Dayton, they blew away a formidable Maryland team with Buck Williams and Albert King, 99–64, surprising themselves as much as anyone else. Risley had been so sure they would lose, he had packed for spring break, planning to leave from there.

Everything else was going their way, too. The Mideast regionals were in Assembly Hall, where the Hoosiers faced two underdogs who had pulled off upsets, No. 7 seed UAB and No. 9 St. Joseph's. While the Hoosiers were dispatching them by 15 and 32, respectively, the nation's No. 1– and 2–ranked teams, DePaul and Oregon State, were upset.

The Hoosiers advanced to the Final Four in the Spectrum in Philadelphia, where they had won their 1976 title. Their semifinal opponent, LSU, was 31–3 and ranked No. 4 but the Hoosiers broke open a close game and drilled the Tigers by 18. Turner outscored LSU's star forward, Durand Macklin, 20–4.

"I didn't start," says Risley, "but I was sitting on the bench and I was talking to one of the players, let's say Grunwald, I can't remember. But I said, 'Look what happens when these guys run down court.'

"The LSU players would actually swerve away from Knight. They were so intimidated by him and his presence that you would start laughing about it. They would be coming down court and right as they got across center court, nine out of ten times, when they came close, they'd swerve to the center of the court. I mean, we were 10 points up before the game ever started. So LSU battled us tight in the first half, and we end up blowing them out."

That night Knight celebrated by stuffing an LSU fan into a garbage can, at least according to the legend that grew up around it.

Knight had headquartered his team across the Delaware River from Philadelphia in the New Jersey suburb of Cherry Hill to get away from the revelry, only to find the hotel loaded with hard-partying LSU fans chanting "Tiger bait!" at everyone else. After the Hoosiers beat LSU, Knight was walking through the lounge of the Cherry Hill Inn when his path crossed that of a medium-sized accountant from Baton Rouge named Buddy Bonnecaze. Bonnecaze was drinking with friends, and on his way back to the bar to buy another round when he saw Knight and congratulated him.

Knight said he answered "Well, we weren't really Tiger bait after all, were we?" Bonnecaze said Knight actually said, "goddamn Tiger bait." Bonnecaze acknowledged calling Knight "an asshole," after which Knight chased him down and asked him what he had said. Bonnecaze repeated it, thinking Knight wouldn't do anything in front of everybody. Knight said he shoved Bonnecaze against a wall and walked away. Bonnecaze said Knight grabbed him by the throat, squeezed it so hard he had bruises around his neck and pushed him backwards over—but not into—a plastic garbage can.

"I walked over," Knight said. "I did a little more than walk over. I walked swiftly over and I said, 'Would you like to say again what you just said?'

"If being called an asshole three or four times, and going over and grabbing the guy that did it in public and then shoving the guy up against a wall is something I've done that's wrong, then so be it because if it happens again tomorrow, I'll be wrong again tomorrow."

Bonnecaze wanted the incident forgotten so no one was arrested or sued. However, it did burnish Knight's growing legend.

Two days later, hours before IU was to play North Carolina in the finals, President Ronald Reagan was shot by John Hinckley, who said he was trying to impress actress Jodie Foster. Hit in the chest by a ricochet, Reagan underwent surgery as the nation came to a halt.

The Academy Awards scheduled for that night were called off. The NCAA tournament committee, led by Wayne Duke, debated until an hour before game time when they heard Reagan's surgery had been successful.

The game had been billed as a showdown between Knight and Dean Smith, who were actually friends with great respect for each other. Smith's team, with Al Wood, James Worthy, and Sam Perkins, had finished second in the ACC to Ralph Sampson's Virginia, but had beaten the Cavaliers by 15 in the NCAA semifinals behind Wood's 39-point breakout.

The favored Tar Heels jumped into a 16–8 lead and stayed ahead through a low-scoring first half. Randy Wittman hit an 18-footer on the baseline just before the horn, giving IU its first lead at 26–25.

Thomas then took over at the start of the second half in one of his Mighty Mouse numbers, stealing the ball twice, assisting on two baskets and scoring 10 points in the first seven minutes. He wound up scoring 19 points in the second half, 23 in all. Landon Turner had 12 points, standing in against Worthy and Perkins, and was named to the All-Final-Four team. Indiana won, 63–50.

That made two NCAA titles and one Pan-American gold medal in six seasons for Knight, to go with all his other headlines. He might be a tempestuous genius, but the genius was as real as the tempest.

Now, however, the war was won and the tempest had blown itself out.

"I just remember coming into the locker room after the celebration," says Glen Grunwald. "I was, I think, the first player in off the floor in the locker room and Knight was really—I was surprised how subdued he was. He was just sort of just relaxed. He was just sitting there and I shook his hand. . . .

"He was obviously happy, but he was very subdued. I was just surprised that that's the way he would be. Knight often said that the pain he suffers from losing does not equal the joy he gets from winning."

The two-year Knight–Thomas tug-of-war was over. Shortly afterward, Thomas entered the 1981 NBA draft and became the No. 2 pick. Knight later said he encouraged Thomas to leave. If Knight did, however, he never said it in public.

Knight had mixed feelings. If Thomas stayed, it might mean more titles. It would surely mean a continuation of their battle of wills.

"I got the impression that Knight didn't really shed any tears when Isiah left," says Russ Brown, "because he couldn't take credit for Isiah. Isiah was a great player when he got there."

In the end Thomas' decision had little to do with Knight and everything to do with Mary Thomas. Isiah got a contract starting at $400,000 with a $600,000 bonus, and bought his mom a house in the suburbs where heat, food, and gangs would never be a problem again.

Normally, when IU players completed the course, things changed for the better. However, Knight's relationship with Thomas, his greatest player, took years to develop. Knight had hated being left to dangle while Thomas decided his career path, and Knight inspired contrary feelings in Thomas.

A year after Thomas left IU, he was honored by the Fort Wayne Mad Anthonys as their Hoosier celebrity of the year at their annual charity golf tournament at the Orchard Ridge Country Club. By then Thomas had money, but still wasn't used to country-club sensibility. For their part, the Mad Anthonys had never honored a black athlete, not Oscar Robertson, George McGinnis, Steve Downing, Quinn Buckner, or Scott May.

Flying up from Bloomington with Knight, Thomas asked what he should say. Knight told him to make jokes at his expense. Taking Knight at his word, Thomas proceeded to tell the Mad Anthonys what Knight had taught him, including the imaginative curses Knight came up with, like "sunt," which was a combination of "sissy" and "cunt."

The Mad Anthonys were outraged. The story got into the newspapers, whereupon Thomas apologized to all concerned. Knight maintained a stony silence but gave Thomas the old unperson treatment, starting the next time he saw Isiah playing in a pickup game in Assembly Hall and ordered him out.

Nevertheless, Knight was as drawn to Thomas as Thomas was to Knight. Knight was and always would be a father figure to Isiah.

"I didn't believe that would ever happen," says Thomas. "I was, 'Hey, screw you, I hate you, blah, blah, blah.' Right?

"He said, 'Just like your parents tell you, one day you're going to come back and you're going to thank me for everything I tried to do for you.' And I did.

"When you're under his tutelage for those three or four years or two years, you come to realize that every single thing that he was talking about in basketball wasn't about basketball. It was about life. When he corrected a mistake out on the floor, it really wasn't about a passing angle. It was about you were too lazy to really go over there and make the proper pass. . . .

"I wouldn't have had the success that I had, and I wouldn't have become the person that I am had I not played for Bobby Knight. I would have been a totally different player and person and everything else. It was probably one of the hardest experiences I've ever had but now that I'm on the other side of it, it was just what I needed to be what I am today."

That was how it was for them all. The program *was* about love, at least after you got through it, assuming you did.

EIGHT

THE VIEW FROM OLYMPUS
INDIANA AND LOS ANGELES, 1981–84

When he walked into the gym, it was like the second coming, you know. Everybody was like, "oooh." He was bigger than the players, actually almost bigger than the program, it seemed like. . . .

We played them in Evansville, Indiana, and when he walked into the gym, it was as though God had come in.

—Olympian Wayman Tisdale,
on his first encounter with Knight

Bobby was recruiting Joe Hillman, so he's shooting one day after the practice was over and Michael [Jordan] is out shooting, too. And he kind of dribbles the ball over to Hillman and he says, "Is it true you're going to Indiana?"

And he says, "Yes, I'm going to go to Indiana." Jordan says, "Do you know what you're doing?" He says, "Yeah, I think so." And Jordan just laughed and he dribbled the ball away laughing.

—Pete Newell

In the summer of 1981, coming off his second NCAA title, Knight almost got out when he was ahead. CBS, taking over the NCAA Tournament from NBC, wanted him to become its lead commentator. They had been signaling each other back and forth in the final months of the 1980–81 season, and the more trouble Knight had with Isiah Thomas, the better CBS looked.

"There were all those rumors," says Phil Isenbarger, a junior in the spring of 1981, "and it was not atypical for him to take that situation or some other situation and use it in the middle of practice. We'd start practicing—'I don't know why the fuck I do this, you know? I could be sitting in a goddamn booth making more fucking money and not have to deal with you fuckers. It's beyond me why I'm here trying to get something done with you people that don't want to help yourselves. I don't need this shit. I won championships. Why do I do this?'"

Nancy Knight was all for a career change that would bring him home from the war that was always going on in his head. CBS would give him twice what he was making at IU, which was $200,000, counting summer-camp money. Then there were all those *situations* Knight kept waking up and finding himself in.

"These things make me wonder if it's worth it or not," Knight told Dave Kindred. "I wanted to win a national championship and then another with an entirely different team. Now what?"

Knight talked about John Updike's famous account of Knight's hero, Ted Williams, bowing out with a home run in his last at-bat:

> *Like a feather caught in a vortex, Williams ran around the square of bases at the center of our beseeching screaming. He ran as he always ran out home runs—hurriedly, unsmiling, head down, as if our praise were a storm of rain to get out of. He didn't tip his cap. Though we thumped, wept, and chanted "We want Ted" for minutes after he hid in the dugout, he did not come back. Our noise for some seconds passed beyond excitement into a kind of immense open anguish, a wailing, a cry to be saved. But immortality is nontransferable. The papers said that the other players, and even the umpires on the field, begged him to come out and acknowledge us in some way, but he refused. Gods do not answer letters.*

That was how Knight wanted to go, with a flourish and a fast trip around the bases, without tipping his cap. He didn't intend to answer letters, either. All he had to do was quit, and he was trying.

Then, on the night of July 25, on State Road 46 outside of Columbus, Indiana, 30 miles from Bloomington, Landon Turner lost control of his car, which flipped over, fracturing his spine. Knight, who was on his annual fishing trip, flew home and rushed to Turner's bedside.

"I was with him when all that happened," says Kohn Smith, Knight's assistant. "He and I and a guy named Elliot Anderson were fishing up in Montana when Landon Turner got in his accident. So, anyway, I ended up driving him to the airport so he could fly back to do everything.

"But for a solid week prior to that, every night in a hotel or whatever, he was listing all the pluses of going to CBS and all the minuses and all the pluses of staying at Indiana and going. So, he absolutely was thinking about retiring and doing the CBS thing. . . . I guess the thing with coaching is that once you're at the top there's no place else to go but down, you know?

"But when Landon Turner got hurt, at first he was really mad. 'That dang kid, I tried to get him to pay attention to stuff and what's he doing, taking off in a car?' But then as the next hour and the next hour passed and the next hour after that, then he started like, 'Jeez, I gotta help this kid.'

"The only thing I know, he said to me personally, he said, 'There's no way I cannot coach this year because I've got to take care of this kid. If I'm not back there they'll just let this go. If I'm back there I can take care of this kid, I can raise money for him, I can take care of his family.' He absolutely was totally heartbroken that this kid with all this talent and future lost it all in a second there."

Knight said nothing ever affected him like the sight of Turner lying in a coma. Knight started the Landon Turner Trust Fund, staging benefits and dinners all over the state, which would eventually raise over $500,000. Turner was in a wheelchair for life, although he regained use of his hands. Few stories would ever illustrate the two sides of Knight as clearly: Six months after placing a tampon in his locker, Knight had devoted himself to Turner's care and saw Landon as his charge. "I'm a coach," Knight said. "I think that's a coach's responsibility."

Knight made Turner the 1981–82 captain. The next spring Knight got his friend Red Auerbach to make him the Celtics' pick in the tenth round of the NBA draft. Turner sent Auerbach a telegram thanking him, adding: "When do I report?"

There was more than Turner keeping Knight at IU, however. Knight said later the CBS people didn't come up with all the money they talked about, and he didn't like the drift he was getting that he was supposed to be their Howard Cosell.

Even before those issues arose, Knight was coming to grips with the central problem: No matter how much he suffered and how often he wished he was out, it wasn't easy to walk away. He had a love–hate relationship with coaching, but there was nothing he cared about remotely as much. The pain was part of the bargain. When Bill Parcells' NFL teams struggled, Knight would call, knowing how nice it was to hear from a friend who knew what he was going through. Knight did the same thing with Tony LaRussa, the baseball manager, once noting, "I spend half my life trying to keep Parcells and LaRussa sane."

So, Knight stayed, although as he told Kindred later, "It's the only time I've ever been close to doing something other than coach here."

With Turner, Isiah Thomas, and Ray Tolbert gone, the 1981–82 team went 19–10 and tied for second in the Big Ten, which was an achievement under the circumstances. And then in the spring, as if the gods wanted to reward Knight or test him or both, he got the call he didn't dare to hope for, telling him he had been named the U.S. Olympic coach.

He could scarcely have been given a greater honor. The 1984 Olympics would be in Los Angeles, the first on U.S. soil since 1932. The Americans might get their first shot at the Soviet Union since 1972 in Munich, where Hank Iba's team lost after a controversial ruling gave the Soviets extra chances at the end.

Knight had been in line to coach the U.S. team at the Moscow games in 1980, since the Pan-Am coach usually coached the next Olympic team. However, after the Puerto Rican misadventure, Providence's Dave Gavitt beat him out in the vote taken by the U.S. basketball federation. It was a crushing blow to Knight.

The federation was again down to two candidates, Knight and Georgetown's John Thompson, but Knight had the support of the most influential members, executive director Bill Wall, Big Ten Commissioner Wayne Duke, and Pete Newell, who had coached the legendary 1960 U.S. team. They believed Knight's story, which was backed up by all the U.S. players and coaches, that he was blameless for the incident in Puerto Rico. Even the people who thought Knight might have conducted himself in a more diplomatic manner didn't want to see him remembered that way.

"I was on the Olympic Committee on the time," Newell says, "and of course we had a lot of anti-Knight guys on that committee who believed every bad thing that was written. . . . But we wanted to know what happened and we got it from the people who were right there and Mike [Krzyzewski] was one of them and he told me. And Bill [Wall] really gave a great report to this committee and we heard from him exactly what happened. And Fred Taylor, all of their stories are exactly the same."

Most of all, they were coaches, and wanted to win, which was no longer a slam dunk. Despite the highjinks the Soviet Union needed to win at Munich, there was no doubt the Soviets were becoming a threat.

Knight would never receive a compliment that meant as much to him. It not only moved him as an American, it showed that the most respected of his peers and the basketball establishment were behind him. He called three friends: Newell, Hank Iba, and Bob Hammel, the sports editor of the *Bloomington Herald-Telephone*.

"He was like a little kid," Hammel told John Feinstein. "I had been at a track meet in Minneapolis and when I called my office, they said he had called, which wasn't unusual. What was unusual was that he had left his home phone number with the desk. Usually, he's very sensitive about giving strangers his number but he had just changed it and he wanted to make sure I reached him.

"When I called, the first thing he said to me was, 'You'll never guess what happened. They've named me Olympic coach. . . .'

"I knew he felt that the scars of San Juan would be too much to overcome. In fact, I didn't even know that was the weekend they were picking the coach because he never mentioned it to me. He was as private about that as he had ever been."

Knight, whose father attached so little significance to the field of endeavor his son chose, often said he wasn't sure he had ever done anything important in his life. This, Knight said, was important. If it was duty, it was personal, too. As Knight noted, "I am not the ugly American and I do not wish to be remembered that way."

Wrote Feinstein: "He loves to bristle and give off an aura of toughness. He enjoys his bad boy image. But deep down one senses that Bob Knight still has a simple dream: to be an American hero.

"This is his shot."

The heroism thing got off to a slow start. Barely had the protests of his selection died out when Knight told a story about mooning Puerto Rico out of his airplane window. It got out and the press arose again, as one.

Knight had been speaking at a dinner dance in Gary to raise money for Methodist Hospital when the emcee jokingly presented him with a one-way ticket to San Juan. Knight, king of the last word, whether appropriate to the occasion or any occasion, said that when he left "that island, I stood up, unzipped my pants, lowered my shorts and placed my bare ass on the window because that's the last thing I wanted those people to see of me."

Whether or not it was true, it wasn't amusing to at least one man in the audience, Carmelo Menendez, a Puerto Rican who had settled in Indiana after his wife graduated from IU. He produced a weekly TV show called *Our People—Los Hispanos*, and reported Knight's words in a column on the Hispanic Link News Service.

The story was picked up and created a furor. William Simon, the former Treasury Secretary who ran the U.S. Olympic Committee, told the *New York Times*' Dave Anderson, "I don't know if Bobby actually said what I heard third-hand but if he did, it was the grossest of bad judgment and he ought to be told to quit it."

Not that Anderson seemed surprised by Knight's sense of humor, noting that Knight liked to tell women, "There's only two things you people are good for, making kids and frying bacon."

Knight was obliged to apologize and did to almost everyone involved, saying he meant it only as a throwaway line. "I have no problem with Puerto Rico in general," he said, "only with certain people."

Now, if he could just keep his big mouth shut long enough to make America proud.

With the mission of his life ahead of him, the two-year run-up to the Olympics would be among the most peaceful seasons in Knight's career, giving his friends hope he was, at last, growing up and settling down.

Knight even summoned the patience to do a radio call-in show, as his friend Dean Smith had suggested. Of course, with all the dumb questions, Knight soon stopped taking calls, and listeners had to mail their questions in. The show devolved into Knight sitting at his desk in his Assembly Hall office, chatting about anything that occurred to him with the host, IU play-by-play man Don Fischer. "His job was to keep Coach interested for the whole hour, which wasn't easy," wrote Steve Alford in his book *Playing for Knight*. "Coach would open his mail during the show, look at tapes, read catalogues—whatever he felt like doing."

Not a lot was expected at IU in the fall of 1982. Knight had fifth-year seniors Randy Wittman and Ted Kitchel back, and a 7-1 freshman named Uwe Blab, a German who had attended high school in Effingham, Illinois, and was highly rated, if no Kent Benson. Blab's hands were so bad that years later when he had his first child, Knight told his wife, "Don't ever let your husband hold this kid over anything but a bed."

Nor was Blab as impressed with Knight as Benson had been, even daring to yell back at him during a game. With Kitchel, a tough 6-8 forward who was known for glaring back when Knight glared at him, it turned out to be one of Knight's most surprising teams.

Fighting for the Big Ten lead, they went into a game against Illinois with Knight, concerned with making the Illini play defense, ordering his players to make at least four passes before anyone looked for a shot.

On the first possession, they made one pass to Kitchel, who shot and missed, whereupon Knight yanked him.

"Coach grabs me to put me in the game," says then-assistant Kohn Smith. "You know, he just grabs the first guy, 'Get in for Kitchel.' Then he grabs whoever is next, 'Get that son of a B out of there.' So, we get somebody in for him and it's the first timeout and Coach is mad as heck at Kitchel—'That son of a B, he'll never play another second at Indiana.'

"You know, he's going on like this. So we have a TV timeout or something and Coach is just chewing on Kitchel. 'How many passes do I want?'

"'Four.'

"Coach says, 'Well, you either are so damn dumb you can't count to four. All right, Kitchel, you coach the team. It's your team, you coach, and it's your offense.'

"So, in a CBS timeout, Kitchel is down there sitting with the team, telling them, 'We gotta make four passes.' And all of us coaches are like, 'Holy hell, this is a real big game for us.'

"It probably means the Big Ten championship, and we've got all this chaos going on in the first three minutes of the game. So we go along and we're going back and forth with them all the time and Coach says, 'What do you think?'

"And I said, 'You gotta get Kitchel back in the game.'

"'I wouldn't play that son of a bitch if I never win another game. Don't give me that shit, I don't want Kitchel. Don't even talk to me about that.'

"So, we go on like this all the way into halftime, and he tells Kitchel he's going to have to turn in his uniform, that he's off the team. He's raising hell with everybody and it's a real tight game. We go into the second half and he asks me again, 'What should I do?'

"'Hey, Coach you gotta get Kitchel.'

"'Goddamn it!' And he starts yelling at me again, you know. But then in about a minute he puts him in. Kitchel goes on and outscores Illinois by himself. I mean, it was like unbelievable. I mean, he scored 30 points or 29 points in the game and ends up beating them about by himself."

They won the Big Ten at 13-5, finished the season ranked No. 5 in the nation, but lost to Kentucky in the second round of the NCAA Tournament after Kitchel's back went out. Knight often said he didn't care about winning and, for once, he acted as if he believed it. He was so proud of his team, he broke tradition by raising a banner in its honor for winning a mere Big Ten title, next to the ones celebrating IU's NCAA championships.

In the fall of 1983, with Wittman and Kitchel gone, Steve Alford, the All-American boy next door in the flesh, entered Knight's life, and vice versa.

Handsome, polite, and polished, Alford was such a Hoosier archetype, it was a wonder they didn't stop giving out the Mr. Indiana award after he won it. With him came two more hotshots, Marty Simmons, Mr. Basketball in Illinois, and Daryl Thomas, a widebody from Chicago who was a McDonald's and *Parade* All-America.

The Hoosiers started 9–3, winning their first two in the Big Ten but, on January 19, they lost to Purdue at home. Knight evicted the players from their dressing room, ordering trainer Tim Garl to take up the carpeting and remove the players' names from their stalls. Knight announced he wasn't going to the next game at Michigan State, told Garl not to make travel plans and ordered his assistants to make no preparations, either.

The players dressed in the hall the rest of the week, taped their own ankles, and ran their own practices while Knight rode a stationary bike and looked uninterested. The players had to make their own travel plans, calling the hotels and the bus companies. Knight kept it interesting until game time, waiting until they were about to go on the floor in East Lansing before making a dramatic entrance. The Hoosiers won in overtime, 70–62.

On February 26, after losing to the Spartans at home, Knight marched into athletic director Ralph Floyd's office and resigned. Floyd spent the next three days begging Knight to come back. The team bussed up to West Lafayette to play Purdue without him but, once more, Knight returned in the nick of time. The Hoosiers won that one, too.

Compared to Knight's mind games, college basketball wasn't so tough. With the precocious Alford leading them in scoring and the precocious Simmons third in scoring and second in rebounding, the Hoosiers went 20–8 and finished third in the Big Ten, a nice start for a young team that sometimes started the sophomore Blab with four freshmen: Alford, Simons, Daryl Thomas, and Todd Meien.

As No. 4 seeds in the East bracket, they beat Richmond in the first round of the NCAA Tournament but that brought them face to face with the No. 1 team in the country, North Carolina. With Michael Jordan and Sam Perkins still there from the Tar Heels' 1982 NCAA championship team, and 6-11 freshman Brad Daugherty, they had gone 28–2. Virginia's Terry Holland called them "the finest basketball team I've ever seen put together."

In a pregame meeting at the hotel in Atlanta, Knight told Dan Dakich, a senior guard, he would guard Jordan. Dakich couldn't have come within a foot of Jordan's vertical leap, but Knight told him to lay back and make Jordan show he could shoot from the outside. In what would become a Hoosier legend, Dakich went back to his hotel room and threw up.

"I had really not felt well but I didn't want anybody to know," Dakich says. "He had had me practicing on the red team, which meant I was going to have a chance to start. It wasn't guaranteed. So, I didn't want anybody to know that I was sick.

"He didn't tell us until the pregame meal, three-and-a-half hours before. And I ate and when I was sitting in the meeting I was just feeling awful, just bad. And this is the truth, and I tell it in speeches, I go up to the hotel room and, honest to God, I went in and I just threw up.

"Long story short, Jordan gets the first two buckets of the game, I think. I come down the court—and I swear to God this happened—and I look at the clock and there's like a minute gone in the game roughly and I'm running down the floor doing the math. And basically four points in one minute, there's 40 minutes in the game, so he's going to get 160 points if I don't slow his ass down here a little bit.

"But he started missing shots. They took him out with two fouls for most of the first half and he never got in sync in the game."

Jordan scored 13 points and IU shocked the Tar Heels' world, winning, 72–68. Alford had 27 and Blab, standing in against the Carolina big men, had 16.

The way to the Final Four seemed to yawn before them, with only a post–Ralph Sampson Virginia team that had finished fifth in the ACC in their way. The Cavaliers were No. 7 seeds who had surprised everyone by reaching the Elite Eight.

It was starting to feel like the Hoosiers' 1981 title run, when no one expected anything and everything fell into place. Knight told the players, "Just get me to the Final Four and I'll win it."

Instead, Virginia beat them two days later, 50–48, with freshman Olden Polynice neutralizing Blab. Knight's dream ended that fast but he had no time to mourn. The Russians were coming.

Finally, he got to take on the world, officially.

Knight intended his Olympic team to crown his career. Representing his country had real meaning to him and he would have his pick of every player in the nation. He had a model: Newell's 1960 team with Oscar Robertson, Jerry West, Jerry Lucas, and an alternate selection named John Havlicek. They overwhelmed all opponents in Rome, winning by 44 points a game and were remembered as the greatest amateur team ever. Knight meant to surpass Newell's team and he had Newell's blessing.

Part of every day since Knight had been chosen had been devoted to the Olympics, setting up tryouts, exhibitions, a spring training site in Bloomington, and a summer training site in San Diego. He kept a file box on his desk with a card for all the best U.S. players, updating them frequently, calling a network of coaches. He had a file cabinet full of scouting reports of international teams—especially the Soviets, who were even better than everyone thought.

In the fall of 1982, the Soviets had toured the United States, going 7–1 against major college teams, losing only in overtime at Virginia to

Ralph Sampson's team. The Soviets were massive, sometimes playing a front line that went 7-4, 7-0, 6-11. The seven-footer was 18-year-old Arvydas Sabonis, whom college basketball maven Billy Packer compared to Bill Walton.

Happily for Knight, this wasn't like 1968 and 1972, when racial and antiwar tensions had led U.S. players like Walton and Kareem Abdul-Jabbar to stay home. Everyone wanted into these games, and Knight wanted to see every last one of them he thought might be qualified.

In April of 1984, Knight's 72 hand-picked invitees flew into Indianapolis and were bussed to Bloomington with lumps in their throats at the sight of all the players there with them. Joe Kleine, a 6-11 center from Arkansas, remembers sitting next to Walter Berry, who was then known only to insiders, coming out of San Jacinto Junior College. Terry Porter of little Wisconsin–Stevens Point had been invited, as had John Stockton, another unknown from Gonzaga. If Slippery Rock had had a good player, Knight would have known about him.

Knight had organized every last detail, as a press corps of 200 found out on day one. The first press conference was on a Tuesday morning in Assembly Hall, where members of the media were read the rules in no uncertain terms by Kit Klingelhoffer, the IU sports information director. Klingelhoffer, who was small and slight, barked at the press people as if they were privates and he was their sergeant. This was routine behavior in Knight's program: Whether out of admiration or fear of what would happen if they screwed up, the people around him often adopted his manners.

All practices but those on Wednesday would be closed.

There would be no one-on-one interviews with Coach Knight.

There would be no one-on-one interviews with the players. Anyone who tried would have his credential pulled.

Players could not be contacted in their dorms. Anyone who tried would have his credential pulled.

Press people would be allowed to watch Wednesday's practices but couldn't make noise or move around. If anyone did, he would be ejected and his credential would be pulled.

Klingelhoffer then announced no players would be available until Thursday. A writer from Louisiana who had been covering Joe Dumars of McNeese State since he was in grade school, and whose editor had only sent him to follow the local guy, would have to wait two more days just to ask Joe how it was going.

Newsday's Greg Logan, managing to be heard above the subsequent outcry, asked Klingelhoffer why three or four players couldn't be made available, say, Wednesday. At the back of the room, a figure in a red sweater who had gone unnoticed leaped to his feet.

"Hey, hold it up a minute!" he yelled. "Let's don't debate all this! We set this thing up this way and that's the way it's going to be!"

Those who hadn't seen him in action had just had their first Bob Knight experience. However, that was the closest the press would come to seeing Knight get upset all summer. Behind the scenes, he raged at everyone, as usual, but he was discreet enough not to go off where the media people could see him. The last thing he was going to do was serve himself up to the world's press, like a pig with an apple in its mouth.

That night, a group of writers heading into town for dinner saw a police car, gumball flashing, next to a car it had pulled into a culvert.

"They must be pulling his credential," said one of the writers.

Welcome to *Survivor: Bloomington.* Knight's tryout camp that spring on the IU campus was more like boot camp than basketball. Big East Commissioner Dave Gavitt, who headed the selection committee, walked around Assembly Hall with two Indiana State Police escorts, one at each elbow, as if someone was afraid the Soviets might kidnap him to get a copy of the roster.

On Wednesday, the press was allowed in for all three grueling practices. Knight oversaw everything in lordly isolation atop a scaffold, à la Bear Bryant. Below him, his 72 players scrimmaged—to the death, it looked like—on three tartan courts marked off side by side in the dark, cavernous old fieldhouse.

"It was crazy," says Sam Perkins, the North Carolina star who was one of the 72. "It was just like cattle, you know, a lot of people in a barn.

And Bobby Knight was at the top of this, it was almost like a tower, looking down on everybody."

In 1979, Knight had told his IU players to rough up his Pan-Am team, but he would not have wanted his Hoosiers to fool with this group. The candidates included Perkins (6-9, 230), Kleine (6-11, 260), Patrick Ewing (7-0, 250), Jon Koncak (7-0, 240), Tim McCormick (6-11, 250), Ed Pinckney (6-11, 230), Karl Malone (6-8, 250), Wayman Tisdale (6-8, 252), Michael Cage (6-9, 250), Antoine Carr (6-8, 250) and Lorenzo Charles (6-7, 252).

Knight told the referees to let them go, sat back and watched the collisions. "You could tell who wanted to make the team and who didn't," says Kleine. "And everybody pretty much did. It was kill or be killed."

Or as Villanova's Pinckney put it: "The Big East did not prepare me for Charles Barkley in the morning, Patrick Ewing in the afternoon, and Lorenzo Charles at night."

The star of the show wasn't Jordan, who cruised through the trials, but the 6-6, 284-pound Barkley, an Auburn junior whose legend was only in its infancy. He was already known for his girth and his explosive jumping ability that belied his pumpkin-shaped body. Fans on the road threw pizza boxes on the floor and called him Boy Gorge, the Round Mound of Rebound, and Bread Truck.

Even for Barkley, 284 was heavy. He called Knight to ask what he wanted him to weigh, but Knight hadn't called back. Barkley then went on a crash diet, eating only fruit, wound up in the hospital and had to eat his way back to health.

"When he got here," Knight said, "I told him, 'I wanted you to report at 215 but I didn't think you could make it so I didn't call you back.'"

Even in this gargantuan mode, Barkley had stunning ability, making plays like a guard, and rocketing off the floor like Jordan himself. Barkley was not only great but brash. With the word around that Knight thought dunking was for hot dogs, everyone laid the ball up on breakaways until Barkley went down and dunked backwards. When Northeastern's 6-6 Steve Halsel tried to challenge one of his dunks, Barkley moved him aside with his left arm and jammed with his right. "After that," said Halsel, "me and Charles—I been trying to be his *friend*."

Syracuse coach Jim Boeheim went to dinner with some Big East writers and told them, "If they cut Charles Barkley, they better mail it in." Washington Bullets GM Bob Ferry said, "If they cut the Bread Truck, I'm rooting for the Russians."

That night, Knight took more than 20 coaching friends to Pedaler's Pressbox, one of his favorite pizza places. He sat at one table with Newell, Hank Iba, and NBA pals Wayne Embry and Jerry Colangelo. At another table sat Knight's former assistants: Krzyzewski, Dave Bliss of SMU, Bob Weltlich of Texas, Bob Donewald of Illinois State, Gerry Gimmelstob of George Washington, and Tom Miller of Cornell. At another table were the Midwest coaches: George Raveling of Iowa, Gene Keady of Purdue, Johnny Orr of Iowa State, Don Donoher of Dayton, and Lou Henson of Illinois.

It was Knight's idea of heaven. All the best players were here with his mentors and his favorite peers. For once, it was all about basketball and nothing else. And at the top of the pyramid was him.

"I've never seen as many coaches having as much fun in all the time I've been coaching," said Knight. "Each guy now, it's like he has this little corporation. He runs it and he doesn't have time for anything else."

By the third day of the trials on Friday, the players were so exhausted, Knight only made them practice twice. On Saturday he cut the 72 to 30, dismissing Syracuse's Pearl Washington and six members of the 1983 Pan-Am team, including Pinckney and Cage. Knight had his own profile, as he cheerfully explained, noting that at his Pan-Am trials in 1979, he cut Mark Aguirre, Buck Williams, Darrell Griffith, Larry Nance, and "never even considered" future NBA All-Star Jeff Ruland.

That night there were two practice games in Assembly Hall before 17,128 fans, an impressive turnout for a town of 34,000 with school out. Nine players who were on the injured list played, including UCLA's Kenny Fields, who had a stress fracture in his foot.

Knight cut the 32 to 20 on Sunday, the last day of the first phase of the tryouts, and let the survivors go home. He brought them back a few weeks later and, with no press corps around, cut Barkley.

"You ask anyone," says Jon Koncak. "Jordan, Ewing, whoever, you ask them who the best player was the first week of the trials, and 79 out of the 80 guys there, or 80 would say Charles Barkley. He dominated the trials. I mean, he kicked everybody's ass."

Knight didn't care how good Barkley was, he was too free-spirited for Knight's taste. Of course, Knight was too authoritarian for Barkley's.

"Charles didn't like anything about Coach Knight," says Alvin Robertson. "There were a lot of confrontations with Knight. They would talk about being on time. He was telling us to be punctual, and then he showed up 10 minutes late. Charles got up and said, 'It's 10 after 5, where the hell have you been?'

"And Knight went off—'Let me tell you something you fat SOB, there's only one leader in this army!' He just went totally nuts."

In all, Knight would cut eight first-round NBA draft picks. The 12 players he kept included modestly gifted but dutiful players like Kleine, Koncak, Jeff Turner, and his own Steve Alford, along with the stars, Jordan, Ewing, Perkins, and Chris Mullin.

Knight loved Perkins, who did everything and picked things up as fast as the coaches could tell him. Wayman Tisdale couldn't guard a wall, but made it because he was such a great low-post scorer. Vern Fleming, a Knight-style point guard (he didn't dribble too much) became the starter. It appeared that Leon Wood, who was not a Knight-style point (he dribbled a lot), made it only as a favor to Pete Newell, who liked him.

Robertson was a greyhound who excelled on defense. Knight took the 6-11 Kleine and the 6-11 Koncak to be on the safe side: if the Soviets threw three seven-footers at them, Knight wasn't going to get caught short on beef to back up Ewing, Perkins, and Tisdale. Alford was there to bust the zone defenses that international teams liked to play, and to explain Knight to the guys. Teammates didn't think Alford belonged, but the day he squared off against the feared Robertson, the guys began to see how tough he was.

If Knight's style was different for his new players, there was no doubt his program had direction and purpose. It would be a great team, but a long summer.

*   *   *

In May, just as Knight was preparing to fly to Paris to watch his looming rival in the European qualifying tournament, the Soviet Union withdrew from the Olympics. It was payback for Jimmy Carter's boycott of the 1980 Games in Moscow after the Soviet invasion of Afghanistan. For Knight, it was a great personal loss: To properly defend American basketball against all enemies, foreign and domestic, he needed a foil. The Soviets had been just as keen. They weren't intimidated by the prospect of facing Knight's all-stars and were as devastated as he was.

"I know Bobby Knight prepare for my team press defense," said their talkative little coach, Alexander Gomelsky, "but I have countergame for press."

Gomelsky also insisted that Knight didn't have a big center. Asked about Ewing, he sniffed, "How big, seven feet? That not 7-4."

Knight never uttered a word, but it was a blow. Now, as the *Los Angeles Times'* Jim Murray noted, "it was like assembling an aircraft carrier to ply the waters between Staten Island and the Battery."

Knight would have assembled his aircraft carrier in a bathtub if that was all the water he had. He stopped trumpeting the Soviet menace and began trumpeting the Italian menace without missing a beat. Like Don Quixote lining up his windmill if he couldn't find a dragon, Knight was obsessed with his mission and was surprised that everyone didn't see it that way.

Koncak, who was surprised to find himself on the team, returned to his home in Kansas City with one pressing piece of business, his forthcoming marriage, which had to be moved up from June 22 to fit Knight's schedule. Happily, the church was available on June 1 and the event was hastily rebooked.

However, Knight had his own plans for Koncak and flew to Kansas City on May 30, two days before the wedding, to tell him. Koncak, whose rehearsal dinner was the same night, had to drive 30 miles to the airport and pick him up at six o'clock.

"I get to the gate and I pick him up," says Koncak, "and he says, 'I want to go to the Marriott Hotel over there and get something to eat, I haven't eaten dinner yet.' So, we drive to the Marriott. I'm looking at my watch, it's like 6:15, and I'm 45 minutes away, you know, I'm going to be late for my own rehearsal dinner. And he orders French onion soup. Don't ask me why I remember that but it's just one of those things.

"We're sitting there and his soup comes and he's taking a couple of spoons of soup and he says, 'Jon, I don't know how to tell you this, but I don't think it's in the best interest of our team and our country for you to get married tomorrow night.'

"And he says, 'I really think it's going to be a distraction for you. You're an integral part of this team. If something happens to Patrick, you're our main guy.'

"And I'm looking at my watch and it's 6:30. And I looked at him, and I said, 'Coach, I can guarantee you, there's nothing more that I want to do than play on this team and win the gold medal, but I'm getting married tomorrow.'

"He said, 'okay, that's all I needed to hear.' He said, 'You can drop me off at the airport.'

"So we got up, got in the car, I drove him over to the terminal, he got out and I sped to the rehearsal dinner. And to this day, I still don't know what this was about."

Knight drove them all summer, from the trials in April, through a rough exhibition tour against NBA stars with a no-foul-out rule so the pros could have at his Olympians, to the Games in August. Of course, the real action was behind the scenes.

"Practices were like murder," says Tisdale. "I mean, it was very physical, very competitive, just probably the hardest practices that you'd ever seen. And this one practice one of the big guys made a comment to Jordan and he fouled him real hard, and Bobby didn't call the foul. And Michael was pissed and his eyes got fire-red, and the next play Michael just went up and did one of the most incredible dunks over the guy that I had ever seen in my life.

"In fact, I think Knight stopped practice after that. He just called practice and told us to go home. Now Bobby Knight being amazed by that, that let me know right then that this guy [Jordan] was going to be a megastar."

Knight later said coaching Jordan had been "a thrill," which might have been the greatest compliment of even a career as great as Jordan's. At the other end of Knight's scale was Ewing, who was used to being treated gently and playing a different role. At Georgetown, John Thompson had Ewing sitting in the lane and blocking shots as Bill Russell had in Melbourne in 1956, heralding the dawn of a new era. Knight didn't play that way; he wanted Ewing out pressuring his man like everyone else. Knight had so little use for Ewing, he turned him over to Raveling in the trials.

Knight liked the effervescent Tisdale, but Wayman had never been asked to play defense, and Knight bore down on him like a tropical storm. In a practice in San Diego, Tisdale took a charge and Knight stopped the drill, got a marker, and wrote the date on the floor.

"The first time I saw him blow up was at the second trials," says Tisdale. "He blew up and I called home that night and said, 'Wait a minute!'"

"He marked the spot, 'Wayman Tisdale takes first charge,' something like that. It was hilarious, man, and just really boosted my confidence. Because before then I thought my name was 'Hey, butthead.'"

Overconfidence wasn't a problem, but getting to the Games was. Knight drove his players so hard, Raveling, Newton, and Donoher finally prevailed on him to take a few days off.

"I mean, there was a two- or three-day period where they sent him off fishing for the weekend," says Koncak. "Probably about a month or three weeks before we went to San Diego to tune up for the Olympics or whatever, but Coach Knight was kind of, I don't know, just stuck in a rut, blowing his top all the time. I don't remember if it was over a weekend or a three-day period, but he basically went fishing or did something for a couple of days and three assistants ran the practices."

Rested or not, Knight was too intense for his players. Away from practice, they stayed as far out of his way as possible, doing everything but posting sentries.

"You can ask all the guys on the team," says Koncak, "not one of them would like to see Coach Knight. I mean, if you saw him walking across the parking lot, you would go turn the other way and walk all the way around the building so that you didn't have to run into him at any time, other than the practice time. He just wasn't very comfortable to be around.

"So, we had this kind of joke where we had Knight radar and if we ever saw him, we'd turn and go the other way. I mean, this is everybody, not just me, it was every guy on the team. Here, I went to the mall and it's in between practices or something so I'm kind of walking by myself. And I've got my Knight radar on and I'm standing in the parking lot and I don't see him and I'm kind of looking around the hotel and I don't see him. . . .

"And I come around the corner and he's standing right there waiting at the elevators, just he and I. And I'm like shocked, you know. I'm like, 'Oh my God, there he is.'

"So, I say, 'Hey, Coach.'

"He says, 'Hey, Jon.'

"So, I hit the button for my floor. I'm standing there and he says, 'Jon, I want to tell you something,' and he puts his arm around me, which was the first time he'd ever even gotten close to me. I'd been playing for him for two months now.

"And he says, 'I really want to tell you how proud I am of the improvement that you've made.' He said, 'To be honest with you, when I sent out the invitations, you were one of the best 80 players, but I hadn't really seen the determination from you and the fight in your game to be a player on the team. But you came into the trials and proved everybody wrong and earned a spot on the team. And you have made as much improvement over these last two months as anybody on our team and I know next week in Los Angeles that I can put you in the game under any situation and you'll do what it takes for us to win.'

"It was like the ultimate compliment, and I'm looking at him and I cannot believe what I'm hearing. And I look at him and I say, 'Well, thanks, Coach.'

"And as the elevator is opening and the little light is flashing, the ding on the elevator door, he looks at me and says, 'Don't fuck it up.'"

The Games started on Saturday, July 28, with the opening ceremonies before 92,655 in the Los Angeles Coliseum, including President Ronald Reagan and his wife, Nancy. Knight's team marched around the track with the rest of the American Olympians and those of 139 other countries.

Athletes from several countries broke ranks to run over when they saw Hollywood stars like Kirk Douglas, Linda Evans, and Brooke Shields in front-row seats, and posed for pictures with them. Jesse Owens's granddaughter ran into the Coliseum and handed the torch to Rafer Johnson, who lit the Olympic flame. Balloons, pigeons, and fireworks were loosed. All the athletes held hands and swayed while Nick Ashford and Valerie Simpson sang, "Reach Out and Touch Somebody's Hand."

With their tribute to brotherhood out of the way, Knight's team began dismantling all comers the next day in the Forum, starting with China. The Americans almost doubled the score, winning 97–49.

Canada was next. Jack Donohue, a New Yorker who had coached Lew Alcindor at Power Memorial, thought he could slow the game down and throw a scare into the Americans because his players knew the U.S. players and weren't in total awe. The Canadians managed to get within 21 points, 89–68.

In that game, Raveling got up and marched to the end of the bench. He said later he had been yelling at the referees, which Knight's assistants weren't supposed to do, that Knight had called him on it, and he had apologized. Actually, Raveling and Knight had been yelling at each other. There had been growing tension between them. Raveling was the assistant the players went to with their problems, and foremost among them was Ewing, whom Knight had put in his care.

"The night before the game, John Thompson was in town," says a U.S. player. "He and Raveling are really tight so he, Thompson, and Patrick just go out and eat dinner, go out at seven, come back at eight-thirty. So Patrick's not playing worth a damn the next day. . . . So he [Knight] looks at Raveling and says, 'Man, you aren't doing shit with him.'

"And, you know, Coach Raveling's a proud person. He says, 'Fuck you.'

"They exchanged words. Raveling got up and walked down to the end of the bench and he said, 'Man, I don't need this.'"

Uruguay was next. The Americans made 15 shots in a row in one stretch and won, 104–68.

The U.S. team was untouchable, but Knight split up the minutes and the points so evenly that no one stood out. Even Jordan, who was on the brink of NBA superstardom, averaged only 17 points as an Olympian. For Knight, the system was everything, but then, the triumph of the system was the triumph of the man who ran the system. Oklahoma coach Billy Tubbs said Knight had to be the best defensive coach in history, noting, "Who else could hold Wayman Tisdale and Patrick Ewing to 12 points a game at the Olympics?"

Oblivious to everything else, Knight drove his players onward. Dreading that they would notice how outclassed their opponents were, he issued a dire warning about their next opponent, France, which he had scouted in the European qualifying tournament in Paris.

"Coach says they beat some of the toughest teams in Paris," said Leon Wood. "He said he was at a loss for words to explain how they could be 0–3 right now."

The French team actually was a collection of squabbling prima donnas. Before the game against the United States, coach Jean Luent suspended three of them for a violation that had occurred a week before. He said he picked this game because it was "a lost cause." Despite Knight's concerns, the Americans squeaked by, 120–62.

Game 5 was against the Spaniards, who *really* had Knight worried. The U.S. fell behind for the first time in the tournament (2–0) but overcame its slow start to win, 101–68.

In game six against Germany, Knight's nightmare scenario came true. The United States ran up a 22-point lead but the Germans kept the game so slow, the American players lost interest. The Germans crept back in garbage time to lose, 78–67. They were so happy to get that close, they held the ball for 20 seconds before scoring their last basket, then let Wood dribble out the clock.

"To me, it's a win," said Germany's Christian Welp. "Before the game, nobody on our team thought we could win. We just didn't want to get beat by 50 or 60 points."

Knight watched in agony on the bench. Photographers sitting courtside heard him railing, "I can't believe this team! They just go out and play the kind of game they want to play!"

He kicked over a cup of water and even got on Jordan, who was 4–14 from the floor with six turnovers, including one in the second half when he tried to drive the baseline and put the ball on the floor two feet out of bounds. Screamed a voice on the U.S. bench, loud enough to be heard upstairs: "*Michael! Get in the game!*"

Knight might have favorites but he didn't play favorites, not even Michael Jordan.

"We went into the locker room," says Koncak, "and he basically goes around the room. Everyone is sitting in their 12 chairs, and he starts with, I don't know, whoever it is, if it's Perkins, he says, 'Sam, I didn't think that you played with the intensity you normally do.'

"And he goes to Tisdale, 'Wayman, you did this.' You know, he's just going around the room. And he gets to Jordan, and he says, 'Mike, of all the guys on the team, I was probably the most disappointed in your play.'

"And that's all he said. He didn't say, 'You son of a bitch,' you know, which was normally what I heard after my name most of the time."

As the players watched in astonishment, Jordan leaped to his feet, as if he intended to go after Knight.

"He told Jordan that he should apologize to each one of us based on how he played, because he played real poor," says Perkins. "Relatively, I think he was trying to motivate Jordan just a little bit more.

"He made Jordan cry, which is the biggest thing that people remember. I mean, you can ask anybody, Wayman, whoever, they're going to say, 'Yeah, Jordan was crying in the locker room.' And some guys like Leon were trying to console him. It was crazy. . . .

"He [Jordan] got mad at him because of the way he was talking. You know how Coach Knight is and the way he talks. When he did get in Jordan's face, I mean, Jordan did jump up and we thought there was going to be some kind of fight but there wasn't."

Says Tisdale, "Knight was just going off. You know, everybody was an MF and a bastard. . . . Mike wanted to definitely tear his neck off. And I knew then Mike was going to be a great player, you know, but when he stood up to Knight I really admired him for that."

The Knight–Jordan confrontation went unreported and the games droned on. The United States advanced to the semifinals—against

Canada, which it had already beaten by 21 points. This time, the Americans won by 19.

They advanced to the finals against Spain, whom they had already beaten by 33. The Spaniards were just happy to be there, having never won a medal in basketball. "The game has to be played," Coach Antonio Díaz-Miguel told the press after Spain upset Yugoslavia in the semifinals, "but some of the players are ready to give you their shirts so you can play in their place."

Knight obsessed to the end. The U.S. team arrived at the Forum for the finals to find Jordan had brought the wrong uniform and several players had the wrong warmups, proof to Knight that his players were already halfway home and primed for the unthinkable. Don Donoher sped back to the Olympic village at USC with a police escort to get the right gear. The coaching staff awaited Donoher's return, as taut as violin strings. Finally, Knight went to the blackboard, ready to give a speech that would singe their eyebrows, but he found a note taped to it, written by Jordan. It said: "Coach, after all the shit we've been through, there's no way we lose tonight."

They won by 31, matching their average margin of victory for the Games. There was nothing more anyone could have asked, although, of course, Knight did. When Wood lost the ball at the end of the first half, Knight kicked over another tray of water cups. When the half ended, Knight railed at Wood on the floor, slamming his right fist into his left palm for emphasis.

When it was mercifully over, the players tried to put Knight on their shoulders but he told them, "Mr. Iba first," so his mentor could have the ride that was denied him in 1972 at Munich. Knight got his own ride while the crowd chanted, "Bobby! Bobby!" Knight wrote in his autobiography that he was so moved at the medal ceremony, he almost cried. If it seemed anticlimactic to some, it was the top of Mount Everest to Knight.

Knight's team lived up to even his expectations, proving itself a worthy challenger to Newell's 1960 squad for the mythical title of best amateur team ever. Nevertheless, if it was great basketball, it was a sideshow in the overall scheme of things.

In their games, the Americans drew an average of 13,520 in the Forum, 1,500 fewer than the Lakers had drawn the preceding season for 41 dates. For the gold medal game, there were only 15,067 in the 17,505 seat building.

ABC would show a minute or two and cut away to something else, like Mary Lou Retton in gymnastics or Carl Lewis' quest for four gold medals, prompting basketball announcer Keith Jackson to complain about air time. Without the Soviets, the United States was Retton without her rival, Ecaterina Szabo, or Lewis without the ghost of Jesse Owens.

As an experience, it was precious for all concerned. Knight kept Jordan's note and showed it to friends years later. He later said of that summer to *Esquire*'s Mike Lupica, "There aren't many things that are a thrill to me but that was."

For his part, when Jordan was asked if he could play at IU, he replied, "Four years with him? I'd have to think about that for a while." Jordan also bet Alford $100 he would never last four years.

All the players except Alford were No. 1 picks, and all but Alford and Wood played at least 10 NBA seasons. No matter where they went, they would always have that summer.

"We had a sense of togetherness," says Koncak. "After the Games were over, I didn't pick up a phone and talk to Leon every week but every time we played a team he was on—and it's been 10 or 12—we'd sit down and talk. It's like Wayman Tisdale. He knows my wife. I know his wife. Every time I see Michael, it's the same way, or Patrick.

"I'll never forget that summer; even though we worked very hard and Coach Knight was very demanding, that was one of the best summers of my life."

NINE

NOT GOING GENTLY INTO THAT GOOD KNIGHT

INDIANA, 1984—87

A writer asked me if I ever woke up the next morning regretting something I had done. I told him, "Oh yeah. Sometimes I regret it when the chair is halfway across the floor."

—Bob Knight, *Knight: My Story*

Bob reminds me of Alexander the Great, who conquered the world and then sat down and cried because there was nothing left to conquer.

—Al McGuire, from John Feinstein's *A Season on the Brink*

In the fall of 1984, at age 44, Knight was officially on top of the world, having just won the prize that was supposed to crown his career. His seasons leading up to the Olympics had been relatively peaceful, engrossed as he was in his vast preparations. His friends hoped he was growing up and settling down at last.

In fact, Knight's life was about to dissolve into tumult once more. Not coincidentally, his marriage to Nancy was breaking up. They had been married for 22 years when they finally filed for divorce in the summer of 1986. They had raised two sons, Tim, born in 1968, and Patrick, born in 1975, but had been fighting almost from the day they were married. Pauline Boop, Knight's next-door neighbor in Orrville, who knew them when they were kids, says they were "the most mismatched couple I'd ever seen."

Bruce Newman, who wrote a memorable profile of Knight for the *Indiana Daily Student*, says Nancy "reminded me a little bit of his mother. She was kind of prickly. . . . I just think that they probably got on each other's nerves. They were both pretty tightly wrapped."

Like Hazel Knight, Nancy Knight wasn't the retiring type. She was outgoing and visible at games, where she was happy to talk to writers, defending Bob, even if she often went further than he would have liked ("There was a time calling him Jekyll and Hyde was a compliment.") Kaye Kessler of the *Columbus Dispatch* says early in Bob's career, Nancy would bake brownies and give them to the writers at the postgame press conference, "and that used to piss him off something fierce."

Knight thought a woman's place was in the home, or at least his woman's was. He told Newman that Nancy was "a great coach's wife." Knight said it in all innocence; he meant it as a compliment.

Nancy's role in Bob's life was strictly defined and didn't include participating in his pastimes. He hunted and fished all over the world, but only with male friends and later his sons. "I told my wife when we got married that there were two things she'd never do with me," Knight told *Indianapolis Monthly*, "play golf and go fishing."

Nor did Knight treat Nancy with great respect when they were together in public. "I remember in '76 when they won their championship," says the *Indianapolis Star*'s Mark Montieth, who was then on the *Daily Student*. "They had a ceremony at Assembly Hall when they got back in Bloomington and they brought Nancy up and gave her some flowers and everybody clapped. . . . They weren't even sitting together, she was sitting three rows behind him and she walked by him and he slapped her on the ass on the way by. And she jumped, she was surprised, and everybody laughed and all that. But he'd do things like that.

"There was a day when I was with the *Daily Student* and we're waiting outside his office and they're leaving on a road trip that day. And he called Nancy, he'd forgotten his tie and he called her to bring over his tie and just the way he talked to her was amazing. No appreciation, 'Now hurry up, damn it.' He ordered her around, just treated her like a slave. I'll never forget that. It was amazing."

Norm Sloan, who was then coaching North Carolina State, and his wife once had breakfast with the Knights in Las Vegas, during the Pizza Hut Annual Classic. "It was very awkward for my wife," says Sloan. "It was difficult for us because there was some conversation that we shouldn't have been hearing. . . . It was embarrassing what he said to her. My wife was at the point of tears when we left. It just bothered her. It bothered me too."

By the fall of 1984, the Olympic exhilaration had faded, leaving the exhaustion. Knight was so spent after putting everything he had into it for two years, C. M. Newton suggested taking a year off on sabbatical, as professors did. Instead, Knight went fishing for three weeks and returned in the fall, revitalized, he thought, but the 1984–85 season turned into the grimmest of his career.

The Hoosiers were ranked No. 5 in the preseason Associated Press poll, coming off their trip to the Elite Eight with Steve Alford, Marty Simmons, and Daryl Thomas back as sophomores. Knight was his usual ornery self before the season, setting off a storm by boycotting the Big Ten coaches' media day in Chicago to protest recruiting violations by a member institution. He didn't say which one, but everyone knew he meant Illinois and Lou Henson.

The long-dormant Illini were keeping more of their in-state athletes at home. For his part, Knight, who had always regarded Illinois as his preserve, was all but retiring from recruiting. Landing Isiah Thomas had required Knight's greatest effort but he no longer wanted to be bothered. Now he sat in his office and waited for his assistants to identify the players they wanted and bring them to see him. Alford, who had attended Knight's summer camp since he was nine, joked that Knight got him for the price of a phone call.

Knight didn't even see some of his players until they suited up at IU. He only saw Delray Brooks play once in high school and Brooks, one of his most ballyhooed mistakes, fouled out early in that one. Assistant Ron Felling said when they asked Knight to get on the phone with a recruit, "A lot of times, he'd say, 'Look, I don't have to call them. I didn't call May and Buckner and, you know, I don't have to call these prima donna son of a bitches, either.'"

Inevitably, IU's talent level began to fall behind that of the other big programs. From 1981, when Isiah Thomas left Indiana, to 2000, North Carolina would get 31 McDonald's All-Americans, and Duke would get 30. Knight would get 16, of whom six would transfer.

No one saw the trouble coming in the fall of 1984. The season started the way it was supposed to with the Hoosiers at 11–3 before going to Ohio State on January 19 and losing, 86–84. Knight hated losing to his alma mater, but it had never triggered anything like the five weeks that followed, starting when he told junior guard Winston Morgan and junior forward Mike Giomi they couldn't fly home from Columbus with the team.

"It was a snowy, icy, cold as heck night," says Giomi. "Coach Knight leaves, the team leaves, and Winston and I are stuck there. About 30 minutes later the athletic director and, I think, Coach Brad Bomba [the team doctor] show up and, you know, we got to get on their plane. Well, Coach Knight was never going to leave us, but that's the whole point: You don't know what Coach Knight is going to do. You know, you have no idea when you're a 20-year-old kid what he was going to do."

Knight said he did it to spare Giomi and Morgan his wrath on the flight home. Dan Dakich, IU's captain that season, says it was no big deal to the players, who would just as soon have ridden in the other plane with Giomi and Morgan.

"To us it was just like, 'That makes sense. Shoot yeah! If he's going to spare us, get your ass on the other plane,'" says Dakich. "You know what I mean? You know how it is. It just wasn't a big deal. Maybe I was just ready to drink the Kool-Aid."

Five days later, the Hoosiers played Purdue, another team Knight hated losing to. Giomi, still banned from the team vehicle—this time the bus to West Lafayette—rode up with Bomba, but Knight kept him on the bench. Without their leading rebounder, the Hoosiers were pushed around on the boards in a 62–52 loss.

Three days later, they played at Illinois. It was a bad time to be going to Champaign, with the Illini, whom Knight had fingered for cheating, ranked No. 6 in the nation, and the game on national television. Over-matched, with his team in a nosedive, Knight left Giomi and Morgan home, benched all of his regulars except Blab, and started four fresh-men: Delray Brooks, Joe Hillman, Steve Eyl, and Brian Sloan.

Since this was Knight, everyone suspected he was up to something. Commentators Al McGuire and Jim Valvano, who were doing the game for NBC, laughed it up beforehand, predicting Alford wouldn't be on the bench for long, but it turned out to be all afternoon. The Hoosiers scored 12 points in the entire first half and trailed by 17 in the second before scrambling back and losing, 52–41.

Knight smirked through the postgame press conference, refusing to answer questions about his lineup, noting, "I'm always really concerned with scoring. I never like a shutout and I'm real glad we got in double figures by the half."

Knight was making yet another point to his players, starting with Alford. In Indiana, Alford's popularity rivaled even Knight's and Knight thought Alford was becoming full of himself. Hoosier fans didn't like seeing their boy next door humiliated, and the idea of giving away a key game didn't go over well, either. As soon as it started, switchboards at newspapers and radio stations lit up throughout the state.

For the first time, there was dissent among the core IU supporters. Even the *Indiana Daily Student* noted Knight's "stubborness and rudeness with the media and the Kremlinlike secrecy which surrounds Assembly Hall and Knight's basketball program. But, God forbid, no one ever questions Knight's decisions on the court. When IU wins, it's because Knight is a genius. When IU loses, some reason other than Knight gets blamed."

Knight was unconcerned, joking about it the next day on his radio show. "When I called my mom last night to see how she was doing, the first thing she said was, 'How come you didn't play Alford?'" he said. "She wasn't particularly happy that Alford didn't play."

Already under fire for mistreating Alford and benching his starters, Knight responded the day after the Illinois game by announcing he was throwing Giomi off the team for missing classes, even though he had a 2.4 average, which met NCAA requirements.

Giomi had been upsetting Knight more than was wise under the circumstances, cutting classes, parking wherever he wanted to, and throwing the tickets away. Knight had taken his scholarship away before the season, but Giomi had come back anyway as a walk-on.

However, just before Christmas, Giomi had gotten a history paper in late and Knight had benched him for the Indiana Classic. Now, Giomi had missed another class.

"Was I a saint?" says Giomi. "No. Was I academically in good standing? Yes. My grades were fine, there were no problems, I was on track. And he said to me, his last parting words to me were, 'I'm sorry. For the rest of you, practice is at three o'clock tomorrow.' And at that time it was over. It was over for him, and it was over for me."

Knight wanted his team to vote on Giomi's fate. Of course, he let his players know where he stood on the issue, which usually settled everything, but not this time.

"He asked me as a captain to have a team vote," says Dan Dakich. "And I said, 'Coach, I'm just going to tell you, I vote he stays.'"

"I remember the next day, he kicks him off, and I met with Coach in his office. And I said, 'Coach, I'll tell you what, I'll move him in with me. I will beat the shit out of him if he doesn't go to class. I'll tell you right now I will physically injure this person if he doesn't go to class and I will make him go to class.'

"And he was great, he was like, 'Dan, I really respect that, but that's not your job.'"

The press split on Knight's motives. Wrote Bruce Newman, now at *Sports Illustrated*: "Knight, who has kept players on his roster after they were caught or arrested for drunk driving, shoplifting, or possessing marijuana, says that Giomi had to be 'separated' from the Hoosiers for missing three classes." Meanwhile, the *New York Daily News*' Dick Young praised Knight for his courage: "Bobby Knight is in trouble at Indiana University because he insists that his basketball players go to school. This peculiar character flaw tells you something about Knight. It should also tell you something about our system of higher education. Knight should stop making such harsh demands."

Young's column was headlined "Paladin in a Savage Land." Unfortunately, Paladin still had the rest of the Big Ten schedule to get through.

With the chastened starters back in the lineup. Alford went 6–18 from the floor and IU lost to Iowa in Assembly Hall by 13.

Knight's closest friends phoned to see if Knight was okay. They all said he must be exhausted after the Olympics but he wouldn't cop to it. Newell says Knight told him, "I'm always tired at this point of the season."

On February 21, Illinois won the return match in Assembly Hall, 66–50, and Knight splintered a chair. The *Peoria Journal Star*'s Gary Childs tried to buy what was left of it from a janitor but was turned down. The writers joked that IU should keep all the chairs Knight broke and auction them off for charity.

The next game was against Purdue in Assembly Hall on Saturday, February 23, 1985, a day that would live forever in Hoosier infamy. It was a warm afternoon and, as Knight later noted, he wore a red-and-white striped IU sports shirt, rather than his usual plaid jacket. Purdue was already ahead, 12–2, when London Bradley, one of Knight's least favorite referees, called a foul on IU.

Normally, Knight said, he would have torn off his jacket and dashed it onto the floor—but he wasn't wearing one. Instead, he picked up his plastic chair and hurled it across the floor, skittering in front of Purdue's Steve Reid, who was standing at the free-throw line.

Knight was ejected, and left to a standing ovation. The Big Ten supervisor of officials, Bob Burson, was at the game and wound up getting both barrels from Nancy Knight, who "really lit into him," according to a conference official.

IU president John Ryan, vice president Ed Williams, and athletic director Ralph Floyd followed Knight into the dressing room. Ryan said Knight was in tears, "remorseful, even contrite. He said he was terribly sorry and he hoped this didn't bring problems to the university. That impressed me. He was genuinely sorry."

To Knight's players, it was more ado about nothing. They saw him throw furniture all the time when there were no TV cameras around. "Basically, it wasn't a shock to us," says Delray Brooks. "I guess it is bad, it was during the game, you know. But we didn't all go *wooooo*, because how many times have we seen him throw something? It wasn't a big deal."

"Quite frankly, and you're gonna think I'm whacked out, but this isn't any surprise to us," says Dakich. "This isn't any big deal to us. This is us and this is Indiana and this is the way it was. . . . Now, these chairs were around the court during practice, they were in stacks. And I think his record was 52 he'd thrown against the wall in a practice. So, we'd seen these chairs go."

There was no question Knight had to be punished. The only question was who would do it. Ryan and Williams wanted to handle it in-house and Knight said he could accept that.

"For Bob's sake and for Indiana's, I thought then and I think now that the university had to take some action," Williams told Feinstein. "It could not publicly condone what Bob did. And Bob needed to be told that. He needed to be told, 'Bob, we love you, we want you here forever, but there is a line, there is a point where we say no more. And you just came close to it."

However, Knight then changed his mind, saying he couldn't accept a rebuke from his employers, even insisting he would resign. Ryan decided to step out of the way and let Big Ten Commissioner Wayne Duke handle it.

Duke had been home, watching the game on television, when Knight threw the chair and says he turned to his wife, Martha, and told her, "Uh oh, there's going to be some hellish days ahead."

"I thought they [Indiana] were going to stand up and be counted," says Duke. "I do remember talking to people at Indiana, intermediaries, and there were indications that it might happen. . . . Indiana was going to suspend him, either with me or without me, and then at some point they backed off and I ended up suspending him myself. I had no other course of action. Indiana wasn't going to do it so I had to do it."

Knight apologized formally in a statement issued by the IU athletic department, managing to simultaneously present a defense that would become familiar: He had been fighting for a cause but had taken it too far.

"While I have been very concerned of the way some things have been handled in the Big Ten, in particular the officiating, which has really frustrated me the past couple of years, I do not think my action in the Purdue game was in any way necessary or appropriate," the statement said. "No one realizes that more than I do.

"I am certain what I did in tossing the chair was an embarrassment to Indiana University. That was not my intention, and for that reason I'm deeply sorry for it. While I certainly take exception to criticism on who I start or play in any game, I feel a criticism of my action in throwing the chair is justifiable. It's something that I will not let happen again."

If there was, in fact, a line at IU, Knight didn't recognize it and Ryan had never enforced it. Ryan knew that Knight had done worse things, like attacking Kit Klingelhoffer, and had never given him as much as a reprimand. Even as the president of the university, Ryan was overmatched. Knight was not only a source of pride and revenue, he could be irresistible in person. Ryan couldn't deal with a contrite Knight at his feet.

Everywhere else in the conference, it was a joke. Michigan State coach Jud Heathcote, whose team was about to play Michigan, saw one of the referees before the game, picked up a chair, and pretended he was going to throw it. Illinois lost at Ohio State, but Lou Henson went out of his way to praise the referees. The Buckeye SID, Marv Homan, who had been there for Woody Hayes' fall, said that IU should go to break-away chairs, like tearaway jerseys.

It wasn't funny in Indiana. Duke suspended Knight for one game. Jimmy Crews coached it, a 20-point loss at Iowa. A week later, in the last home game on Senior Night, IU lost to Michigan and Knight dispensed with the traditional ceremony in which he thanked his seniors and they said good-bye to the fans. Dakich had always told Alford that everything would seem worthwhile when they were finally standing at the microphone. After four long years, Dakich and Blab never made it to the microphone.

IU finished 15–13, 7–11 in the Big Ten and didn't make the NCAA Tournament. Knight accepted an NIT bid—after informing his players they didn't deserve it—hoping to salvage something from this disaster, but lost to UCLA in the finals, 66–64.

At four in the morning, when the plane landed in Bloomington, Knight convened a meeting and told junior Winston Morgan he was off the team. However, when Knight saw Morgan stop on his way out to congratulate assistant Jimmy Crews, who was leaving to take the Evansville head coaching job, Knight was so moved he decided to take Morgan back. Of course, Knight didn't get around to telling Morgan for two months.

"The best thing about that meeting," says Delray Brooks, "is that when it's over, it was going to be over."

For some of them, it was going to be over for good at IU. Giomi transferred to North Carolina State. Marty Simmons went to Evansville with Crews. Simmons, who had played so well as a freshman, had gained weight in his sophomore year. To show him how much added weight slowed a player down, Knight once made Simmons practice with a 25-pound weight tied around his neck.

Knight was like a grizzly with a thorn in its paw. At the Final Four in Lexington, Kentucky, he ran into Wayne Duke, of whom he would later write, "I thought the world of him and still do."

Not at that moment, though.

"Between games we went down to the press room and I ran into Knight," says Duke. "It was the first time I'd seen him and intuitively I stuck out my hand to him. The last time I had talked to him he hung up on me and then I suspended him. He said to me, 'Don't you put your fucking hand out to me in public. And I mean fucking never.'"

After the season from hell came the summer from hell. Knight took the Hoosiers on a five-week tour of Canada, Japan, China, Yugoslavia, and Finland, which may have sounded like fun but didn't turn out that way. Knight drove everyone so hard getting ready, assistant coach Kohn Smith quit before they left.

"We came in after practice one night," says Smith, "and I was just trying to find anything positive to say to keep a little better mental thing going on into practice. I said, 'Well, Coach, you've got to remember now, four or five of these kids, these aren't our best kids.'

"And he went off on me, 'Goddamn it, that's what we got and that's what you're dealing with!' You know, he really chewed me out and walked out of the room. And I told Joby [Wright] and Royce [Waltman], 'You know what, boys? That's it, I'm done.'

"And I grabbed my stuff and walked out. Royce and Joby, they're just trying to say, 'Hey, don't do it,' but I left for a week and I wouldn't let anybody find me. The managers and everything were trying to find me and I basically quit. I was just looking for another job. He finally got me and we talked it all out and I said, 'Hey, I don't want to go to practice hating these kids. I'll work them as hard as anybody will, but this is summer and we're going overseas and I want to have some fun.

"And then we got overseas and in the games and it was kind of the same thing. All of a sudden now, Joby and I and Royce are coaching the team and Coach is up in the stands and he's got Pete Newell and Everett Dean and Henry Iba, you know, they're all up in the stands. And here we are coaching the team and we can only play Alford so many minutes. We've got to play [Magnus] Pelkowski, you know, we got to make a player out of him. Well, hell, we're playing [the Soviet Union's Arvydas] Sabonis and [Alexander] Belostenny.

"And Coach is so competitive and he starts sending notes out of the stands and we get playing in the tournament in Japan and he comes down. And so he takes over the team and it was all hell again, you know. We're sitting there asking what in the hell is going on. And Joby is saying he'll swim back to America."

After they were thumped by the Soviet national team in Hiroshima, Knight fired all the assistant coaches and trainer Tim Garl. They walked the streets of the city late that night, scared he really meant it this time.

Alford kept a diary, which he reproduced in his book, capturing the spirit of the thing:

July 3, Nagasaki (Via Bullet Train)
- Played Japan again and lost. Court and refs were horrible. Coach took us off the floor with 8 minutes to go but we returned.

July 6, Kobe
- Waited and rested all day for Russian game.
- We lost again, 90–70. . . . Coach threatens that when we get back

home, we have two days, then back to Bloomington. (HA, HA, HA, HA).
- Miss home dearly.
- Do I sound homesick? (I am.)

*   *   *

In the fall of 1985, John Feinstein took up residence in Bloomington, on leave from the *Washington Post*. Volunteering to spend a season with Knight wasn't something that occurred to many writers, but Feinstein was a brash young man who was a veteran of the Georgetown beat, where he had dared to stand up to John Thompson, another winning-by-intimidation guy and the father of Hoya Paranoia.

Feinstein wanted to show the inner workings of an elite program that was scrupulously clean. Amazingly, Knight was willing to open up his, granting complete access. For the 1985–86 season, Feinstein would be one of them. The only condition was that he wasn't to write anything about Knight's personal life. Nancy was gone most of that season, spending 10 weeks at the Duke weight-loss clinic. Their older son, Tim, was at Stanford, and Bob looked after the younger son, Patrick, who was in high school.

If Knight seemed like the last coach who would give a writer the run of his program, he actually granted uncommon access to press people he trusted. If Knight saw the press as a whole as a fifth column rather than a fourth estate, he was always appreciative of the writers who appreciated him. By the '80s, he had collected an impressive salon, which included respected men like Dave Kindred, Tom Cushman, Pete Axthem, Frank Deford, David Halberstam, Billy Reed, and David Israel. Knight gave them more than access; he regarded them as blood brothers.

Kindred's friendship with Knight dated back to 1974, when Knight slapped Joe B. Hall in the head. Kindred, then at the Louisville *Courier-Journal*, persisted when Knight tried to avoid talking about it afterward. Knight began confiding in Kindred from that moment, as if they had been pals for years. Kindred would have preferred a cordial professional relationship, but Knight didn't give him a chance: When Knight liked someone, he lavished all his charm on him and overpowered him.

The writers who covered the IU beat on a daily basis got the other side of Knight. They had a name for Knight's confidants: The Kool-Aid Seven. Around the program, "drinking the Kool-Aid" was such a common phrase, even players and coaches like Dakich used it.

However, with their access, Knight's confidants did many of the best pieces on him, even as they confessed to their biases and stuck up for him. Knight even held still if they crossed him in the paper, painful as it was for him.

When Knight had his run-in with that LSU fan at the 1981 Final Four, Tom Cushman, then at the *Philadelphia Daily News*, wrote a column comparing Knight's night out to that of Dean Smith, his opponent in the finals. Smith had been at a restaurant signing autographs for all who asked while Knight was reportedly putting Buddy Bonnecaze in the garbage can. The suggestion was that Knight had overreacted yet again.

Several weeks after IU won its title, Knight called Cushman, saying he was coming back to town to do a clinic and asked him to get him tickets for a Phillies game. Cushman replied that he thought Knight might be mad at him. Knight said he was but was writing him a letter about it.

"So," says Cushman, "we were having lunch in Philly, I said, 'I thought you were writing me a letter.'

"He said, 'I am, I'm not done with it yet.'"

A few days after Knight left, Cushman got the letter. It was seven handwritten pages, painstakingly laying out Knight's position, saying that he knew his friends wished he would try to stay out of trouble, rather than court it. It ended with a line from a poem: "Bullfight critics row on row around the enormous plaza full. Yet there's only one man there who knows, and he's the one who fights the bull."

Knight, who claimed he didn't care what the press wrote, cared enough about being gently chided by Cushman to work for weeks on this letter, but still couldn't bring himself to acknowledge doing anything wrong. It was as close to introspection as Knight could come, even when he tried.

However, aside from Bob Hammel, the local sports editor, the confidants were from somewhere else and were only around for a day or two. Hammel was well liked and respected within his profession, but he had a unique situation; Knight was no one to tolerate dissent and in a town in which IU was the local industry, Hammel's bosses wouldn't have tolerated an anti-Knight line. Hammel and Knight became close friends and, inevitably, Knight's perspective became Hammel's.

Feinstein represented something new. Knight had given him access but didn't consider him a friend like Hammel, Kindred, and Cushman, when Feinstein approached him about spending a season on the inside. Intrigued, Knight checked Feinstein out further, with Kindred, Feinstein's colleague on the *Post*, and with Mike Krzyzewski, who was close to Feinstein. They said Feinstein was a man of his word and Knight greenlighted the project.

The result would be a remarkable portrait of a remarkable man. Feinstein worked hard to present a balanced picture, but his unvarnished reporting carried an impact that no catalog of Knight's principles could diminish. There were incredible fits of rage, like the one after a loss at Louisville, when Knight told Kit Klingelhoffer to say he was skipping the press conference to get his players back for exams and was upset when he found that his explanation wasn't mentioned in a newspaper story.

When Knight saw this reference in a game story in the Indianapolis Star *[Feinstein wrote], he exploded. He called Klingelhoffer down to the locker room. . . . Knight was, to put it mildly, unhappy with Klingelhoffer. "I get enough crap from these people without this kind of thing happening," he said. "Jesus Christ, is that fair, Kit?"*

Klingelhoffer escaped. Knight walked into the bathroom. For a moment, there was silence. Then he began kicking the bathroom stall. He stormed back into the room, kicked the phone sitting on the floor and the garbage can in the corner. "I just can't take it any more," he yelled.

Just as sobering were Knight's fits of despair, like the one after losing the 1985–86 Big Ten home opener to Michigan, which had beaten them badly in the last game of the preceding season.

> *The coaches' tape session was stormy. Knight kept getting up and leaving several times to walk off his frustration. Finally, just after 2 A.M., they went to the Big Wheel to eat. Knight never said a word until he stood up to leave.*
>
> *He looked at his four assistants, each of them bleary-eyed with exhaustion. "I waited nine f_____ months to play this game," he said. "Nine months. I can't tell you how sick of basketball I am right now. If I never see another basketball game in my life, that will be just fine."*

With Knight, the show never stopped; those around him just never knew what was playing that day. After the Hoosiers beat Purdue with a stirring comeback, Knight went to the interview room, delivered a long discourse on fishing, took no questions, and left.

"I asked him why he did it," Feinstein wrote. "He said he just felt like it."

There was something else new at IU in the 1985–86 season: junior college players. The previous season had been such a debacle, and Knight was in such need of players, he had reevaluated his principles against taking jucos.

"We were playing up in Wisconsin, and Wisconsin had better athletes on their team than us," says assistant coach Kohn Smith. "We always had real good kids but we needed to have good kids that were good athletes. . . .

"Coach after the game says, 'Wisconsin has better athletes than us.' So he told me—you know, I was the part-time assistant coach then, Joby [Wright] and Jimmy [Crews] were the recruiters—but he wanted me to start listing every junior college kid that's available. He

said we gotta get some athletes in here, and so we started really search-
ing out every junior college kid that had the grades to be able to come
in and play.

"Joby was always that way. He always felt like we needed to have
guys that could run and jump. Of course, he was black and he felt like
we needed more. [Laughing] He didn't want to be the BYU of the
East."

In the fall of 1985, Knight brought in two junior college players,
Andre Harris and Todd Jadlow. Neither had much impact, though, and
Harris left at the end of the school year for what were announced as ac-
ademic reasons.

In comparison to the 1984–85 nightmare that preceded it, the
1985–86 season was merely hard, though Delray Brooks, who was starting his sophomore year, wouldn't be around for the end of it. Brooks had
been one of Knight's most acclaimed recruits, coming out of Rogers
High in Michigan City, where he had not only been Mr. Basketball but
USA Today's national player of the year and the governor of the Indiana
Boys State Convention. At 6-4, with long arms, Brooks was supposed to
be the complement Knight had never had for Alford, handling the ball
while Alford came off screens. As usual, Knight wore his players out before Brooks arrived, telling them how Delray would kick their asses.
Knight even invited Brooks to the Olympic trials right out of high
school; the only other prep there was Danny Manning, who would be
an All-American at Kansas.

Brooks was a special young man, intelligent, tough, and poised, but
he wasn't a special player. He had slow feet and had trouble guarding
people, much less shutting them down. Knight liked him, but it wasn't
hard to tell Brooks would never be of much use to him.

Brooks made the starting lineup for the Hoosier Classic during the
Christmas break but the following week in practice, he traveled during a scrimmage and Knight demoted him to the second team on the
spot. Brooks, who still expected to start the next game, didn't even
get in.

"That was the breaking point for me," Brooks says. "I called my
parents and told them that I would be leaving. They wanted me to stay

and finish out the year if I can. I said, I'm going to lose my mind if I try to stay here."

Brooks transferred to Providence, where he wound up starting on a team that made the Final Four under another tough coach, Rick Pitino.

The Hoosiers started the 1985–86 season 8-2, but began Big 10 play losing at home to Michigan and Michigan State. Knight was still playing 6-7 junior Darryl Thomas at center, where he was always facing taller opponents. Thomas was a 240-pound widebody with good hands and nimble feet but he wasn't tough enough for Knight.

"That was Daryl's name—Pussy," says Rick Calloway, a freshman forward that season. "Daryl's name wasn't Daryl, his name was Pussy. . . . He [Knight] put tampons in his locker. He'd put Juicy Fruit bubble gum and tell him he was a fruit. You know, just stupid shit like that."

Being torn down didn't work with Thomas, who was still making only halting progress in his junior year. Knight's reaction was volcanic, as in a videotape session that season, described by Feinstein in *A Season on the Brink*:

> "Honest to Christ [*Knight says*], I want to just go home and cry when I watch this shit. Don't you boys understand? Don't you know how bad I want to see Indiana play basketball? I want to see Indiana play basketball so bad, I can f_____ taste it. I want a good team so bad it hurts. I want to go out there and kick somebody's ass."
>
> *He looked at Winston Morgan. . . . "Do you?" Morgan nodded assent.* "Bullshit. Lying son of a bitch. Show me out there and I'll believe it. I come out here to practice and see this and I just want to quit. Just go home and never come back."
>
> *Knight was hoarse from yelling. His voice was almost choking with emotion. He stopped. The tape started. It ran for one play.* "Stop, stop it," *Knight said.* "Daryl, look at that, you don't even run down the floor hard. That's all I need to know about you, Daryl. . . . You never push yourself. You know what you are, Daryl? You're the worst f_____ pussy I've ever seen play basketball at this school. The absolute worst pussy ever. You have more goddamn ability than 95%*

of the players we've had here but you are a pussy from the top of your head to the bottom of your feet. An absolute f_____ pussy."

Even if it wasn't enough for Knight, Thomas averaged 14 points and shot 56 percent in the 1985–86 season. Alford averaged 22.5 points and shot 56 percent, which was a remarkable accomplishment for a player who rarely got anything closer than a 15-footer. Calloway, a lithe 6-6 forward, surprised everyone by starting as a freshman and becoming the Big Ten rookie of the year. The Hoosiers won 13 of their last 16, finished second in the Big 10 and went 21–7 overall.

They were seeded No. 3 in the East region of the NCAA Tournament. They would open with the No. 14 seed, Cleveland State, a little nobody from nowhere. No one knew it better than Coach Kevin Mackey, a brash, fast-talking New Yorker, who was making the most of his moment onstage. His team had gone 27–3 in the Association of Mid-Continent Universities, known as the AMCU-8. "What's that?" asked Mackey, "A motor oil?"

Mackey even dared to joke with Knight before the game, telling him, "Hey, take it easy on me, big guy."

"I'll paraphrase his answer for you," said Mackey afterward. "He said, 'I'm not gonna give you any breaks out there.'"

Mackey didn't need any breaks. He had a deep roster of playground stars who had fallen through the cracks. Their full-court press put the slower Hoosiers back on their heels and IU never recovered. In a shocking upset, the Hoosiers fell, 83–79.

As far as Knight was concerned, a season's worth of progress was wiped away. In the final meeting at Assembly Hall, the team's three seniors, Winston Morgan, Stew Robinson, and Courtney Witte, were sitting with their teammates when Knight walked in and dismissed them coldly.

"He said to the seniors, 'You are no longer associated with this program,'" says Witte, "which I thought was pretty low."

Two months later, in May 1986, Bob and Nancy divorced. In *Knight: My Story,* he writes, "I blame myself for it far more than her because I spent so much time trying to develop a career in coaching. I was gone so much and so oriented to making a success out of coaching that there was an inevitable strain in our marriage. I look at our two sons now and know she did a really good job with them, probably far better than I. For as much as I was gone, she obviously did well with them."

It's the only reference to Nancy in his 375-page autobiography.

No IU class had ever failed to win a conference title under Knight but the once-celebrated Class of '87, with Alford and Thomas, went into its senior year in the fall of 1986 without one. Knight brought in two more jucos, 6-11 Dean Garrett and Keith Smart, a cat-quick 6-1 guard.

Garrett was from San Francisco City College, a long way from Knight's Indiana-Illinois-Ohio recruiting area, showing how wide he was now obliged to cast his net. Smart was even farther out of profile, and not just because of geography. Growing up in New Orleans, he was 5-6 when he graduated from high school. He then broke his arm in a motorcycle accident, got a single offer from a small school in Iowa, and spent a year, as he put it, "flipping burgers."

Smart proceeded to grow into a hot prospect. Knight, coming off three subpar seasons, was back on the recruiting trail himself, and it led all the way to Smart's school, Garden City Junior College, on the prairies of western Kansas. Unfortunately, no one had told Smart that Knight was coming to see him.

"All the players had these fake gold chains," says Smart. "We went out to a little strip mall and the chains were just real fake but they were gold. And we went in the locker room with the gold chains on. And here's my hair cut with a little part that went all the way around my head and then an arrow pointing down to my number—No. 12.

"So I walked in there [the dressing room] and he's sitting there and he looked at me—he gave me that look like, this can't be a guy that we're recruiting. . . .

"At that time he wasn't allowed to talk to you so he said to my coach, 'Is that the way you let your dah-dah players wear their hair?'

"I said to myself, 'I probably won't go to Indiana.'"

On the other hand, Knight didn't often see someone as fast as Smart, with a 42-inch vertical leap. Looking for a way to reconcile

Smart's fashion sense with his own principles, Knight remembered a note Clair Bee had sent him before he died. It said, "Clair Bee and Bobby Knight do not believe repetition is gospel."

Smart came to Bloomington to meet the players, who were aghast. As Alford wrote in his book, "Somehow I couldn't see a guy who dressed like Mr. T playing at Indiana." However, they found out Smart had been a Boy Scout and were impressed to hear him say he was looking for discipline. Against all the odds, Smart became a Hoosier.

Knight had always known he needed a guard to handle the ball and take the pressure off Alford, and he finally had one. Alford and Smart couldn't have been more different but they got along famously, calling each other Ebony and Ivory, from the song by Paul McCartney and Stevie Wonder.

Alford needed the help, after carrying a heavy burden on his narrow shoulders for so long. With no one else to turn to, Knight had spent two seasons trying in his inimitable style to get him to take over as if Alford were Quinn Buckner or Isiah Thomas. Alford wasn't like the commanding Buckner or the gifted Thomas. He was a small-town kid who grew up shooting baskets in his driveway until he never missed.

IU players would always wonder if Knight had it in for his Mr. Indianas like Dave Shepherd and Alford, who arrived in Bloomington with such fanfare. Knight always bore down on his upperclassmen, but Alford, who was now a senior, had been getting the treatment since his sophomore year.

"You know, Steve Alford, for example, was the head of Fellowship of Christian Athletes," says Kohn Smith. "Since he was a little kid, he'd been taught to be a real good Christian, church-minded and everything like that. So, when he came to Indiana, he was president of the Fellowship of Christian Athletes. One time Coach was getting on him about playing harder, and everything and he said, 'What, do you think Christ is going to come down through the roof and make jump shots for you?' And Steve was totally crushed. So, that was one time when I got Steve after the game and he was ready to quit."

"He said, 'I've been taught that since I was a little kid.'

"I said, 'Steve, that's fine. Coach isn't right there with you. That's your religion. When he's talking about basketball, then listen. But you don't have to listen to him about what you believe religiously. Don't ever let anybody take that from you.'"

It was common practice for Knight, the card-carrying iconoclast, to shock his religious players, as when he would tell Alford, "You couldn't lead a whore to bed." Alford could take it, though; he often said his father, who had coached him in high school, had thrown him out of more practices than Knight.

Unfortunately, that meant Alford became a lightning rod for Knight's rage. Years later, Ricky Calloway would claim that Knight had even punched Alford, although Alford denied it.

"Of course, Steve's not going to say he did," says Calloway. "And a lot of other different guys on the teams are not going to say he did. Because unfortunately a lot of my old teammates are still brainwashed. But we were coming out of a practice and we were in a locker room and Coach Knight was going off. And he blamed the whole thing on Steve because we had not practiced well and we were just all standing there. And he was talking and he just turned around and just punched him in the stomach.

"And Steve knelt over, kind of lost his breath a little bit. But that was the end of it. Of course, when he left, Steve said he was okay. It wasn't surprising because he had done it before. . . . We were out there at practice after a game, I can't remember exactly which one it was. And Daryl [Thomas] didn't play good and Coach was calling him names and calling him a pussy and that he was soft and stuff like that. And we were all sitting on our stools. Coach knelt down in front of Daryl and was yelling at him. And then he just hauled off and slapped him in the face.

"And it was really kind of surprising to everybody because Coach Knight kind of regretted what he did. So, what he did is he told Daryl, 'Now, hit me back. Show me you can be tough. Hit me back.'

"You know? Which he had never done before after hitting a player. And of course Daryl kind of barely touched him. And we're all teasing Daryl like, 'You're stupid. You had a chance to stomp the shit out of him because he hit you.'"

*   *   *

In December 1986, *A Season on the Brink* came out and began rocketing up the charts, eclipsing everything else at IU. The book had a small first printing of 17,500 copies but took off when Knight blasted Feinstein, calling him a "pimp" and a "whore."

Replied Feinstein: "I wish he'd make up his mind so I'd know how to dress."

Feinstein's motives would be questioned but he wasn't out to rip Knight and when he was done, he didn't think he had. In his acknowledgments, Feinstein recalled a column Kindred wrote about Knight, in which he said he often wondered if the end justified the means. Kindred decided it did. To which Feinstein added, "I agree."

Knight saw the book as an attack, but the IU players and some of Knight's best friends thought it was an accurate portrayal. The book flew off the shelves in stores throughout the state of Indiana. For the first time, Hoosier fans found themselves wondering if it was enough that Knight graduated all his players and didn't cheat to get them if he tortured them for four years.

"Until that time, everybody kind of saw Knight as an old-school disciplinarian who made his kids go to class and say 'Yes sir, no sir,'" says IU grad Rick Bozich of the Louisville *Courier-Journal*. "Then when people read the book, there was a natural tendency to focus on some of the more outrageous stories. Some people didn't embrace that kind of behavior. They scratched their head and said, 'This guy is a little bit off the wall.'"

Of course, no one was more interested in the book than Knight's players. Todd Meier got the first copy and put a different jacket on it so he could take it on the team plane.

"Even then, he was careful not to read it in Coach's view," wrote Alford. "None of the players thought Feinstein was unfair to Coach and we certainly didn't perceive the book as an attack on the team. . . . I could sit back and laugh out loud at some of the incidents that had been painful at the time. I didn't find the book at all threatening. When people came up to me and said, 'Is that book true? Did those things really happen?' I'd laugh and say, 'It's 100 percent fact. I know. I lived it.'

Knight claimed to be upset because he said Feinstein had broken a pledge not to quote him using the word, "Fuck." Feinstein actually used "f___" and said there had been no such arrangement.

"Well, I told Bob that I thought it was pretty much on the mark," says Tom Cushman. "His whole concept of the book was that the book was not to be about him, it was to be about his players. His concept was that, 'We'll do this book so that you'll see that a program on this level can be run honestly where the kids go to class, where they work towards graduation, where they don't get anything, where it's completely on the up and up. And it's possible to do this, so I'm going to give this writer the kind of access where he'll be able to see that. So it's not to be about me.'

"Well, I told him up front, 'You're not going to get by with that because there's no publisher that's going to do it. I mean, you dominate your program.'"

Knight dominated more than the basketball program at IU, a fact that was distressingly clear on campus. In response to *A Season on the Brink*, the Bloomington Faculty Council adopted a "statement of rights," safeguarding athletes from "physical or verbal abuse, intimidating, coercive or degrading behavior," and urging them to report violations to university authorities. Knight didn't even feel threatened enough to get upset.

"I'd like to thank the Bloomington Faculty Council," he said on his radio show, "for tabling their debate on whether they will plant petunias or daffodils in a flower bed behind the old library long enough to send me the starting lineup."

Amazingly, the furor over the book didn't touch them. Knight told his players it had been a mistake to let Feinstein come and let it go at that.

Ironically, while readers recoiled at the descriptions of how mad Knight's methods could be, Knight was as calm as he had ever been. His 1986–87 team picked up everything as fast as he could say it. When an early upset at Vanderbilt was followed by a shaky win over UNC-Wilmington, Knight said it was his fault for being too tough after the

Vandy game and cut his players some slack, even if it almost killed him to do it.

"For the first time in my career, I said, 'Oh well, what the hell, we won,'" he told the *Courier-Journal*'s Bozich. "You have no idea what that took for me to say that. Nobody does. That's not me. That was really hard for me to do, maybe the hardest thing I've ever done in my life."

The Hoosiers were a jerry-built collection. Alford was the only starter from Indiana. They didn't have anyone who would be a No. 1 pick in the NBA. However, all five starters averaged in double figures and shot over 50 percent. They executed precisely, running their offense all the way to the very last option. They weren't overpowering, but in games decided by three points or fewer, they were 7–0.

Fortuitously, that was the season the NCAA put in the three-point shot. Knight, a purist, hated the idea, even though he always loaded up on shooters and stood to benefit. Now the rule was in, and he had the greatest deadeye around. That season, Alford made 56 percent of his threes.

The Hoosiers went 24–4 and became Big Ten co-champions, sparing the celebrated Alford-Thomas Class of '87 the indignity of being the first under Knight at IU to go four years without winning a conference title. There were two other Big Ten teams in the nation's top ten, but the Hoosiers blew through the conference, winning 14 of their first 15, losing only at Iowa, which was then ranked No. 1.

IU then won the return match at Assembly Hall, with the players following Knight's instructions to throw the ball off an Iowa player if they had trouble getting it inbounds against the fierce Hawkeye press. Daryl Thomas, who was getting tougher all the time, banked one off Brad Lohaus' nose.

The Hoosiers were lucky, too. They went into their last game needing a win and a Purdue loss for a share of the title and the No. 1 seed in the Midwest. Sure enough, IU won and Purdue lost, making the Hoosiers Big Ten co-champions. Now they could play their first two NCAA Tournament games in the Hoosier Dome, with the regionals in nearby Cincinnati.

The Hoosiers buried Fairfield, 92–58, and beat Auburn, 107–90, moving into the Sweet 16 against Duke in the first meeting between

Knight and his foremost disciple, Krzyzewski. Knight had never lost to a former assistant in six games, and he won this one, too, 88–82.

Then came Knight's old favorite, LSU. The Tiger fans turned the air purple, screaming at him, although this time they were careful to keep their distance. The Tigers, a No. 10 seed, had reached the Elite Eight with a gimmick defense Coach Dale Brown called "the freak," which confused the Hoosiers, who led only 48–47 at halftime. Knight raged up and down, drawing a technical foul, and yelled at an NCAA official sitting courtside, Notre Dame athletic director Gene Corrigan. Hammering the table to make his point, Knight flipped a telephone receiver into the air.

With the "freak" looking like a box-and-one that took Alford out of the offense, the Tigers led, 66–57, with 5:07 left. However, Brown elected not to kill the clock at that point and the Hoosiers rallied, pulling to within 76–75 and getting the ball back with :26 left.

IU came down and set up without calling timeout, which was how Knight did it. When the game was underway, it was in his players' hands. This time the Hoosiers couldn't find anything and Daryl Thomas took a desperate eight-footer that missed everything . . . except Calloway, who grabbed the ball out of the air and laid it in off the board for the game winner with :07 left.

LSU called time and set up a last play, but Nikita Wilson's short jumper, which missed, was ruled too late anyway.

"I was worried about losing," said Knight in one of his favorite punch lines in speeches afterward, "until I looked down the floor and saw Dale Brown. Then I knew we had a chance." For his part, Brown says Knight cursed at LSU fans afterwards, including his daughter. Brown says his daughter told him Knight had yelled, "LSU, I stuck it in your fucking asses again."

Knight was fined $10,000 by the NCAA and the flying telephone went into IU lore, along with the chair and Jim Wisman's jersey. Knight's team, which was 28–4 and ranked No. 2, went into the Final Four to play 37–1 University of Nevada–Las Vegas, the No. 1 ranked team, in what was presumed to be the real title game.

The Final Four in New Orleans was like a Knight festival. He was in his charming incarnation, dropping in "we writers" references at press conferences, since he was doing a daily syndicated diary.

"Do you think I'm unyielding?" he asked Dean Garrett, sitting next to him at one session.

"No," said Garrett, meekly.

"See?" said Knight, triumphantly. "He doesn't think I'm unyielding."

Everyone expected the Runnin' Rebels to push the pace and IU to choke on their fumes. UNLV's Jerry Tarkanian had taken the running game to a new level, letting his players fire at will, so the new three-point rule was like hitting the lottery for them. The flashy UNLV point guard, Freddy Banks, who had his uniform No. 13 cut into his hairdo, had taken more three-pointers (339) than the entire IU team (241). He did it in this game, too, taking 19, making 10 and scoring 38 points.

Surprising everyone, Knight didn't slow the game down at all, daring to run with the Rebels. Even if his players weren't as fast as the Rebels, Knight knew they could outexecute them. Unlike other UNLV opponents, the Hoosiers wouldn't get rattled by the Rebel press and forget to run their offense, and they knew what to do with open shots. Alford took only four threes but scored 33 points. IU shot 62 percent, broke the game open in the second half with a 12–2 run and held off the Rebels to win, 97–93.

Said Tarkanian, lamenting their inability to contain Alford: "White guys are never as slow as they look."

The Hoosiers were through to the finals, where they were a solid favorite against Syracuse. After all they had been through in recent seasons, finding themselves in this position was as much a surprise to Knight and his staff as anyone.

"I can just remember turning off the film that last film session," says Kohn Smith, "and Bobby turns to me and says, 'This has got to be the worst team that ever played for a national championship.' He said, 'I don't know how the hell we got here but it's been a hell of a ride.'

"And he did say we coaches had done a great job with the team, and all of us felt like a million dollars then. But yeah, he said that this has got to be the worst team that has ever played.

"[Laughing] But that's us. That's him. It was never ever good enough, you know, we were always trying to get a little better."

The game would be one of the classics of the Final Four. Alford hit seven of his first eight three-pointers, but the Orangemen stayed with the Hoosiers all the way, led by their brassy little sophomore point guard, Sherman Douglas, and their big front line with 6-10 senior Rony Seikaly and 6-10 freshman Derrick Coleman. When Alford cooled off, Smart, who had been out of it in the first half, got back in, scoring 12 of IU's last 15 points.

Syracuse led, 73–70, with :38 left, after forward Howard Triche made the front end of a one-and-one and missed the second. Smart took the ball the length of the floor before the Orangemen could get back and hit an eight-foot leaner to cut it to 73–72.

With :28 left, Coleman, a 69 percent free-throw shooter, was fouled and went to the line, only to have Knight call time out to "ice" him. When they returned, Coleman barely grazed the front of the rim with the front end of the one-and-one.

The Hoosiers brought the ball up without calling timeout again, looking for Alford, but couldn't find him. With :10 left, Smart threw it inside to Thomas, who started to go baseline but encountered the hulking Coleman. With :07 left, Thomas threw it back to Smart on the wing. With his options dwindling, Smart cut to his left toward the baseline to get away from Triche and, still moving laterally, got off a 16-footer. Smart's momentum had carried him out of bounds when it fell with :05 left.

Smart would later remember telling himself to get his legs into it, to make sure he got some arc, and thinking it felt good when it left his hand. But that night he said, "I just threw it up. I didn't know where it went."

The stunned Orangemen let the clock run down to :01 before calling timeout. That was just enough time to try a desperate length-of-the-court-inbounds pass that Smart intercepted.

It was perfect as perfect could be. The Academy Awards were pre-

sented that night with Dennis Hopper up for best supporting actor in
Hoosiers, the paean to Indiana high-school basketball. Writer Angelo
Pizzo and director David Anspaugh were former IU students, who had
given their coach, played by Gene Hackman, several lines right out of
Knight's mouth. Pizzo and Anspaugh skipped the dinner before the pre-
sentations to watch the game at Anspaugh's house.

For Alford, the Indiana archetype, who had taken so much to play
for the Indiana icon, it was a storybook ending. At one of the Final Four
press conferences, he had been asked what Knight was really like. While
he grimaced, Knight jumped in as usual, reminding Alford, "You little
SOB, keep one thing in mind—you aren't *ever* going to be out from
under the umbrella."

Insiders said Alford had suffered more at Knight's hands and was
more angry about it than he cared to admit in public. Nevertheless, Alford also ached for Knight's approval. Their moment together after the
title game, described in Alford's book, was like the scene in *An Officer
and a Gentleman*, in which the tough sergeant played by Lou Gossett
salutes Richard Gere, the maverick he has kicked through the training
course.

> During a lull, [wrote Alford] I looked around for Coach Knight. I
> finally spotted him sitting calmly in a folding chair with his sons,
> Patrick and Tim beside him. I guess he could be calm; it was his
> third championship, our first.
>
> He waved me over and sat me down on his right. He put his
> arm around me and leaned toward my ear. "I want you to know,
> Steve, that I really appreciate all that you've done since you've been
> here. You've gotten everything you could out of your ability."
>
> I had tears in my eyes and I think he had tears in his. We both
> knew what the moment signified; the end of our relationship as
> player and coach. . . .
>
> He gave me a little squeeze. "Steve," he said, "I've never been
> prouder of a player than I am of you."
>
> I had waited four years to hear that. It was worth the wait.

Knight was back atop college basketball. He had just won his third NCAA title, moving him out of the pack of greats tied at two (Hank Iba, Branch McCracken, Phil Woolpert, Ed Jucker, Denny Crum) into an elite circle with John Wooden and Adolph Rupp.

Years later, Knight would say he stayed too long at IU and would remember this night as the perfect one to have left on. He said it occurred to him at the time and he might have, "except I'd seen Damon Bailey."

TEN

THE HONEYMOONERS

INDIANA, 1987–93

*When I was introduced to Bobby's second wife, someone said
to her, "Tom worked for your husband for fourteen years."
And she said, "And he survived?"
She's a good gal. Good for Bobby.*

—Former IU sports information director Tom Miller

As usual, in Knight's career, the biggest triumphs preceded the greatest falls. It wasn't long after the Hoosiers won in New Orleans that the bad news started rolling in, and the 1987–88 season became like the hangover after the party.

Then, something different happened. After that season, Knight's life took a turn for the better. For once, it wasn't something that happened in a basketball game. It was a woman.

In the spring of 1988, Knight would marry 41-year-old Karen Edgar. Unlike his first wife, Nancy, who seemed confined to sitting in the grandstand of his life, Karen seemed to bring him companionship and joy. A new, mellower Bob Knight would emerge, noted, it seemed, by every writer who passed through Bloomington.

Happiness would become him as a coach. In the five seasons after he and Karen married, he would win or share three Big Ten titles, make the NCAA's Sweet 16 twice, and the Final Four once.

Of course, right up to the day he brought Karen to Bloomington, it was tumult, as usual.

* * *

In August 1987, four months after the Hoosiers won their NCAA title, a story surfaced in the Louisville *Courier-Journal*, detailing a stormy night at one of Patrick Knight's games at Bloomington North High School the previous spring, in which his father had railed at Coach Mike Lord.

Patrick was a brash, engaging young man who worshipped his father, but was one of the few who wasn't intimidated by him. While everyone else tiptoed around Knight, Patrick would be the one laughing at him for locking his keys in the car. Nevertheless, with Bob and Nancy separating during the 1986–87 school year, the family had gone through difficult times. Even before the incident with Lord, there had been a scene between Patrick and his mother after one of his games.

"I walked into the dressing room after the game," says Lord, "and Patrick is slamming lockers and stuff and I blew up: 'Stop it now!' I had no idea why he was upset. Well, what it turned out to be is his mother. He wanted to go out with the guys after the game. His mother said no, go home. So, he had that tantrum. . . .

"I'm walking out to go home, it's 9:30 or 10. . . . Patrick is in the car with Nancy. This was around when they [Bob and Nancy] were getting ready to go through their divorce. And he [Patrick] opened the door and then it started.

"So, I wind up staying. We got them separated and I had some of my coaches talk to Pat, and I talked to Nancy. We'd bring them back and when we brought them back they'd just boom, blow up. And so I left there about one or two in the morning to go home. We counseled them all night. . . . You know, Patrick was probably a little bit spoiled, but he wasn't a bad kid, you know."

Patrick was a sophomore in the spring of 1987 when Bloomington North was eliminated from the state tournament in the Martinsville Sectional by Edgewood. During the game, according to Lord and Greg Miller, a local writer, Patrick was taken out, argued with the coaches, and started to leave before sitting back down.

Lord says his assistant told Patrick, "Get yourself under control," and the response was, "Fuck you!"

"When I went to sit him down, he sits down, he has like a

tantrum," says Lord. "And some of my seniors got mad. They were going to—I mean, I had to break up a fight on the bench, after 30-some years of coaching and I'd never had this happen. We got everything settled down and Patrick started to take his jersey off. He looked up in the stands. Well, Bob was up in the stands, and he signaled for him to sit down, which he did. . . . In the meantime, [Nancy] was yelling and cussing at my wife at that time. She said, 'Do something, Bob.'

"So, anyway, we go in the dressing room after the game. We wind up losing because this is an emotional thing. . . . And Patrick said he'd go home with his dad. I said fine. Well, then I'm waiting in there, and my assistant coach comes in, my freshman coach, and he's in tears. I say, 'What's the matter?'

"He said, 'I feel about this tall,' and held his fingers about four to six inches apart.

"I said, 'Why? It didn't matter. It's only a game.'

"'It wasn't that,' he said. 'I just got bitched out by Bobby Knight out there.'

"I started to go out and my principal came in. I said, 'Bob Knight's out there and he's madder than hell, so let me go out and talk to him.'

"So I start out, stop at the basketball court, and Bobby came up about four or five feet behind me, 'Hey, Mike!'

"And I turned around and, 'What?'

"'That's the poorest fucking coaching of a bunch of kids I've ever seen.'

"And that stunned me. So I stood for a minute and then said, 'Let me tell you something. You haven't done so great your whole career.' I said, 'You'd have a chance to have a pretty good athlete there if you work on his attitude.'"

Only after the Louisville *Courier-Journal* broke the story four months later, did the local *Herald-Telephone* report it. Lord had already resigned as coach by then, and the *Courier-Journal* story reported that Bob and Nancy Knight had been "in part responsible." Lord insists he didn't say that, but nonetheless he was soon fired from his other job as athletic director.

* * *

Three months later, in November 1987, with the IU opener still weeks away, the Soviet national team came to Bloomington for an exhibition. Knight had a lot of feelings about the Soviets, whom he never got to meet in the '84 Olympics. Now here they were, with their cocky little coach, Alexander Gomelsky, who had even dared to sneer at the Americans in 1984 ("Soviet team no come, Bobby Knight win"). The antagonism between them went back years; in a 1977 exhibition between IU and the Soviets, Knight took off one of his shoes and pounded the scorer's table with it, imitating Premier Nikita Khrushchev's performance at the United Nations.

Knight's Olympians might have been able to handle the Soviets but his Hoosiers couldn't, even with Keith Smart, Ricky Calloway, and Dean Garrett back from their championship team. The Soviets led, 66–43, when Knight got two technicals, was ejected, and refused to leave, obliging referee Jim Burr to declare the game over. Knight claimed he was only appealing the injustice of getting a technical for wandering outside the coaching box, insisting Gomelsky had done it all night. However, Calloway says Knight told them that he just couldn't stand to watch any more.

"He was getting pissed off so he just told us to leave the floor," says Calloway. "But when we got in the locker room, he said the reason why he did it was because we weren't playing well. . . . Of course, he said it was the referees. But when we got in the locker room and he told us it was that he couldn't watch it anymore. We were playing that bad."

Since quitting isn't the American way, not even Hoosier fans rushed to Knight's defense on this one. Nor was the new IU president, Thomas Ehrlich, as forgiving as his predecessor, John Ryan, who had never taken action of any kind against Knight. Ehrlich, a former Harvard law professor, had served in the State Department in the Ford and Carter administrations but that didn't prepare him for Bob Knight.

In a departure from Ryan's old hands-off policy, Ehrlich announced that he had "strongly reprimanded" Knight for causing "great embarrassment not only to himself . . . but also, and most importantly, to the entire university and its supporters." Ehrlich apologized to the U.S. federation that arranged the game, the Soviets, and Gomelsky.

Knight issued an apology in his usual unapologetic style. Claiming he never expected to win the game, he told IU fans he was sorry for ruining "what should have been a good evening," and acknowledged it was wrong to pull a team off the floor. He didn't mention the Soviets or Gomelsky.

The 1987–88 season that followed was a disappointment. Indiana was ranked No. 6 before the season but went 19–10, finished fifth in the Big Ten, and was upset in the first round of the NCAA Tournament by Richmond, after which Calloway, a three-year starter, transferred to Kansas.

Smart, considered a rising star after his historic shot, plummeted back to earth. Michael Jordan, who had hit an NCAA title-winner at North Carolina, told Smart it would change everything and it was true. Jordan's shot launched the game's greatest career. Smart's shot set him up for a fall. He became an ordinary player as a senior and lasted just two games in the NBA. Without Steve Alford, the Hoosiers were no longer cool in the clutch. With no Alford to hit from the outside, they couldn't prevent opponents from sitting back in zone defenses. "We didn't have that top guy," says Smart. "I guess I had been thrust into that role of being that top guy, but I really wasn't ready for that role."

Knight tried to get Calloway to take over, but Calloway wasn't like Alford, who tried to assume any burden Knight put on him. The Hoosiers were 9–6 and 1–4 in the conference when Knight blew up at Calloway at a shootaround before their game at Ohio State for playing one-on-one with freshmen guards Jay Edwards and Lyndon Jones.

"So, he comes to the locker room [before the game] and he tells me that I can't dress with the rest of the team," says Calloway. "He tells me to go into the other locker room and get dressed. So, I stood there for a minute and he said to me, 'I thought I told you to go into the other locker room?'

"But I still didn't leave. So he gets right up in my face and he tells me that I'd better leave right now before he does something that we both were going to regret. And that was one of the times that I really wanted him to do something to me, because I was actually fed up with it.

"And then that night, he didn't allow me to eat the pregame meal with the team. I had to order room service. So, that night Quinn Buckner came up to my room and wanted to talk to me. Of course, I don't like Quinn because Quinn is just another yes man for Coach Knight.

"I said to Quinn, 'Get the hell out of my room because I've been here three years and you've never had one word to say to me. You never came up to me to talk to me before. And the only reason why you're up here now is because Coach Knight told you to come up here, so I really don't have anything to say to you, so I would really appreciate it if you got out of my room.'

"I didn't play in the game. So, I said in the newspaper that I just had to be ready to play when called upon. The next day at practice Coach Knight comes up to me and tells me, 'I saw what you said in the paper. But you don't have to worry about it because you won't ever play again.' And just all this old bullshit."

Calloway finished his junior year chained to the bench. When the Hoosiers got back from the first-round loss to Richmond, Knight told him he was through at IU.

Knight often played out such scenes after bad seasons, whether out of actual anger or to test the players or both. After Alford's junior year, Knight had told him he would start his best defensive players next season and he wasn't one. Alford told John Feinstein, "I was convinced that he had never been more serious in his life."

Alford had been determined to prove Knight wrong, which was what Knight intended. Calloway began thinking about leaving, which was not what Knight intended. It was late in Calloway's college career—after his junior year—to transfer, but he had had enough.

"I came up to talk to him," says Calloway. "So, I knocked on the door. And at this particular moment, I just wanted to talk to him. No cameras around. No coaches. No players. Nobody that he could try to impress. So, I walked into the locker room and the first thing he says to me is, 'What the fuck do you want?'

"So, already I'm on the defensive because I just came in to talk to

Knight as a teenager in photos from his yearbooks at Orrville High School, where he was a good student and a great athlete. Below, Knight is No. 9, second from right in the second row. (*Courtesy of Orrville High School*)

Knight celebrates a victory at home over Ohio State en route to the Hoosiers' undefeated 1975–76 season, which ended with an NCAA title. (*Courtesy of* The Bloomington Herald-Times)

Knight with his best player and greatest test, Isiah Thomas. *(Courtesy of* The Bloomington Herald-Times*)*

In the signature blowup of his career, Knight throws a chair onto the floor during a 1985 game in Assembly Hall against Purdue. (*Courtesy of* The Bloomington Herald-Times)

In another celebrated explosion during Indiana's 1987 NCAA Tournament win over LSU, Knight hammers the scorer's table so hard, he sends a telephone receiver flying. (*Courtesy of* The Bloomington Herald-Times)

Knight and his players, en route to their 1987 NCAA title, laugh it up with CBS' Brent Musberger and Billy Packer after coming from nine points behind in the last six minutes of their elite eight win over LSU. (Courtesy of *The Bloomington Herald-Times*)

Knight chats with Soviet Union Coach Alexander Gomelsky before an exhibition. In a less convivial moment during a previous meeting in 1987, Knight pulled his team off the floor. (Courtesy of *The Bloomington Herald-Times*)

Knight with Pat Graham, who played valiantly for him but remained a Hoosier loyalist when Knight's move to Texas Tech split the ranks of his former players. *(Courtesy of Brian Spurlock)*

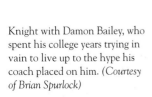

Knight with Damon Bailey, who spent his college years trying in vain to live up to the hype his coach placed on him. *(Courtesy of Brian Spurlock)*

Knight with his son Pat, who had a special challenge: playing for his father, who was even harder on him than he was on the other players. (*Courtesy of Brian Spurlock*)

BELOW: Calbert Cheaney pretends to whip Knight with a towel at the end of their 1992 NCAA Tournament rout of UCLA, making a joke of the furor that erupted when Knight pretended to assail Cheaney with a bullwhip. (*Courtesy of The Bloomington Herald-Times*)

Knight makes one of his forceful points with Neil Reed in January 1997. Not long afterward, Knight was captured on a videotape of a practice with his hand on Reed's throat. (*Courtesy of* The Bloomington Herald-Times)

BELOW: Knight takes his team in at halftime, giving someone yet another piece of his mind. (*Courtesy of* The Bloomington Herald-Times)

Knight with Luke Recker, an Indiana icon in his own right, who fled the IU program after his sophomore year. *(Courtesy of Brian Spurlock)*

Knight yells at referee Ted Valentine, before Valentine, who had already given him a technical foul, ejected him in the spring of 1998. *(Courtesy of The Bloomington Herald-Times)*

Purdue fans taunt Knight in 1999, after an off-season incident in which he accidentally shot a friend on a hunting trip. (*Courtesy of* The Bloomington Herald-Times)

Knight greets his former star and future conference rival, Steve Alford, then coaching Southwest Missouri before his move to Iowa. (Courtesy of Brian Spurlock)

As Mike Davis, Knight's assistant and soon-to-be successor winces, Knight diagrams the Assembly Hall ticket lobby, giving his version of the Kent Harvey incident. (Courtesy of *The Bloomington Herald-Times*)

Indiana VP Christopher Simpson, Myles Brand's right-hand man, holds up a fish he caught on an outing with Knight a few months before Knight was fired. (*Courtesy of Christopher Simpson*)

Simpson's 12-year-old daughter, Sara, in the boat with Knight, who later called her father a "double agent," insisting that Simpson had never fooled him. Actually, they were friends until the firing. (*Courtesy of Christopher Simpson*)

Part of a rowdy crowd of students, estimated between 2,000 and 4,000, which marched to protest Knight's firing by IU President Myles Brand. (*Courtesy of* The Bloomington Herald-Times)

A party atmosphere prevails amid the demonstration in which some coeds bared their breasts and several of the 1,500-pound iron dolphin statues were torn off their moorings in Showalter Fountain. One of the statues was carried to Assembly Hall, a mile away. (*Courtesy of* The Bloomington Herald-Times)

A wan-looking Knight, wearing blue instead of IU red, bids a painful farewell to IU students overflowing Dunn Meadow. At one point his wife, Karen, gave him a kiss and put her head on his shoulder. (*Top: Courtesy of* The Bloomington Herald-Times; *bottom: Courtesy of Brian Spurlock*)

The darling of the Lubbock business community, Knight, who once scorned commercialism, takes the court emblazoned with logos representing Adidas and O'Reilly Auto Parts, as well as Texas Tech. (*Courtesy of Brian Spurlock*)

Knight with Pat, his son and designated heir as Texas Tech coach, on the Red Raider bench. (*Courtesy of Brian Spurlock*)

the man. I've been here three years now, I'm 21 years old, I felt like we could talk. So, he says to me, 'Before you even say anything, I just want to let you know, you might as well transfer because you're one of the worst players I've coached, and you can't even play here anymore.'

"So, right now, what I said to myself, is, 'You know, fuck you, too.' That's what I wanted to say to him. So, I said, 'Well, Coach, evidently you don't want me here, and I don't want to be here either. So, I just want to thank you for all you've done for me, but I just can't play for you anymore.'

"So, I go to walk out of the room and he says, 'Wait a minute, Goddamn it! What do you mean you don't want to play here?'

"And I said, 'Well, Coach, you just told me that I might as well transfer. So, what am I supposed to say?' I said, 'Coach, let's be real. Let's just talk, man. There's no cameras around. There's nobody else in here. Just let me and you talk.'

"Then he started calling me selfish. Just all this stuff. So, he's going off on me, and I said, 'Coach, I don't really mean to cut you off, but you know what? I don't have to listen to you talk to me like this anymore.'

"And I just walked out. And that's the last time I actually talked to him."

Calloway transferred to Kansas, sat out a year, became a starter for one season, and had a great time playing for Coach Roy Williams, a former Dean Smith assistant.

"Somebody asked me that," says Calloway, "you know, 'Yeah, you transferred to Kansas but Kansas didn't win a national championship and Indiana did.'

"You know what I told them? I said, 'I'd give that championship back if I could have played for Roy Williams for four years.'"

In the spring of 1988, Connie Chung of NBC News arrived in Bloomington. NBC was doing a special on stress management and had asked to interview Knight. This should have been a no-lose situation, allowing Knight to show off his wit for a national audience. However, when Chung asked him, "There are times when Bobby Knight can't do it his way—what does he do then?" he answered, "I think that if rape is inevitable, relax and enjoy it."

Sensing he had said something that might get him in trouble, Knight then added, "That's just an old term that you're going to use. The plane's down, you have no control over it. I'm not talking about the act of rape. Don't misinterpret me. But what I'm talking about is, something happens to you, so you have to handle it."

It was an old term Knight had used before, as he did in the 1980–81 season when he reluctantly turned Isiah Thomas loose, which, to Knight, was like being raped. This time, however, he said it on national TV and the furor was immediate. The NBC switchboard lit up. Campus women's groups picketed Assembly Hall, carrying signs that said "Rape Is Every Woman's Knightmare" and "Rape Is No Game."

Through the local *Herald-Telephone*, Knight said he had asked Chung not to use the remark and she had agreed. The paper also reported that Chung herself "had used the most objectionable of four-letter words several times in a lively back-and-forth discussion on camera," which NBC "did not elect to use."

It was common for sportswriters and sportscasters to allow coaches ex post facto privileges to say something and then declare it was off the record. However, a network news operation wasn't dependent on Knight's good will and played by tougher rules.

"I'm sure the producer and I told him that we're aware of it," Chung says. "We understand that he doesn't particularly want us to use it, but we can't promise him anything, that we'll go back, we'll look at it, we'll see what he said, and we'll make a decision with our executive producer's input as well.

"That's what we always say unless there were any preconditions that were set. . . . Once it's on tape, you know, it becomes part of the record."

This was a different kind of controversy for Knight. It didn't happen because he was angry. He was just talking and wound up revealing more of himself than he intended.

Knight was sexist to his core, although he didn't confine his stereotypes to women. Despite his intelligence, he was given to incredible generalizations and insulted everyone, regardless of gender, race, and national origin.

Knight had spent his life in the company of men. They hung out during the day, watched videotape until the early hours of the morning, went out and got something to eat before finally going home, and then, in the off-season, went hunting and fishing.

Knight constantly demeaned women, or demeaned men by comparing them to women. He routinely called his players "pussies," asked them if they were having their period, and put tampons in the locker of more than one. If women appeared anywhere in the workplace, Knight let them know they were on his turf, as when he spoke at a clinic in Louisville attended by then–North Carolina State coach Norm Sloan.

"It was one of the first clinics where we had some women coaches," Sloan says. "There were four or five of them there, I guess. And he just made it a point of letting them know that this is a man's world and you don't have any business being there. And the way he tried making his point was with about three really, really off-color jokes. Then he said, in essence, if you can't take that then you don't belong here.

"I just thought, here's a guy who's so accomplished and capable at his business. Why do that? And it's always been a puzzle to me as to why Bob would go over the line when it wasn't necessary. And I still don't know. I have no idea."

Showing he was the pure strain, Knight didn't even consider sexism unseemly. In front of *Sports Illustrated*'s Frank Deford, who was there to do a story on him, Knight asked the IU women's coach, Maryalyce Jeremiah, if she knew what a "DAB" was. The answer was "dumb-assed broad."

In Bruce Newman's memorable *Indiana Daily Student* piece, Knight declared, "I don't like people very well because most of them lack fortitude or they lack integrity. Women, in particular, bother me. I don't like women at all. I can't bear all the small talk and social amenities that women put you through."

In Knight's program, wives weren't allowed at the kind of get-togethers other coaches would have considered family affairs. While

Feinstein was there, graduate assistant Murray Bartow, the son of Gene Bartow, told Knight how much his wife was looking forward to the annual party at the Indiana Classic, with the coaches of all four schools. Knight replied that she wasn't invited.

Mike Krzyzewski, another taskmaster, credited his three daughters for softening him, and once mused that having a daughter would have been good for Knight. When Feinstein ran that past Patrick, he replied, "I think if I had come out a girl, he would have pushed me back inside."

Knight didn't care about Connie Chung's audience but he was intensely concerned about the new IU administration. Ryan was gone and his vice president, Ed Williams, who was close to Knight, was about to retire, too. As far as Knight was concerned the new president, Ehrlich, had already hung him out to dry once for that misunderstanding with the Soviets.

Now Ehrlich declared that Knight had embarrassed the university again, telling the *New York Times*, "Coach Knight was not speaking for the university. His reference to rape and his coarse language were in very poor taste. Period. That's all I really want to say."

Ehrlich had already figured out he had to tread lightly around Knight. A president had to be concerned with fund-raising and the school's relationship with legislators, and Knight might have been the greatest resource on any campus in the nation. Knight technically served at Ehrlich's pleasure, but Ehrlich was about to learn what a technicality that was.

No one in the state could imagine IU without Knight but, all of a sudden, everyone had to, in Technicolor. Within days of Ehrlich's comments, Knight was talking to officials at the University of New Mexico about their vacant coaching job, which he suddenly seemed to regard as an attractive option.

Knight knew the job was open, having recommended his old assistant, Dave Bliss. Now Knight told the Lobos they could have the sorcerer rather than his apprentice. On May 10, sixteen days after Chung's interview aired, Knight was in Albuquerque. The *Dallas Times-Herald* reported he was offered a $350,000 salary and the use of a $150,000 house, reporting it was a "done deal."

Knight said the package included a cabin on the best fishing stream in the state. A rich New Mexico booster, worried that Knight would miss the forests around Bloomington, volunteered to build him his own seven-acre preserve on the butte. Knight enthused about New Mexico, saying it was "part of the country that I enjoy very much," calling the Lobo officials "awfully nice people" and adding that changes at IU had "really concerned me for some time."

Knight's friends were more pointed. "The clash at the university has caused him to rethink his entire existence," said Quinn Buckner.

"Speaking from experience," said Pete Newell, "if you feel the president doesn't totally subscribe to you or the program, you'd better start looking around because eventually either he'll go or you'll go. And, most of the time, it's the coach."

Indiana, both the state and the university, was shaken. Students picketed Bryan House, Ehrlich's residence, with signs making fun of his bow ties. Fans bought full-page newspaper ads begging Knight to stay. Governor Bob Orr issued a statement, saying he "would hate to see Bob Knight go" because he "exhibits what it means to be a winning Hoosier—bright, tough, loyal, a little stubborn, confident." Lieutenant Governor John Mutz praised Knight as a "tremendous salesman for the state." A shanty erected by IU feminists to protest the lack of a campus rape-crisis center was torn down by two male students, who wrote to the school paper saying they did it in support of Knight.

The whole state awaited Knight's decision breathlessly. On Friday, May 13, two days after Knight's return from Albuquerque, Athletic Director Ralph Floyd told a crowd of students who marched to Assembly Hall, "No news is good news. I've not heard a thing today and the media has followed me to the restrooms."

On Sunday, Knight met with Ehrlich, who made it clear *he* didn't want Bob to go anywhere, either. On Monday, Knight announced he was staying.

"In my view, he's an outstanding coach and I want him to stay," said Ehrlich. The president also noted, "I have come through the last week with a new appreciations of what it's like to be in the middle of a press blitz."

Knight, whose closest friends had spent a week listing his problems with Ehrlich, issued a statement, announcing, "The thing that aggravates me is that so many remarks have been made and inferences drawn by people who have not either taken the time to look at this situation or have any understanding of my thinking right through to where I was supposed to be upset with a president who emphasizes academics. I think it's obvious I would be that kind of a president's biggest supporter. Nothing could please me more."

Only a year removed from the winner's circle, Knight was still the king of Indiana, whether he pulled his team off the floor and insulted women or not. If his move in the direction of New Mexico looked like a ploy designed to show Ehrlich who was in charge, the entire state went for it.

Grateful for Knight's support, Ehrlich spent the rest of his seven years at IU worrying about the rest of the campus and letting Knight run the basketball program.

In the irony of ironies, that was the spring when the nation's foremost male chauvinist pig married again and, as far as anyone could see, found happiness.

Knight's second wife wasn't a homemaker like his first, but another basketball coach, and their romance was more out of a playbook than *Modern Romance*. Karen Edgar Knight, then 41, had been a scoring champion in high school in Kingfisher, Oklahoma, before she became a coach, winning three state titles in Lomega, Oklahoma. They met at a basketball clinic. They began corresponding after she wrote him asking about some X-and-O nuance, and were married without fanfare in the spring of 1988.

Nancy had a defined role in Bob's life, taking care of the home and the kids while he obsessed on his job. Karen was a partner. Knight said proudly she knew enough basketball to carry on an intelligent conversation with Pete Newell. Knight told stories about his bride's sharp eye, like the time she was giving him a hard time after a game and he told her, "Hey, lady, why don't you bake a cake, or something?"

And she responded, "You can bet one thing, buster, if I did bake a cake, it would be a lot better than your zone defense."

Suddenly, Knight had a new sunny image. He went half the 1988–89 season before drawing his first technical. Even opposing players remarked on it. "He's been like a teddy bear this year," said Illinois' Nick Anderson. "Last year, I never saw a coach like him. Maybe he's getting too old now and can't take it." Knight treasured a letter he got from Bob Hope, who wrote, "I haven't heard anything about you for a couple of months so you'd better throw a table."

Patrick was now a star on his high school team. His older brother, Tim, had just graduated from Stanford and was back home, working for his father, coordinating his clinics and speaking appearances and handling the rest of his business affairs. Everything seemed to have turned out for the best. Of course, Knight insisted he hadn't changed, claiming he had always been like this but had been misunderstood.

"Anybody who sees me game after game, year after year, knows that I've screamed less than many guys I've coached against," he told Hubert Mizell of the St. Petersburg Times. ". . . But now, in the cable TV era, a dozen of our games are shown nationally every season. People see that I'm not always in a rage. They begin to think, 'He must've changed.'

"My opinion is that I'm not really different. I'm not any more relaxed or calmer. Games can upset me as much as ever. Marrying Karen has been great for me but I don't think it has caused me to change in ways my players or the public can see.

"What I was, I still am."

Coincidentally or not, his 1988–89 team surpassed all expectations. The team had lost Smart, Garrett, and Calloway and wasn't ranked in preseason polls, but it went 27–9 and won the Big Ten with a 15–3 record.

It was as unorthodox as it was unexpected. Knight started the season with a big front line of 6-9 freshman center Eric Anderson, 6-9 Todd Jadlow, and 6-7 Chuckie White, a high-jumping McDonald's All-American. After six games, including a 101–79 pounding by

Louisville in the Hoosier Dome, they were 2–4 and the Louisville *Courier-Journal*'s Rick Bozich wrote, "If dunking is inevitable, sit back and enjoy it."

Knight decided to start his five best players, even if three were guards. This meant playing 6-2 Joe Hillman at forward with the highly rated sophomore guards, Jay Edwards and Lyndon Jones, who had won three state titles together and had been co–Mr. Basketballs at Marion High School.

Hillman had broken scoring records at Hoover High in Glendale, California, but now he was a fifth-year senior, and it was almost too long ago to remember. A highly regarded prospect in baseball, he had been drafted by the A's and played minor league ball in the summer but, as a basketball player, he was still on the bench in his fifth year at IU with a career average of 3.8 points.

At 6-2, the feisty Hillman was like Knight at Ohio State, a hard-nosed tweener who had to go against better athletes. Knight had never found a role for him until the Louisville loss, when he started thinking about playing three guards. Hillman was the last to find out. He had made a key error against the Louisville press, had gotten the usual roasting and was in one of those I-can't-take-it-anymore moods Knight's players went through.

"So he's livid with me afterwards," says Hillman. "You know, 'We've never had a fifth-year senior. That's so bad. Da, da, da, I wish you were just going to play baseball. And, da, da, da, da, da.'

"I mean, this was the whole ride home from Indianapolis. I'm thinking, 'Goddamn it.' So I get on the phone with my dad and I said, 'This is it. This is just bullshit. I'm out of here. I'm going to go lift weights. I'm going to get ready for baseball next year with the A's. Screw this crap.'

"My dad says, 'Nah, hang in there. Just go.'"

Knight started the three-guard lineup at Notre Dame. The Hoosiers lost but instead of the usual blowup, Knight said it looked pretty good to him.

"That was all he said," says Hillman. "Which I thought turned the whole season around right there. Because if he blows up and goes off and we start a whole new lineup and all this crap going into the next few games, I think we'd stink. And we came back and we built off of that game and we won like thirteen in a row."

Edwards became the Big Ten player of the year, averaging 20 points. Anderson, the first freshman to start right away under Knight since Isiah Thomas, was their No. 3 scorer and No. 1 rebounder. The key was Hillman, who was their No. 2 scorer at 12.6 points and held his own against bigger Big Ten forwards. He crowded Michigan's 6-8 All-American Glen Rice, held him to a total of 26 points in two games as IU won both by a point.

Hillman's leadership was just as important. A natural take-charge guy, he couldn't say anything as a lowly reserve, but now he was someone. When they trailed Minnesota at halftime in Assembly Hall and Knight locked them out of their dressing room, it was Hillman who gathered the players together and gave the speech.

On Senior Night, Knight announced to the crowd, "The most valuable player is not the best player. It's the player who has done the most to get the team where it is. It's an absolute clear-cut situation that Hillman is the MVP. Period."

Making their season more remarkable, the Big Ten was loaded that season. Illinois and Michigan finished behind the Hoosiers and then made the Final Four. The Wolverines won the NCAA title.

IU lost in the Sweet 16 to Seton Hall but Knight took it in stride, knowing how remarkable it had been to get that far. His Illinois archrival, Lou Henson, said it might have been "his best coaching job ever."

In the fall of 1989, Knight's last great class arrived. There were two Mc-Donald's All-Americans: Pat Graham of Floyd Central, who was also Mr. Basketball, and Greg Graham of Indianapolis Warren Central. Knight said 6-10 Chris Lawson of Bloomington South was "better than Kent Benson at the same level." Almost unnoticed was a left-handed late bloomer from Evansville named Calbert Cheaney.

The most famous, or notorious, was 6-8 Lawrence Funderburke of Columbus, Ohio, who had been ranked among the nation's top prospects until he was thrown off his high-school team his senior year with his coach citing his "lack of respect for my authority as coach."

Knight signed Funderburke, anyway. "Maybe his troubles aren't his own doing," said Knight. "I like the kid. . . . There's something there that's really worth working with."

For all Knight's principles, he never met a star he didn't think deserved a second chance. He stuck with Jay Edwards over the course of Edwards's two-year career at IU, while Edwards was suspended for academic reasons and had his scholarship taken away. When Edwards tested positive for smoking marijuana in the summer before his sophomore season, Knight took him back the next season. (When asked about his fiery antidrug proclamation in 1978, Knight insisted he threw those three players off the team not for smoking pot, but for lying to him about it). Now Edwards was gone, having just ignored all advice and entered the NBA draft his sophomore year. He went in the second round and lasted one season with the Clippers.

The surprise was that Funderburke wanted Knight, but he was a different young man. He had been in the middle of a recruiting war with allegations of payoffs, but he was also pleasant and a good student. Thrown off his high-school team, he says he decided to sign with Indiana or North Carolina, whoever called first.

"Coach Knight is a very intriguing personality and I know I was as well at that time," says Funderburke. "I know people said, 'Well, didn't you know what you were getting into when you went there?' But really when you're recruited, you're naive to a lot of things as a 16-year-old, 17-year-old, 18-year-old. You're not aware of things. And I think more than anything else, I wanted to prove to others that I could play there."

Six games into his college career, Funderburke was averaging an impressive 12 points and 7 rebounds and the Hoosiers were 6–0. Knight was cutting him unprecedented slack, even letting him live off campus in an apartment because Funderburke said he didn't like being around a lot of people.

Funderburke was coming off his best game, a 26-point outing in a romp over Long Beach State. At the next practice, he says, Knight came up to him and put his arm around him.

"He said to me, 'Lawrence, just think about all those a-holes'—I don't cuss now—he said, 'Think about all those a-holes who said that you would never make it here,'" says Funderburke. "And he said, 'We've proven them wrong.'

"Ironically, the same day, he kicked me out of practice. He said to leave and never to come back again."

To that point, Funderburke had been the only freshman who hadn't been thrown out of a practice. After the other newcomers learned their career wasn't over, they found out it was just Knight's way of making a point. Funderburke didn't stick around to find out what the point was. An IU player who was kicked out was supposed to wait for one of the assistants to cheer him up, but when Joby Wright arrived in the dressing room, no one was there. Wright had to go to Funderburke's apartment to find him. When Funderburke said he was leaving, Wright became more forceful.

"He came in there, he said, 'I'm not going to let you leave,'" says Funderburke. "He was standing in front of the door, and blah, blah, blah, and then he kept talking to me over and over again. We must have talked for an hour or so or more. And then that's when he said, 'No, I'm not going to let you leave.'

"I said, 'What you going to do?'

"So, he kind of pushed me and shoved and stuff like that. Roughed me up. I mean, Joby was 6-7, 240. I was 6-8 back then and I weighed 200 pounds."

With the martial spirit of Knight's program, there was lots of aggressive behavior as staffers imitated their leader. Publicists barked at press people and threatened to withhold credentials. Assistant coaches threw their weight around. Behind it was the fear a displeased Knight would unleash his wrath upon them next.

Wright first denied roughing up Funderburke but subsequently told *Sports Illustrated*'s Curry Kirkpatrick, "Yeah, I did grab him by the arm and put him on the chair. I cared about him. I wanted to talk to him face-to-face. I'm just so screwed up over this kid."

Funderburke wanted to transfer to Kentucky, but Knight wouldn't grant him his release. Funderburke dug in his heels. He stayed at IU to finish his academic work that semester, ultimately transferred to Ohio State, where he had a solid career, and played six seasons in the NBA.

Without Jay Edwards and, after six games, without Funderburke, the Hoosiers still started the 1989–90 season 13–2. However, Knight told his young players that Big Ten play would be different and it was. The Hoosiers lost nine of their last 14 and tumbled to seventh in the Big Ten.

"We went to Ohio State," says Pat Graham, "and Jimmy Jackson and Treg Lee and those guys, I mean, they beat us, not only on the scoreboard, they beat us senseless. I mean, they just pounded us. They treated us like junior high kids. That's when we kinda woke up. We went 8–10 in the Big Ten that year. We were not very good, and we, luckily, fell into the NCAA tournament."

They fell right out, losing to Cal in the first round, but Knight took it with relative calm. Young was young and no one knew it better than he did. Besides, the Damon Era was finally at hand.

Damon Bailey hadn't even been in high school when Knight first saw him as an eighth grader in little Heltonville, 20 miles south of Bloomington. Even at 14, Damon already had such a reputation that Archie Dees, an IU star from the '50s, had told Knight about him. With Knight at his grade school game, watching every move he made, Bailey, who was already a sturdy 6-1, reached down and palmed a basketball out of the rack. "I looked at him," wrote Knight, "and saw Jerry West."

Knight's assessment, which appeared in John Feinstein's book, made Bailey famous: "He's better than any guard we have right now. I don't mean potentially better. I mean right now." Right then, in the spring of 1986, the Hoosiers had Alford. Knight's assistants knew he was prone to falling head over heels for high school stars who would become dismayingly mortal when they played for him.

Knight never fell harder than he did for Bailey. He organized a three-car caravan to go see Damon again, with assistants Ron Felling and Royce Waltman and several of Knight's professor friends, which Feinstein described in his book.

Knight led the way, speeding down the back roads of southern Indi-ana. . . . When a third car suddenly appeared, cutting between Knight and his followers, Waltman drew back in mock horror. "Oh my God!" he cried. "It must be the Purdue staff. They're going to beat us to Damon. . . ."

"Yeah, I can see it now," Felling said. "Tomorrow's paper will have a headline, 'Bailey Signs With Indiana, Will Choose High School later.'" . . .

Felling began going on in lyrical tones: "This is what basketball is all about. A boy, a dream, a hoop. The backroads of southern Indiana on a cold winter's night. Coaches flocking from all over to see the young wonder. The gym appearing in the gloaming. Hearts skip a beat. Could it be, yes it is. The Home of Damon." . . .

[Bailey] was very, very good. But still, just a 14-year-old boy . . . In the stands, Waltman turned to Felling. "What do you think?

"I think," Felling said, "the mentor has skipped a cog."

The mentor hadn't lost it completely. Even with the expectations Bailey carried, he had one of the most storied careers in the overheated history of Indiana high school basketball. His school, Bedford North Lawrence, played before an estimated 800,000 fans in his four seasons and reached the Final Four three times. He was All-State all four sea-sons and broke the state scoring record. In his senior year, the finals were moved to the Hoosier Dome, where they were televised by ESPN and drew 41,046, a record for a high school game that still stands. Bailey scored 30 points, including his team's last 11 in a come-from-behind victory over favored Elkhart Concord, and ran into the stands to hug his parents. When the press asked about joining Knight in the fall, Damon announced, "Now, I'm his boy!"

By then, Bailey was 6-3 and 190 pounds, a polished all-around player but not a great shooter like Alford. With his elfin looks, Bailey had a similar boy-next-door appeal, but he took it to a new level. "There's no comparison," Knight said. "As popular as Alford was, he wasn't even close to this kid."

Knight had made the oldest mistake in the business, overrating a teen who matures early and has a physical advantage that will fade as his peers catch up. Had Knight seen Jerry West in high school, he would have seen a scrawny kid who was years away from wowing people.

Arriving at IU in the fall of 1990, Bailey started as a freshman and became the Hoosiers' third leading scorer, averaging 11.4 points and shooting 51 percent. He would get better through his four years at IU, and he would never stop being a cult figure. He just wasn't a great player.

"You know, Coach Knight mentioned him in that book," says guard Todd Leary, who was a year ahead of Bailey. "And I remember reading about it in the Indianapolis paper and seeing a picture of him when I was in junior high. From then on, people just followed him. . . .

"And I'm not saying that Damon Bailey wasn't a good player. He was an outstanding player and he could do some things that a lot of players don't do. He saw things happen, I think, a lot of times before they were happening. . . . As far as the physical talent, I just don't think he had what everybody expected him to have. And when Coach Knight mentions you like that—I mean, to compare him and Calbert Cheaney, you're talking two different leagues. Calbert Cheaney is just a physically talented individual. I mean, he's got not only physical jumping ability and strength but he's a great basketball player. And he can do things on the basketball court that just not very many people can do.

"And Damon Bailey wasn't that way. I mean, he's six-foot-three. He was a reasonable athlete. He couldn't jump out of the gym, but he was a reasonable athlete. And it just doesn't allow him to compete, I think, at a level that a lot of people, including Coach Knight, expected him to compete at when he got to the college level."

The players liked Damon and so did Knight. They all admired Bailey's poise and his toughness. They all felt bad for him, too, because he never had a hope of living up to the kind of expectations that Knight had placed on him.

"We were all very good friends in college, and we played AAU together and we played some other tournaments together, and Damon and I were always very, very good friends," says Pat Graham. "Damon was a very good basketball player but Damon wasn't as good as Calbert. But there actually were people in the state of Indiana who believed that, truly, an eighth-grader in Heltonville, Indiana could play in front of Steve Alford.

"I've had a guy come up to me—honest to God truth, Leary was there—and ask Todd Leary and me if Damon Bailey could eat a light bulb. Eat a light bulb. I mean, that's how absolutely asinine some of the people were.

"Damon Bailey in high school, supposedly he ran eight miles to his grandmother's, ate breakfast, ran eight miles home, and went to school. Well, we always laughed at him about that and he said, no, that never happened. But he was just this small-farm-town basketball player in the state of Indiana, he was the greatest thing since sliced bread and it was all made because Bob Knight said that in a book and the state of Indiana went with it.

"And it's still to this day that way. I mean, Damon never played pro basketball. And I don't know who's a bigger name in this state, Larry Bird or Damon Bailey. To this day."

In the fall of 1990, expectations sat heavily on the shoulders of the entire roster as everyone soon realized Bailey couldn't carry them. The Hoosiers did well—they went 29–5 and were Big Ten co-champions—but Knight wanted more and, in a relapse, blew up when he didn't get it.

At Iowa State, sophomore center Chris Lawson said he saw Knight punch a player in the dressing room at halftime. Lawson wouldn't name him, and didn't make the accusation until years later, when he told the *Nashville Tennessean*. The paper reported the player was sophomore forward Matt Nover. Nover issued a nondenial denial, saying he wouldn't talk about it.

"It was up at Ames," says Lawson, "and a teammate made some mistakes and didn't get some rebounds or whatever it was and then we came in at halftime and he was jumping all over him," said Lawson. "And he just went right upside the head. . . .

"I was really amazed, I mean. It was kind of the same situation [which happened once] in a practice and the guy didn't set a screen. He [Knight] went out and grabbed him by the shorts and kicked him right in the butt. And then, I mean, the following day there were bruises."

Being around Knight was like being in a cage with a grizzly bear.

There was no way to avoid contact. What would have been corporal punishment anywhere else was just the way things were at IU. The prevailing attitude among his players was: so what? Pat Graham says Knight got him once with a two-handed shove at halftime of a game at Northwestern. "I mean, he drills me pretty good from behind," says Graham. "Again, I didn't take it as really that big a deal. . . . Did he get my attention? Yes. Did we win? Yes. Did I play well in the second half? Yes."

The Hoosiers were 14–1 in January when Knight exploded at a practice before their game at Purdue. Unlike his other harangues, someone taped this one, which was replayed gleefully by radio stations and was still circulating a decade later on the Internet. Screaming throughout with more rage than the written word can convey, Knight told them:

IF YOU WANT TO PLAY, GET OUT, GET THE FUCK OUTA HERE! I MEAN, IF YOU'RE NOT GOING TO RECOVER, GREG GRAHAM, IF THE REST OF YOU ARE GOING TO LET HIM DRIVE RIGHT BY YOU, IF THE REST OF YOU ARE GOING TO LET HIM CATCH THE BALL OUTSIDE THE THREE-SECOND LANE AND DRIVE ALL THE WAY IN HERE WITHOUT ONE GUY CHALLENGING HIM, THEN I'M LEAVING AND YOU FUCKING GUYS WILL RUN UNTIL YOU CAN'T EAT SUPPER! NOW I'M TIRED OF THIS SHIT! I'M SICK AND FUCKING TIRED OF AN 8–10 RECORD! I'M FUCKING TIRED OF LOSING TO PURDUE! I'M NOT HERE TO FUCK AROUND THIS WEEK! NOW YOU MAY BE, BUT I'M NOT! NOW I'M GONNA FUCKING GUARANTEE YOU THAT IF WE DON'T PLAY UP THERE MONDAY NIGHT, YOU AREN'T GONNA BELIEVE THE NEXT FOUR FUCKING DAYS! NOW I'M NOT HERE TO GET MY ASS BEAT ON MONDAY! NOW YOU BETTER FUCKING UNDERSTAND THAT RIGHT NOW! THIS IS ABSOLUTE FUCKING BULLSHIT! NOW I'LL FUCKING RUN YOUR ASS RIGHT INTO THE GROUND! I MEAN, I'LL FUCKING RUN YOU, YOU'LL THINK LAST NIGHT WAS A FUCKING PICNIC! I HAD TO

*SIT AROUND FOR A FUCKING YEAR WITH AN 8–10
RECORD IN THIS FUCKING LEAGUE AND I MEAN, YOU
WILL NOT PUT ME IN THAT FUCKING POSITION AGAIN
OR YOU WILL GODDAMN PAY FOR IT LIKE YOU CAN'T
FUCKING BELIEVE! NOW YOU BETTER GET YOUR HEAD
OUT OF YOUR ASS!*

Besides all the expletives, there were 13 first-person references in 13 sentences. With Knight, it was always about Knight. His players proceeded to win at Purdue, 65–62, showing this group could handle anything Knight threw at it.

The Hoosiers were Big Ten co-champions at 15–3 and 27–4 overall, ranked No. 9 in the nation. They were seeded No. 2 in the Southeast bracket and advanced to the Sweet 16. However in the regionals in Charlotte, No. 3–seeded Kansas hit six three-pointers in the first seven minutes, ran up a 23–4 lead and won, 83–65. The Hoosiers were on their way; it just wouldn't be this season.

In May 1991, Knight was inducted into the Hall of Fame, an overdue honor that had been deferred in 1988 when he was voted down, presumably because of the incident with the Soviet team. Knight was so stung, he demanded that his name be withdrawn from consideration forever.

Nevertheless, three years later, he received the honor he had earned many times over. Clearly touched, he was at his disarming best at the press conference, prompting a new round of stories reporting how much he had mellowed.

"If there was one change that has taken place with me over the years," Knight said, "things today that might have irritated me years ago amuse me."

Talking about Red Auerbach, a friend of many years, he almost broke down. "To my everlasting appreciation, for whatever reason, Red liked the way my teams played," said Knight. "If you were to ask, uh, if you were to ask him, I would imagine that Red saw some of him in me . . . [a pause, with his eyes seeming to shine in the TV lights] when he was about my age. He was just great to me."

In the fall of 1991 Knight began again with two more promising freshmen, 6-9 Alan Henderson of Indianapolis Brebeuf and 6-8 Brian Evans of Terre Haute South. Knight would never again have as much talent on one roster. Four Hoosiers—Cheaney, Henderson, Evans, and Greg Graham—would be No. 1 NBA draft picks. (In comparison, Knight's 1987 champions had none.) Of the 15 McDonald's All-Americans Knight landed in the '80s and '90s, six came between 1987 and 1991.

Bailey was still mortal, and Lawson never came close to becoming the next Kent Benson before transferring, but everyone else lived up to expectations or exceeded them. Cheaney, the quiet left-hander from Evansville who had been an afterthought coming out of high school, became a major star and everyone's favorite. "I mean, Calbert Cheaney, you can't meet, talk to, or be around a better person," says Pat Graham. "Best person you'll ever meet. Best teammate I ever had."

The Hoosiers went 22–4, and were ranked No. 2 nationally with three games left when the bottom fell out. They lost two of their last three, including one at Purdue, after beating the Boilermakers by 41 points in the first meeting.

That cost the Hoosiers the Big Ten title and the No. 1 seed in the Midwest bracket of the NCAA tournament, and marked the return of the old Bob Knight, who was caught by TV cameras yelling at assistants during the game at Purdue. Still fuming when their plane landed in Bloomington, Knight started walking the four miles home although the word going around was that he wound up getting a ride.

"He claimed he walked home," says Todd Leary. "I'm not sure I ever believed that or not. It's a pretty long walk. I know when we got on the plane there was a lot of yelling and screaming and ranting and raving. And I can honestly remember sitting there thinking, 'I wish he would sit down because he might unbalance this plane.' He was running around the plane and throwing himself from side to side on the plane, up against the walls. . . .

"That time he lost control. You know, when you get older, when you're in your third and fourth and in my case fifth year of playing there, you can tell what's calculated and what's not calculated. But I can honestly tell you that was one of the times he lost control of himself."

The next day Knight no-showed for his own radio program: *Due to circumstances beyond our control, Coach Knight will not be with us for the Coach Knight Show.*

Then he cancelled the team's annual banquet, a bombshell in Bloomington, where the event was the highlight of the social season. Knight insisted it had nothing to do with the Purdue loss. IU officials hurriedly backed him up, saying attendance had been dwindling and they had been thinking of doing it for years.

The local organizers were devastated. Kiwanis President Craig Tenney told *USA Today*, "He just announced, 'We're not having it, period. This is it.' . . . It's a crying shame." The players were embarrassed. They didn't care about having one less appearance to make, but they suspected it was indeed because they lost.

"We could have cared less about that banquet," says Graham, "when it was cancelled, I can remember almost feeling like, 'Oh, my gosh.' People were looking at us like, you all basically cancelled it. Coach Knight did no wrong. . . . That hurt us. We're talking about 18-, 19-, 20-, 21-year-old kids, and, I mean, we were just like appalled."

Instead of being the top seed in the Midwest Regional, the Hoosiers were placed in the West and sent all the way to Boise, Idaho, where they ran over Eastern Illinois, 94–55, and beat LSU, 89–79. They moved on to the regionals at Albuquerque and beat Florida State, 85–74.

Then Knight brought the thunder down on his own head once more, pretending to menace Cheaney with a bullwhip at a shootaround that was open to the press. A photograph ran in papers all over the country. As a cavalier allusion to rape had inflamed women, the image of a white man whipping a black man pressed buttons throughout the nation.

Nevertheless, it may have been the most overblown controversy in Knight's life. He had pretended to do the same thing to a white player, Pat Graham, too, and the players knew it was a joke, since it started out as *their* joke. Pat Graham and Knight's son Patrick, who had enrolled at

IU and was now on the team, had bought the whip and given it to Knight.

"It was totally not any big deal," says Graham. "There were some big deals and that was not a big deal. Coach Knight had taken us to an area where bullwhips and stuff like this are made, handmade, and pottery. It was kind of like an Old Mexico area. They had food and little restaurants. . . .

"So, Pat Knight and I were in a little shop and we saw this bullwhip. We kind of got laughing about it. Well, Pat Knight buys it, I don't know, five, ten bucks, whatever. When things were going good as far as wins and losses, when you were on a roll, hey, Coach Knight was a nice guy, and you might be able to kind of joke with him a little bit. Normally, you couldn't. So, we got on the bus and we got back to the bus, and here Pat Knight jumps up. He's going to give Coach this thing from the team.

"Very few times do you see ever Coach Knight kind of let his guard down to where he just kind of starts laughing, where he can't control his laughter. He's cracking up. And this, for whatever reason, got him. He thought this was the funniest thing in the world.

"And so we went to the shootaround from there. It wasn't a practice because we never practiced in front of the media and fans and everything. So, we get there and he's kind of walking around with this bullwhip. He's kind of being a showman and everyone's laughing and he's kind of walking around whipping this thing. Of course, again, we don't really think anything big about it. We're kind of getting a cracking joke out of it. . . .

"So, that night, we're sitting around our hotel. I can remember Alan Henderson being in there playing cards with everyone. And all of a sudden, we've got the NAACP on this thing. And I mean, we're a team, half black, half white, never had any problems with that. . . . I mean, we're all just thinking, you've got to be kidding me. We were just mortified."

The Albuquerque chapter of the NAACP protested. The leader of the Indiana General Assembly's black caucus wrote a letter to Thomas Ehrlich, calling for Knight's ouster. However, Ehrlich's forthright response to the Connie Chung incident had resulted in Knight threatening to leave, and the IU president didn't want to go through that again. Ehrlich issued a personal apology, saying Knight had been joking, although he conceded it "wasn't perceived that way by some and I'm sorry. I don't want to offend anybody ever. Indiana University certainly doesn't want to and our coach doesn't want to."

Ehrlich's coach wasn't staying up nights worrying about whom he offended. Asked about it, Knight said, "Don't bother me with that shit."

All Knight cared about was his opponent in the regional finals, the same UCLA team that had beaten the Hoosiers by 15 points in the season opener. Knight didn't need a reason to be excited about an NCAA Tournament game and if he had, the sight of the Bruins' powder-blue uniforms would have sufficed. Just to make it perfect, the outspoken Bruin players leaped into the bullwhip debate. "If that had happened in L.A.," said guard Darrick Martin, "there would be riots by now."

The next day, the Hoosiers routed UCLA, 106–79. On the sideline late in the game, Cheaney pretended to whip Knight with a knotted towel, which was, finally, the last word on the subject.

Now, Knight was no longer Simon Legree but Machiavelli. He was "an unabashed bully and a master manipulator" in the *Atlanta Constitution* and "crazy, loco, nuttier than a Nestlé's Crunch bar [and] also a genius" in the *Chicago Sun-Times*.

Two weeks after canceling the banquet and failing to do his own radio show, Knight was on top of the world. He barely seemed to notice the bullwhip controversy and, for once, just let it go. He disarmed his critics in his press conferences in Albuquerque by demonstrating various comic game faces, providing another memorable snippet of videotape. When it was just Knight and his players in practice, he was just as relaxed.

"He really made it fun for us," says Leary. "You know, we had a really bad end of the year and then all of a sudden he just kind of flipped it around. And he was a lot of fun to be around and he made things fun to be at and, you know, our shootarounds were fun and our film sessions were kind of fun."

Nevertheless, recess was over. Now they were in the Final Four, matched up with Duke and Knight's godson, or, at least, his former godson.

Coach K, as Krzyzewski was now known, had been one of the closest players to Knight, who brought him to IU as a graduate assistant, got him the job at Army, and then the one at Duke, when Krzyzewski was a mystery candidate coming off a 9–17 season at West Point. Duke athletic director Tom Butters said Knight told him, "He has all my good qualities and none of my faults."

When Krzyzewski appeared in his first Final Four in 1986, he asked Knight to speak to his team and Knight walked around Dallas wearing a Duke button. Now, however, the Blue Devils were defending NCAA champions and the preeminent power in the college game, having been to six of the last seven Final Fours. They had just made this one on Christian Laettner's celebrated last-second shot against Kentucky in the regional finals.

Krzyzewski was doing it the old-fashioned way, with good players. Since his arrival in Durham in 1980, he had landed 14 McDonald's All-Americans to Knight's nine, and now had a star-studded lineup with Laettner, Grant Hill, and Bobby Hurley. Krzyzewski was demanding, too, but in public he was humble and displayed no self-destructive tendencies. Inevitably, he tired of the "disciple" angle and began insisting he was his own man. Knight, ever sensitive to slights, thought success was making Krzyzewski snooty, noting in *Knight: My Story* that Krzyzewski now took his time answering his calls and sometimes didn't call back.

When IU beat Duke five years before in the 1987 tournament, Knight talked about how hard it was to play Krzyzewski. The 1992 meeting wasn't like that; it was for blood and supremacy.

Cheaney and Company were good but Laettner, Hill, and Hurley were better. The Blue Devils won, 81–78, starting the second half on a 21–4 run, going up by as many as 16 points, and holding off a late Hoosier rally as Leary hit three three-pointers in the last two minutes.

After the game, Knight gave Krzyzewski a perfunctory handshake and walked by without looking at him or stopping. Knight then went out of his way to embrace Colonel Tom Rogers, a Duke aide who had been part of Knight's program at Army, slipping him a letter for Krzyzewski. In the letter, Knight told Krzyzewski he ought to remember the people who had helped him.

Krzyzewski said he didn't think anything of Knight's brusqueness after the emotional game. When they met in the interview room, and Knight congratulated Laettner and Hurley, but walked past him without looking at him again, Krzyzewski got the point. Krzyzewski conducted his press conference in a noticeable daze. Afterward, he went back to his locker room with John Feinstein, who was close to him, and hugged his wife, Mickie, who was surprised to see he was crying.

"What is it?" she said.

"Knight," said her husband.

Krzyzewski recovered to beat Michigan two nights later, for his second NCAA title. His protégé days were over. He and Knight would go years without speaking again.

In the fall of 1992, the Hoosiers set out on what would be Knight's last great season. Calbert Cheaney's storied class of '93 was back for its senior year, with sophomore Alan Henderson coming up fast. The Hoosiers started the regular season ranked No. 1 and finished it the same way, going 27–3. They won the Big Ten at 17–1.

In their last home game against Northwestern on Senior Night, Knight broke tradition and stopped play when Cheaney broke the Big Ten career scoring record. "I don't usually get excited about individual achievements," Knight wrote ". . . [That] was special—for our fans and me. It was a great kid achieving a great honor."

However, along the way they lost Henderson, who blew out his right knee in a February practice when they were 22–2. The Hoosiers managed to win six of their last seven games with 6–4 Greg Graham putting up big numbers, but when Henderson tried to return in the NCAA Tournament, he lasted only a few minutes. The Hoosiers still advanced to the Midwest Regionals in St. Louis, where they put away No. 15–ranked Louisville, 82–69, shooting 72 percent in the second half.

Before they played Kansas in the Midwest finals, Knight paid his team the rare compliment of saying he was pleased by its toughness. "And," he noted, "I'm not easily pleased by that."

Nevertheless, he knew that, as in 1975 when they lost Scott May, they would be vulnerable without Henderson deep in the tournament. The '75 team lost in the Midwest finals and so would this one. Roy Williams' Kansas Jayhawks, the No. 2 seed, beat them, 83–77, clamping down on Cheaney when he came off screens. Pat Graham, who had been on fire in the tournament, cooled off. Greg Graham got in foul trouble. IU was leading, 50–48, in the second half, but Kansas turned it around with an 8–0 run, highlighted by guard Calvin Rayford stealing the ball from Bailey and going in for a layup.

Knight, who loved this group, took it as gracefully as he could. In his book, he praised Chris Reynolds' "incredible spirit," Pat Graham's toughness in playing hurt and Greg Graham's assertiveness after Henderson went down. Knight gushed about Cheaney, who was "what any coach wants in every player he coaches," crediting him with a "Jordanesque quality."

In its last three seasons, the Class of '93 had gone 87–14 and 46–8 in the Big Ten, winning two conference titles and reaching the Final Four. Pat Graham and Leary, who had each sat out a season with injuries, would be back, but the rest were moving on. Knight would just have to see if he could find more like them.

ELEVEN

DINOSAUR
INDIANA, 1993–99

Kids are different. The way I was able to play under him was different than the way someone in the '90s would be able to play under him. . . .

I mean, I have a daughter, and I'm completely different with my daughter than my parents were with me. . . . I just think a lot of players came in with all these accolades and are All-American and have been hearing that all their lives and they don't want somebody getting on them and telling them they can't do this and can't do that all the time.

—Wayne Radford, Class of '78

Bob Knight was too old to change and too young to quit.

—Pat Graham, Class of '93

When was it that old school and hard-nosed slipped over the line and became too old and too hard?

It wasn't anything that could be pinpointed. It happened incrementally, so Knight could be seen as a living legend in 1992 at his last Final Four, and hopelessly out of fashion by Y2K. He wasn't winning as much and his way of doing things was from another time. The world kept changing, but he remained Bob Knight.

At 53 in the fall of 1993, it looked like he had reached higher moral ground. It had been eight years since he had thrown the chair, seven since his divorce and the publication of *A Season on the Brink*, five since Connie Chung. His oldest son, Tim, was working with him, and his youngest, Patrick, was playing for him. His wife, Karen, was also his friend. If he was no more sensitive, he seemed more secure. He was so disarming with the press after the bullwhip controversy, it went away quickly. It had always been possible for him if only he felt like doing it. Now, it seemed, he finally felt like doing it.

Nevertheless, his program still ran at the same fever pitch, with everyone driven to their limits, everything dependent on his mood, and his mood dependent on how much he won.

"The bottom line with Coach Knight is if you lost, it was bad; if you won, it was good," says Pat Graham. "I've heard people say a thousand times, 'Oh, he can be mad when you win and there's good losses.'

"No, that never happened."

And now, for the first time, at IU under Knight, the program began to veer off course.

As often as it happened, it was still always a surprise when one of Knight's teams cratered. So it was again in the fall of 1993, coming off a season in which the Hoosiers had gone into the NCAA Tournament as the nation's top-ranked team. With Alan Henderson, Brian Evans, Damon Bailey, Pat Graham, and Todd Leary back, they were ranked No. 9 in the preseason Associated Press poll. So the entire state was stunned when they opened with a 75–71 loss to little Butler.

The Bulldogs were just happy that the lordly Hoosiers had deigned to come to Indianapolis to meet them. The game was in Hinkle Field-house, the storied barn in which Milan won the 1954 state tournament and the movie version, *Hoosiers*, was shot.

Afterwards, Knight threw a fit that lasted from the time the players got on the bus back to Bloomington in the afternoon to the early hours of the next morning when his team meeting finally let out. The bus driver, a Bloomington resident named Bob Eakle, was so shocked, he turned into a Knight critic for life, writing a series of letters to the local paper denouncing him.

Like the other drivers for the IU-owned bus line, Eakle was aware that Knight had more requirements than the coaches in other sports.

Normally, the bus had to be there 15 minutes before the scheduled departure, but with the basketball team it was an hour or more. Knight would board last and the bus would immediately pull out. Once, at a hotel out of town, Eakle parked in a spot where he would have to back up a few feet to pull out, and trainer Tim Garl told him to back up ahead of time. Eakle says Garl told him, "When Coach Knight gets on the bus, he wants it to go *forward*." Knight never talked to the driver but to Garl, who relayed his orders. The players sat silently in back unless it was a long trip and Knight gave them permission to talk among themselves.

The trip home from Butler was only an hour and 20 minutes and Knight did all the talking.

"I think he started screaming at them before we even left," says Eakle. "I don't think the bus had pulled away yet. . . . The whole way home, he'd sit in his seat and fume a little while and after fuming a little while, jump up and start screaming at 'em some more. It was kind of an on-and-off thing. He was definitely being profane. I wish I had a recording. . . .

"I couldn't watch very closely because I had to watch the road, but I could glance in the mirror and see that he was sort of acting as if he might smack somebody. Maybe he didn't actually smack somebody but he was making motions as if he might . . .

"Fans, they know he has a temper and they see him shouting at the referees, but I don't think they have any inkling of what went on in that bus that day. . . . He was screaming at the top of his lungs to such an extent that sometimes his voice escaped him. It kinda trailed off into squeaks. It was a pathetic, embarrassing display and I resented being forced to witness it. . . . It was not an isolated incident. It was the only Bob Knight bus tirade I ever saw, but the other drivers say it was standard procedure when he was displeased with the team's level of play."

At least Eakle got to go home when the ride was over. Knight made the players stay the night.

"We went back and tried to practice at Assembly Hall, but it was against NCAA rules for us to do that so we didn't get to do it," says Leary. "We just watched film for about eight hours. I'm not kidding either. No, it was eight hours. It was at least eight hours. I know we left really, really early in the morning. It was probably two or three o'clock in the morning."

The show was just starting, as the players learned the next day when Knight showed up at practice with a shotgun.

"I mean, anybody with a little bit of common sense knew he wasn't going to hurt you with it," says Sherron Wilkerson, then a freshman guard. "If I recall correctly, he lined us up in a circle and he said, 'If any of you cocksuckers play again like you did, I've got a bullet for every one of you.' He said, 'If I miss once, I won't miss twice.'"

Knight smoldered for a week. He was so angry at his veterans, Leary and Graham, he didn't talk to them. "Wouldn't look at us," says Graham. "Wouldn't even speak our names." Finally, mercifully, the Hoosiers got to play again, even if it was against No. 1–ranked Kentucky in the Hoosier Dome.

Graham says the IU players went into it thinking, "We were going to get our asses handed to us." Instead, they put together an inspired effort. Graham and Leary were on the bench, expecting to stay there, but when the Hoosiers got off to a good start, Knight put them in, too. In a major upset, at the end of the kind of week you could only see at Indiana, the Hoosiers won, 96–84.

Their joy lasted until their next game, a 101–82 rout of Notre Dame in Assembly Hall, in which Patrick Knight threw a crosscourt pass away in the closing minutes. His father yanked him out of the game, grabbed him by the shoulders, threw him into a chair and kicked a leg—either Pat's or his chair's—before the ESPN cameras.

Knight later conceded throwing Patrick into the chair, noting, "I've done this with other players," as if it was of no more consequence than if he had slapped his backside. Knight insisted he had only kicked the chair.

Patrick, steadfastly loyal but with a sense of humor of his own, made a joke of it, saying, "I know he was going for the chair. My leg just happened to be where the chair was." His teammates said they hadn't seen any kick but as Graham says, "We all kind of had an idea deep down and, you know, Pat Knight at the time was pretty angry about it."

Patrick was in his third year at IU and second season of eligibility but still only a fringe player. He had intended to go to a small school like Creighton where he could start, but his father talked him into playing for him. Hoosier fans had been unkind enough to boo Patrick, but his teammates loved him. He was as brash as a star even if he wasn't one. Almost from the day he arrived as the runt of the highly rated class of '94, a year after the vaunted class of '93, he was the one things revolved around. He was Bob Knight at Ohio State all over again.

"To be honest with you, Patrick was kind of the ringleader of the whole group," says Leary. "He's a person that was just a lot of fun to be around. And I'm sure you've got stories about when you were in school, about one guy who was just crazy and nuts and would do all kinds of stuff. Well, that was Pat."

Knight was even harder on Patrick to show his son got no favors, but this incident, in which he appeared to kick him, looked so alarming that the fans behind the IU bench began booing. They were the program's biggest contributors, the prosperous people in the red sweaters, but Knight looked up from Patrick and yelled at them, too.

"From my seats in Assembly Hall, I can see the bench," says then–athletic director Clarence Doninger. "I'm not on the bleachers, I'm in the seats above that, three or four rows up, but I can see onto the bench. And in that game, he got mad at Patrick and Patrick was over the sidelines and Bob kicked. There's no question he kicked. . . .

"And the crowd gasped when they saw that. And there was a chorus of, for lack of a better word, boos directed toward Bob from the IU crowd. They were stunned to see this because it was sort of violent. . . . And Bob turned to the crowd and just spewed out profanity. And I could see it and hear it. Then that caused some other boos and he did it a second time."

The appearance of kicking one's son had especially disturbing overtones, and if that didn't oblige IU to act, cursing at the biggest boosters did. It fell to Doninger, Knight's long-time friend and associate. Knight and Doninger went back years. When Knight got in trouble in Puerto Rico in 1979, he turned to Doninger, a former IU player for Branch McCracken, who had become a lawyer in Bloomington. Doninger flew down to San Juan and appeared in court with Knight.

Doninger understood Knight had to be disciplined and discussed it with Big Ten Commissioner Jim Delaney, who agreed to step back and let IU handle it in-house. In the first action any Indiana administrator had ever taken against Knight, Doninger suspended him for one game.

However, Knight got to decide which game he would miss. It turned out to be the next one, a romp over Tennessee Tech. In a prepared statement read by the announcer before the game, Knight offered no apology for kicking his son, but in the usual grudging style, he said: "If my reaction to the jeering from the stands on Tuesday night offended any *true* Hoosier fans, I am deeply sorry and wish to apologize."

Knight's statement also said, "Given the opportunity to observe each of you, I probably wouldn't agree with all that any of you said or did, either," and added wryly in closing, "We've been working on Patrick's passing."

If it wasn't quite an act of contrition, at least everyone could tell he wrote it himself. It wasn't funny to Knight, though. As far as he was concerned, Doninger was now sleeping with the enemy, as Doninger learned when he gave his old friend the news.

"Have you ever been around Bob Knight when he gets mad?" says Doninger. "What he said to me, no human being should have to ever take. No human being. And Hayden Murray, the faculty rep, and Mary Ann Rohleder, the compliance officer, were sitting there. No human being should have to take it."

Doninger says Knight later apologized. For his part, Knight insisted afterward that his problems at IU started with that incident.

"Their relationship was great up until that incident," says Leary. "I know I saw them together all the time and I saw Coach Knight with his arm around him. . . . Clarence Doninger in no way did that to hurt him or to get any publicity. Because if Clarence Doninger could have crawled under a rock, I think he would have. He was not trying to seek anything out of that. But I think his hands were tied and he had to do something."

Knight couldn't turn around without making contact, or news. On February 8 at Michigan State, there was another incident on the bench when he leaned into Sherron Wilkerson's face and head-butted him. That one was on television, too. Whatever was going on, it was getting physical on the IU bench.

"I still to this day believe that it was an accident," says Wilkerson. "My initial reaction was that it was on purpose. Coach Knight and I did talk after that game and he flat out asked me if I thought he did it on purpose. And at that time I told him, 'At first, Coach, yes I did. But now I don't think that you did it on purpose.'

"And my point being, after we hit heads, he kind of looked at me, and if anybody knows Coach Knight, he communicates a lot by facial expression. And when we conked heads, he kind of looked up at me for a split second, as if to say, 'My fault, I'm sorry.'"

By Knight's standards, he bore that season's furor calmly. He didn't publicly denounce Doninger. He gently chided the press, saying, "Maybe you all lead a very tranquil, passive life, chronicling the problems others have. We all have areas where we don't want to step over the line. But can any of us say that this will never happen?"

On Senior Night, Bailey bowed out, having averaged 19.5 points in his last season. Knight had forgiven him for not becoming the next Jerry West, but still couldn't get over the notion that Bailey had greatness in him. He thought Damon was burned out after his celebrated high school career. "Bailey," he said once, "had a hard time being as good as he could all the time."

Bailey had always carried the expectations placed on him gracefully, but it wasn't easy as he made it look. Like Steve Alford, he was an icon in Indiana who always said and did the right thing and had too much invested to take on Knight, the greatest icon of them all. Nevertheless, Bailey later told friends stories, like one in which he was summoned to Knight's home late at night, to be yelled at, not only by Bob, but by Karen Knight.

At the end of their four years together, Bailey wasn't altogether sad to be leaving. Knight gave him a warm sendoff on Senior Night, noting how well Damon had handled all the pressure on him.

Then, in one of those moments one could only see at IU, Knight recited a poem for the Assembly Hall crowd:

When my time on Earth is gone
And my activities here are past,
I want that they should bury me upside down
So my critics can kiss my ass.

Nevertheless, it had been a good season. The Hoosiers went 19–8, then advanced to the Sweet 16 for the fourth year in a row, the longest streak going in college basketball, before falling to a strong Boston College team led by Howard Eisley and Bill Curley. Getting that far was an accomplishment with Wilkerson out with a broken leg, Bailey playing with a pulled muscle in his rib cage, Brian Evans with a brace on his right shoulder, and Pat Graham taking injections to stay in the lineup with a broken bone in his foot.

The Hoosiers were in it until the end, taking a 64–59 lead on Bailey's fast-break layup, the last basket of his career. But BC ground them down the rest of the way and won, 77–68.

Knight pulled Bailey at the end and gave him an affectionate pat on his head, as if to acknowledge that whatever Damon had, at least on this day, he had given Knight.

Two months later, in May 1995, Knight, his sons, and several friends went hunting in Argentina. Tim Knight came home with a broken nose and a separated shoulder, saying he had fallen in the shower.

If Patrick, the younger son, had a hard time living up to what his father wanted, he was at least accomplished enough to play basketball at the college level. Tim, six years older, but a half-foot shorter, was the mop-haired runt of the family. He was into the game—he was a ball boy for the Hoosiers and he coached in summer AAU ball—but that was as far as he got. Nevertheless, his father saw to it that his oldest son stayed involved in his life: In later years, Tim would be his father's business manager, and for better or worse, he was destined to spend his life in his father's shadow.

The incident in Argentina went unreported, but rumors spread that

Knight had actually beaten his son up in a fight. It would finally sur-face—as an allegation—in the IU trustees' 2000 investigation, and would be reported as such by the *Indianapolis Star*. Tim told the *Star* he and his father had had "an argument . . . that lasted no more than 30 seconds" and acknowledged they had had a "wrestling scuffle" but in-sisted he had slipped on the wet floor.

The details were never confirmed. However, in a 2002 deposition in a lawsuit brought against Knight by assistant Ron Felling, Patrick ac-knowledged that Tim and his father had been arguing in the shower be-fore Tim was hurt.

Q: *What do you recall?*

A: *Got in an argument. It was a family argument between my brother and my father and I. . . .*

Q: *What was this argument about between your father and you and your brother Tim?*

A: *I don't know. I just—I jump out, I heard them arguing and I just jumped out of the shower and just told them to cut everything out. . . .*

Q: *Were they wrestling. Were they physical with each other? What was hap-pening?*

A: *No, they were just in each others' face and so I just got out because, I just, just told them to stop. . . .*

Q: *Was your brother hurt at all from that fight?*

A: *He separated his shoulder.*

Q: *How did that happen?*

A: *I don't know. When I got out to stop it, everything was pretty much done.*

Q: *Did your father ever describe to you what happened in that fight?*

A: *No.*

Q: *Did your brother?*

A: *No. . . .*

Q: *All you know is that they had a confrontation and your brother walked away with a separated shoulder?*

A: *Yeah.*

*   *   *

In the fall of 1994, Myles Brand became the new IU president. One day, he would be hailed as the man who stood up to Knight. For years, however, he was just hoping he could continue Tom Ehrlich's policy of peaceful coexistence.

Brand was a former professor of philosophy who had become president of the University of Oregon and arrived with his right-hand man, Christopher Simpson, installing him as an IU vice president. Showing how central Knight was in any equation involving IU, when Brand told Simpson he was up for the job, the first thing Simpson said was, "How are you going to deal with Bob Knight?"

"First thing I thought of," says Simpson. "When you think of Indiana, you think of Bob Knight. And Brand laughed and said, 'It's a great opportunity.'"

Simpson had once been the press secretary for Senator Strom Thurmond. Knowing that first impressions are important, Simpson began preparing for Brand's first meeting with Knight as if Brand was going before a Senate subcommittee.

"I talked to people at Indiana about him," says Simpson, "and I talked to them about how Knight greeted previous presidents, so I understood the lay of the land. And I was told, for example, and it could be apocryphal, but I was told by a person at Indiana University that when Tom Ehrlich, Brand's predecessor, first met Knight—and I believe it was in Knight's office—Ehrlich walked in and Knight never said a word to him but leaned down and began to tie his shoe and never made eye contact. And Knight began the conversation with Ehrlich without making eye contact while tying his shoe. And throughout that conversation, I am told and I do not know if this is true or not, Knight peppered it with tremendous amounts of profanity. . . .

"I was told many horrendous stories about when presidents had fallen into disfavor with Knight, the way it was described to me. The sum total didn't scare me but it made me understand, because I have a political background, that we needed to approach this whole thing methodically and strategically. . . .

"I didn't lay all that out to Brand but I simply said, 'The guy's extraordinarily volatile, as we all know. He also appears to me to be an icon in the state with enormous clout, probably more than any university president during his tenure, and we need to approach the relationship very carefully. And Myles did not disagree.

"So, from that first conversation until the time we came to Bloomington, which would have been the first of August of '94 as we began to plan to transition, that was one of the three or four things that I kept at the forefront of my mind. . . . I didn't know Bob Knight but my assumption was he got his way eight times out of ten at the university. And I say that as somebody that reads the newspaper. My assumption conversely was that Brand wanted that institution to be known as a great academic institution, a great public institution nationally, not as Bob Knight's university. So, I could see kind of from the very beginning where there was the potential for those two images or approaches or philosophies to collide at some point.

"And my job, I felt like, was a professional devil's advocate and I had to constantly be looking for potholes and problems the president may encounter. . . . That was the big one."

The first problem was finding Knight so they could schedule the meeting. When Simpson asked where he could reach him, he was told Knight went hunting or fishing in August and no one knew where he was. A month later, Brand and Simpson were on a tour of IU's South Bend campus when they got a call from Brand's secretary in Bloomington: Knight was back and wanted to have dinner with them that night.

"You know, it's noon or one o'clock," says Simpson, "we've got a full day of activities and I told the president. And he said, 'What do you think we ought to do?'

"And I said, 'I think we need to get back to Bloomington and have dinner with him.'

"And we rearranged our schedule slightly and the two of us were alone on the university plane going back. And then, for the first time, I walked the president through all these different scenarios I had heard, all these atrocities that Knight allegedly had displayed when he met previous presidents, and kind of laid out what could go wrong in this meeting.

"For example, I said, 'When we walk in there, if Knight looks at me and says, 'I don't know who this guy is, I'm only going to have dinner with you,' if he says something like that or uses lots of profanity or insults you, don't be shocked because apparently he's done it in the past.'

"A car meets us, we go right to Knight's office. Knight is standing there waiting on us and he brings us into his office and he could not have been nicer, warmer, more charismatic, more interesting, more personable. He was an absolute delight. We talked for, I don't remember, 30 minutes or an hour. Then we went out to a restaurant in Bloomington and dinner lasted about three hours and Knight and Brand totally hit it off. What Knight didn't realize before the dinner was that Brand is a pretty avid outdoorsman. His idea of a good time is taking a horse and going out into the outback in Alaska for four to six weeks at a time.

"Despite the image of Brand as this guy from New York with a funny accent, in Midwestern parlance, who was a button-down, three-piece-suit philosopher, it turned out that Brand had gone riding through Montana one time and knew an outfitter and a fishing guide that Knight regularly fishes with. So, immediately, the two hit it off spectacularly."

If Knight was a demigod at IU, the landscape was changing in the Big Ten, where the other schools had begun catching up. Michigan's Fab Five had reached the NCAA Finals as freshmen in 1992 and gone back as sophomores in 1993. Purdue had reached the Elite Eight the previous spring with Glenn Robinson, winning the first of three Big Ten titles in a row.

At IU, replacements for Cheaney, Henderson, Bailey, et al, were proving hard to find. At one time Knight could sit in his office and take his pick of the top players in the state, but now key players were going elsewhere. North Carolina had just won the 1994 NCAA title with seven-foot Eric Montross from Indianapolis, whose father said he sent him to Dean Smith to spare him "Knight rage." Robinson, the best player the state had produced since Larry Bird, had turned down IU for Purdue.

Recruiting now centered on the summer camps run by Nike and

Adidas that were essentially bazaars, where coaches, AAU coaches, agents, and street agents checked out the prospects like beef on the hoof. Knight didn't even like to compete for players, much less hover over them in summer. When his peers were sitting in the bleachers at Adidas or Nike, Knight was usually deep in the woods. Nor did Knight consider it a problem that he was trying to recruit black players with an all-white staff. After Joby Wright left to take the head coaching job at Miami of Ohio in 1990, IU went seven years without a black assistant.

The Big Ten that Knight had so long dominated had changed as the old roll-out-the-balls coaches were replaced by Purdue's Gene Keady, Illinois' Lou Henson and Lon Kruger, Michigan State's Jud Heathcote and Tom Izzo, Michigan's Bill Frieder and Steve Fisher, and Iowa's Lute Olson, Tom Davis, and George Raveling.

Knight was still getting players but was obliged to go farther afield. His freshman class in the fall of 1994 was rated the nation's best, headed by 6-8, 240-pound Andrae Patterson from Abilene, Texas. Knight, who had once spurned junior college players, was now filling out his roster with them. From 1993 to 1996, five of his 12 signees would be jucos.

In the fall of '94, he even took a flyer on a playground legend named Michael Hermon, his first player from the Chicago Public League. Hermon had transferred twice before his senior year, alighting at Martin Luther King High School amid circumstances so suspicious that rival coaches announced they wouldn't play King.

"I just like him," said Knight of Hermon. "I just like being around him."

Knight would only get to be around Hermon for one year. Hermon went AWOL after putting up an airball in a loss to Notre Dame in his fourth game and left for good the following summer for what were announced as academic reasons.

Knight's best freshman guard was a scrawny, 6-2 redhead named Neil Reed, who proved his grit by playing with a separated shoulder. Knight gave him his highest commendation, saying, "We're not tough at any position on our team with the exception of Neil Reed."

Reed looked like the kind of player the program was all about. He grew up in Louisiana but was raised to revere Bloomington as if it were Mecca. When he was a child, his father, Terry, a high school assistant coach, drove up on a lark, hoping to see an IU practice, and was befriended by Knight's assistant Ron Felling. Neil attended Knight's summer camps. The family had a picture of him at nine with his 11-year-old sister, Michelle, taken on the floor of Assembly Hall. Neil went to Bloomington South as a sophomore when Terry, who was between jobs, went to work at the local Budweiser plant.

They moved back to New Orleans where Terry Reed became an assistant at East Jefferson High and Neil became the two-time Class 5A player of the year and a McDonald's All-American. Neil only took one recruiting trip. As Felling told *Sports Illustrated*'s Jack McCallum in Reed's freshman year, "He already knows where he wants to be buried. Somewhere between the McDonald's on campus and Assembly Hall."

Reed was starting by his fourth game and rose to prominence in his ninth, scoring 14 points in an 80–61 rout of No. 3–ranked Kansas. He was featured in an *SI* article headlined "The Frosh Prince."

Reed was in paradise. "It's beyond anything I could have imagined," he would later write in *ESPN Magazine*. "Those first few games, you'd try to look cool, but the whole time you're thinking, 'I'm wearing an Indiana jersey.'"

The Hoosiers went 19–11 in the 1994–95 season, an acceptable start for the young nucleus. Henderson and Patrick Knight bowed out on Senior Night, ending a stellar career for Henderson and a hard five years for Patrick. Booed by Hoosier fans who expected more; driven by his father, who hoped for more; shaken by the breakup of his parents' marriage, Patrick had his own rebellion to get through. When his father heard a rumor that Patrick had smoked marijuana at a party as a freshman at IU, he made his son take a drug test, which he passed. In the spring of 1992, after redshirting in his sophomore year, Patrick had been arrested for public intoxication and disorderly conduct outside a downtown bar, allegedly swore at the arresting officer, and was tossed off the team by his father.

Patrick later said it was a turning point in their relationship. "We did a lot of talking, not only about what happened that night but about life in general," he said. "We really talked about personal things we hadn't talked about before. Father–son things."

For the rest of his IU career, Patrick was an exemplary player, beloved by his teammates for his hardworking, unselfish attitude. He just wasn't very good.

"Todd and I and Damon, we were all good shooters and sometimes Patrick struggled with the shooting," says Pat Graham. "And I can remember Coach getting so angry in practices over this shooting thing. If he could just make some shots, I think Coach felt he could play more.

"Well, one time Coach is on Pat's tail about shooting. Now, you're talking about real pressure, when you feel like you have to hit a shot to even have a chance to play. And he missed a shot and he said, 'Fuck!'

"And of course, Coach goes off on Pat and says, 'If any of you sons of bitches do any more of that again, I'm going to run your ass!' All this stuff.

"Well, sure enough, old habits are hard to break, and the next screwup, Pat says 'fuck' again. With this, he tells him to run the stairs . . .

"Pat's going up these stairs and he's running about four at a time. And [coach] is yelling, 'I want you to say the word the whole way up and the whole way down!'

"So Pat does it. He's saying 'Fuck,' four more steps, 'Fuck.'

"And Coach says, 'I need it louder!'

"I mean, he's yelling this in Assembly Hall and it echoes anyway. Well then, he gets mad because he says, 'Pat, I want you to say it every step.'

"Now it's probably 80 steps to the very top and he's saying, 'Fuck, fuck, fuck,' and I swear to God, we broke up, I mean, the whole team. And actually I think Coach even started chuckling, you know, because it was funny."

All outgoing Hoosiers lived for Knight's benediction, but Patrick's investment dwarfed theirs, so it was nice when his devotion was returned, in public and in kind.

"Look back over the players that we've had and I love Alan Henderson, he's one of my favorite players," said Knight on Senior Night in the spring of 1995. "Cheaney. Woodson. There are a ton of them. But I leave you with this and then I turn it over first to Patrick and then to

Alan. I do leave you with this thought: Patrick Knight is my all-time-favorite Indiana player."

The 1994–95 season ended on a less seemly note. Missouri upset IU in the first round of the NCAA Tournament and Knight harangued the moderator at the postgame press conference. His name was Rance Pugmire, a University of Idaho official who had been told Knight wasn't coming and so informed the press. When Knight appeared, he fumed at the inconsequential misunderstanding, on camera, adding another chapter to his legend.

KNIGHT: *You've only got two people that are going to tell you I'm not going to be here. One is our SID and the other is me. Who the hell told you I wasn't going to be here? I'd like to know. Do you have any idea who it was?*

PUGMIRE: *Yes, I do, Coach.*

KNIGHT: *Who?*

PUGMIRE: *I'll point him out to you in a while.*

KNIGHT: *They were from Indiana, right?*

PUGMIRE: *No, they're not from . . .*

KNIGHT: *No, weren't from Indiana, and you didn't get it from anybody from Indiana, did you?*

PUGMIRE: *Could we please handle . . .*

KNIGHT: *No, I—I'll handle this the way I want to handle it now that I'm here. You [bleeped] it up to begin with. Now just sit there or leave. I don't give a [bleep] what you do.*

Nobody at IU felt like tangling with Knight over it, although Christopher Simpson says Brand thought about it. Knight did tell his secretary to send Pugmire a red IU sweater, which was as close as Knight came to apologizing of his own volition.

"I don't know if he sent it under the context of 'I'm sorry' or if he sent it under the context of choke on it," says Pugmire.

The NCAA fined Knight $30,000. To Knight, a televised, expletive-filled harangue of a defenseless functionary was part of his right of free speech. He complained forever after that the NCAA was "playing golf on my $30,000."

Incidents were nothing new for Knight. However, a downhill trend that kept on going would be.

Knight placed great faith in what he called "the system" and for all the turmoil within, it had been remarkably stable. With the notable exception of Ricky Calloway, most of the players who had left or been encouraged to go had been reserves. But now, the turnover rate began to include prize recruits.

Sherron Wilkerson, who had been Indiana's Mr. Basketball in 1993, was thrown off the team as a sophomore in the 1994–95 season after being arrested for assaulting his girlfriend. Knight was widely praised for coming down swiftly on Wilkerson while the supposedly high-minded Nebraska football coach, Tom Osborne, found a way to keep tailback Lawrence Phillips on the team after a similar charge.

Unfortunately for IU, more players than Wilkerson were going. In the summer of 1995, Michael Hermon and a part-time starter named Michael Hart left for academic reasons and a highly regarded red-shirt freshman named Rob Hodgson transferred to Rutgers. With Knight's new reliance on junior college players, who were only there for two years, the program no longer had the old sense of solidity, with the older players teaching the younger ones how to endure Knight.

In the fall of 1995, there were only two seniors on the team, Brian Evans, the left-handed sharpshooter, who would become the Big Ten MVP, and backup center Todd Lindeman. The Hoosiers started 7–5, including a loss to DePaul in Assembly Hall, the Hoosiers' first at home to a nonconference foe in 11 years. Knight, who rarely conceded anything, pointed out how young the team was, noting, "I'm no miracle worker. I can't put kids just here into the third year."

The Hoosiers still managed to go 19–11 and 12–6 in the Big Ten, tying for second place and getting a No. 6 seed in the NCAA's Southeast Bracket. Then for the second year in a row, they were upended in the first round, this time by 11th-seeded Boston College.

The 1996–97 season looked promising with Patterson and Reed, now juniors, joined by freshmen A. J. Guyton, a tough little guard in the

Keith Smart mold, and Jason Collier, a seven-footer from Ohio who was rated the nation's top prep big man. The Hoosiers won the Preseason NIT in Madison Square Garden, beating Duke and Mike Krzyzewski, with Patterson going for 39 points in a breakout game that seemed to announce his arrival. They were 12–1 going into conference play, ranked No. 8 in the nation, their highest in four seasons.

However, they unraveled again, losing six of their first 10 in the Big Ten. Knight's mood dove with their fortunes. That spring, in an incident that went unreported, he grabbed Reed by the neck in a practice.

Reed did what an IU player was supposed to do: keep his mouth shut and suck it up until the bitter end, which came shortly thereafter. The Hoosiers wound up 9–9 in the Big Ten, dropping to sixth place. Seeded No. 8 in the NCAA's Southeast bracket, they were beaten by 9th-seeded Colorado, 80–62—the third year in a row they had been knocked out in the first round. A disconsolate Knight walked the two miles back to the hotel in a driving rainstorm through a bad neighborhood in Winston-Salem, North Carolina.

Back in Bloomington, Knight called in his three top juniors, Patterson, Reed and Richard Mandeville, and gave them his you're-not-going-to-play-so-you-might-as-well-transfer speech.

This was a standard ploy, but with the wrong player in the wrong mood it could backfire, as it had with Calloway in 1988, and was about to now with Neil Reed.

Reed had already thought about leaving after his sophomore year. His junior year had been worse, and an invitation to transfer was one insult too many. As Reed later wrote in *ESPN Magazine,* "One of those players started crying, telling Coach Knight what he wanted to hear. The other rocked back and forth in his chair, talking nonsense. It was ugly. Then it was my turn.

"'Well, what do you think?' Coach Knight asked.

"'I think Indiana isn't what it used to be,' I said.

"That was the last time we ever spoke."

Knight didn't consider the case closed. With papers around the state picking up on his public suggestions that some of his players might not be back, the IU athletic department released a statement: "Despite rumors, no changes have been made. At the end of each season, Knight talks with players, especially upperclassmen, as to what he expects of them, what their roles might be and what options he feels might be best for them."

Reed had his own idea of what was best for him. He announced he would transfer to Southern Mississippi, where his father had become an assistant.

Knight acted unperturbed, making sure everyone knew he had kicked Reed out before Reed quit, telling an Indianapolis radio station, "Neil's father has indicated they will accept our invitation for him to go elsewhere and that's fine. We'll take that and go from there."

Reed knew what it meant to pick a fight with Knight but he wasn't backing down. From the office of a New Orleans law firm, Reed faxed a statement, saying Knight "has continued his longstanding tradition of verbal attacks and physical attacks on his players and coaches. I have personally been at the forefront of those personal attacks." Terry Reed told the *Chicago Tribune*'s Gene Wojciechowski that Knight was an "out-of-control egomaniac," claiming for the first time that Knight had put his hands around Neil's neck.

Until Reed left, all the serious charges had come from outside the program. Now, after 25 years of shoves, kicks, grabs, and head butts, an IU player had called it abusive for the first time.

Serious charges against Knight meant orchestrated responses, but this one went above and beyond. Knight convened a team meeting, read the indictment against the absent Reed and got the players to return the desired decision, voting their already departed teammate off the team. Knight had once cheerily announced he could override any vote—"That's part of our democratic process, too"—but now, under fire, he wanted his chorus to chime in. The chronology made the ploy transparent—no one had said anything about a vote when Reed left, until Reed made his statement—but now player after player stepped forward and took the podium to denounce Reed.

"As far as the allegations," said freshman guard Michael Lewis, "I was here when he was voted off the team. He didn't leave by choice, he was voted off the team. By playing a year with Neil, I learned that anything that he did wrong, it was never his fault. Whether it was a bad pass or being out of position, it's never his fault, always somebody else's."

"That just shows that he has not developed into a man," said Guyton, "and I think that's why, the main reason this guy, you know, Reed is coming out with these statements."

Joe Hillman, the true believer from the '80s, said the current players had told him, "Neil Reed was the problem, we've got to get rid of Reed, he doesn't work hard, he doesn't lift weights, he doesn't run."

An IU spokesperson said the university had no comment and was planning no investigation into the claim that Knight had grabbed Reed by the throat. Nevertheless, there was blood in the water now and it wasn't all Reed's. Two months later, *Sports Illustrated*'s Gerry Callahan took a hard look at the program's decline in a story headlined "Has Knight Lost It?"

Setting the tone, an unnamed friend of Knight's told Callahan, "I told Bob a long time ago, if you're going to alienate so many people, then you'd better win and win big. Because when you don't, they're going to be lined up to shoot you. . . . And that's what's happening." Reed talked to Callahan but wouldn't discuss Knight's attack, saying, "I don't want them to take me to court." Reed wouldn't even say anything to Doninger in two exit interviews.

"I said, both to Neil and to his father, 'If you feel you've been wronged, you've got to tell me how you've been wronged,'" says Doninger. "And Neil's response was, 'On the advice of my counsel, I'm not going to say anything.' Or words to that effect.

"I called every player on the team and every coach, other than Bob himself, into my office, either individually or, in some instances, there may have been two players at one time. But I called every single one of them, the trainer, everybody connected with the program, and asked them, 'Now, if there's something I need to know about, you need to tell me. They all said, hey, everything's fine."

The *SI* story prompted another IU press conference to respond. The players also signed a letter to the magazine, which was released to the wire services: "We all came here to succeed on and off the floor and Coach Knight's record in this area has been proven over and over again. . . . There is not one of us who regrets the decision we made in coming to Indiana."

Whoever wrote the letter may have missed a regret or two. One of the signatories, Jason Collier, would leave a month into the following season.

It would take more than Reed's sad tale to threaten Knight's security. Nevertheless, the class of '97 had become his first at IU not to win a Big Ten Title, the Hoosiers had just been eliminated in the first round of the NCAA tournament for the third season in a row, and his program was slipping. A *Sporting News* story said, "Knight's Indiana University basketball program now ranks No. 2. Not in the country . . . in the state where Gene Keady's Purdue Boilermakers are beating Indiana on the court, in recruiting and in the Big Ten standings." The story also noted, "Some fans have already begun the vigil on [Knight's] successor, with the hope it will be native son and former IU All-American Steve Alford, the coach at Southwest Missouri State."

In the unkindest cut of all, the *Indiana Daily Student* ran a story headlined: Has the Game Passed Coach Knight By?

For all the talk about the players he couldn't get, Knight was still assembling impressive rosters. The mystery was what was happening after they arrived.

Once more, the Hoosiers came back looking good on paper in the fall of 1997. Andrae Patterson had been allowed to return for his senior year, starting at forward alongside the seven-foot Collier. Guyton had been the Big Ten freshman of the year. Joining them was freshman Luke Recker, the reigning Mr. Basketball and Knight's most heralded recruit of the '90s, the latest, biggest (6-6, 210), and most gifted in IU's line of Hoosier icons like Alford and Damon Bailey.

Like Bailey, Recker was approaching legend status before he got to Bloomington. IU fans had been awaiting his arrival since Knight broke precedent and signed him as a sophomore at DeKalb High School. Before Recker's senior year at DeKalb, his mother, Marti, a nurse, was tending to a dying 90-year-old woman named Alice Girardot, an avid IU fan, who asked to meet her son. When Luke came to the hospital, Marti said the old lady took his hand, told him "I'm going to be with you," and passed away 20 minutes later.

However, the Hoosiers' promise faded once more, starting when Collier quit the team in mid-December, complaining he had lost 20 pounds, wasn't sleeping, and was seeing a psychologist. "People tell you it's going to be tough," Collier said later. "People tell you it's the hardest thing to do for four years. But you're 18 years old, coming out of high school, and you're thinking, 'Yeah, whatever, I can do it. Guys have done it before me.' But you don't know what you're getting into until you do it."

Knight thought Collier was spoiled by all the publicity he got in high school and said his decision "was in his best interest as well as ours." Collier quickly joined the ranks of the unpersons at IU; the numbers from his nine games in the 1997–98 season aren't even included in the team statistics in the media guide. Collier went on to play two seasons at Georgia Tech and was a first-round NBA draft pick, but never lived up to his high school billing before dying tragically of a heart rhythm disturbance at 28.

Knight wished out loud for the good old days before players came to him with reputations and attitudes. "I wish I could've coached when nobody heard of these kids," he said. "I remember when I was a sophomore in high school in the summer of '55. I lived in Ohio and somebody told me of this great team in Indiana. They had this great player. His name was Oscar Robertson. Nobody heard of him one state over."

Unfortunately, it was now the '90s, and with Collier went any illusion of a quick return to greatness. The 1997–98 Hoosiers lost four of their last six games. On Senior Night in the last home game, an 82–72 loss to Illinois, Knight went off on referee Ted Valentine, who hit him with three technical fouls, one more than it took to eject him.

Valentine had already earned his own wing in Knight's doghouse by calling a technical foul on him in the 1992 Final Four loss to Duke. In this game, Valentine gave Knight a technical in the first half. He then ejected Knight in the second half, giving him two more technicals for going onto the floor and circling him menacingly (Valentine's version), or just happening to pass within an inch of him on his way to visit his injured player (Knight's version). In the hue and cry that followed, the Big Ten fined Knight $10,000, but also censured Valentine.

Christopher Simpson says Brand had been uneasy about Knight's behavior since he harangued Rance Pugmire three years before. Now Brand finally entered the fray—on Knight's side. The deliberative process, as described by Simpson, suggests how much the top officials at IU feared Knight.

"I remember the president being very troubled [by the Pugmire incident] because that's not behavior anybody would endorse of a university coach," says Simpson. "But the dilemma was, the people who had been at the university for a long period of time during that conversation said, 'Now before you say or do anything, remember if we say or do anything to anger the coach, he may blow up. We don't know how he will react. He could even quit.'

"Coach Knight had enough power to where, if the president said, 'This is unacceptable and I'm going to blast him publicly,' you could have alumni, donors, even legislators that could—there could be a backlash, and that's not in the university's best interest.

"But the president didn't want the tail to wag the dog. Meaning, he did not believe Coach Knight should get away with anything or everything on President Brand's watch because President Brand truly believed we always have to do what's best in the university's interest and that's not to be known as Bob Knight U."

Brand intended to back Knight while demonstrating there was oversight at IU. He co-authored an op-ed piece with John Walda, a prominent Fort Wayne lawyer who was the head of the board of trustees and a friend of Knight's, which ran in the *Indianapolis Star.* They not only defended Knight against Valentine, but also against suggestions that he had lost the support of the administration, and that the game had passed him by. They repeated Knight's claim that the press never mentioned his graduation rate and his clean program. Actually, as any Nexis search would show, those things were mentioned ritually.

Curiously, it seemed, Brand and Walda hauled Woody Hayes into the affair, noting Ohio State had "acted correctly in dismissing" him for punching an opposing player. Simpson says they were drawing a line that Knight couldn't cross.

However, Walda and Brand then concluded with a flattering letter from Dean Smith ("I am not aware of any player who has graduated from Indiana who is not grateful to Coach Knight for his experience with the Indiana basketball team"), which they decided was good enough for them. They closed with: "We agree. IU is most fortunate to have Knight as our head basketball coach."

If Brand thought this was a warning, Knight, who didn't take such things lightly, missed it.

The IU administration knew how far out of control Knight really was, but kept that to itself. The same month Knight had his run-in with Valentine, he raged at Doninger's diminutive 64-year-old secretary, Jeanette Hartgraves. Knight's secretary had called, asking for Doninger, and when Hartgraves asked the purpose of the call, she said that Knight grabbed the phone and told her it was "none of your goddamn fucking business."

Hartgraves said Knight then stormed into the office, called her a "fucking bitch," and was advancing on her when Doninger stepped between them. The story wouldn't come out for two years, but Doninger reported it to Brand's office in yet another incident that was referred up the chain of command and never came back down. No investigation ensued and no action was taken against Knight.

"We were having a budget meeting and we had a big group in there and I had asked if we could not be interrupted, this is one that's going to take some time," Doninger says. "And Bob wanted to see somebody in the room. And so Jeanette indicated to Bob's secretary when she called, 'Well, look, they're in this meeting. I'm not supposed to interrupt them. What's this all about?'

"So, that's when Bob got on the phone and called her names. . . . Jeanette does come into the meeting and she's white. And she says, 'Clarence, I'm sorry, I've just got to talk to you.'

"And so, I come out. I see that she's really distraught. And she's beginning to tell me what happened and Bob walks into the office and he goes at her with this look . . . and calls her the names again. And I jump in front of him and her. I said, 'Bob! Bob!' And I guess he finally came to his senses and he walked out, stormed out. . . .

"Jeanette didn't want to pursue it. And I personally should have, I think as I look back on it. I should have insisted we go over to Human Resources and go beyond just reporting it.

"You've got to understand, that's the climate that was there. And so when Bob says that he wasn't being backed, I mean, it's the other way around."

Unfortunately for Knight, coaches' reputations are not made or salvaged in the editorial pages. Despite the stirring defense by Brand and Walda, another of Knight's teams had just gone splat in the Big Ten in the 1997–98 season, finishing in a tie for fifth at 9–7. The Hoosiers were then spared the indignity of a fourth consecutive first-round exit in the NCAA Tournament by beating Oklahoma in overtime before UConn sent them packing.

At IU, struggle begat gloom, which begat departure. The Hoosiers who were leaving now represented the program's highest hopes. Of the last five McDonald's All-Americans who would play for Knight at IU, three—Reed, Collier, and Wilkerson—had already transferred. Worse, No. 4 was warming up on the runway.

Recker had lived up to his billing as a freshman in the 1997–98 season, averaging 12.8 points, second on the team, shooting 49.9 percent, and impressing everyone with his flair and his hard-nosed play. Recker could take the heat, he just didn't want to. In addition to everything that was going on, Knight needed him at forward and Recker wanted to play guard, which would be his NBA position.

Knight wasn't going to sit back and let Recker go, as he had with Reed and Collier. When Recker confided his concerns to Knight after the season, Knight said he would quit if he left. Recker's teammate, Richard Mandeville, later told CNN/SI's Robert Abbott that after

Recker talked to Knight, "He came to my house and was just a mess. Luke was a mess. Oh my God, he felt like he was going to ruin all the assistant coaches' lives in the program, the state of Indiana. He thought if he left, he would never be welcomed back to Indiana."

Recker stayed for now, but morale was a problem across the board as the ballyhooed Class of '98 went out with a whimper, becoming the second under Knight that didn't win a Big Ten title. Patterson, a preseason All-American, finished his senior year on the bench, alongside his fellow seniors Mandeville and forward Charlie Miller, who had also arrived as a highly regarded prospect.

"Andrae was the man," said Recker's father, Clair, in Rich Wolfe's book *Oh What a Knight/Knightmares*. "He was chiseled and stuff and Charlie was a good ball player. And by the time they were done, Andrae was sitting on the bench and Charlie was hardly ever getting off the bench, and, of course, Neil went someplace else. Richie Mandeville, another story, never got the opportunity.

"Were all these guys overrated in high school? I don't think so. It's just that I think Coach Knight tried to break them down and build them up again . . . and today's players are different in that regard. If you're a really good ball player, you've got to think twice about whether or not Indiana is the right place for you.

"Andrae Patterson and Charlie Miller are not bad kids. I met those kids, great kids. That's what they were—they were kids. I think there have been some kids who have had some real issues with that . . . who struggle with, 'Am I really as bad as Coach makes me out to be, am I really that bad of a person?'"

The 1998–99 season was more of the same. The Hoosiers started well, going 13–2 in nonconference play, but struggled in the Big Ten. Michigan State won the NCAA title that season, Ohio State made the Final Four, and Purdue, Wisconsin, and Iowa were nationally ranked. The Hoosiers went 9–7 in the conference, tying for third. Illinois then bounced them out in the first round of the Big Ten tournament, beating them by 16 points.

The Hoosiers did get out of the first round of the NCAA Tournament, beating George Washington, 108–88. Then St. John's bombed them, 86–61, IU's worst loss ever in the tournament. In Knight's last five seasons, he had won two games in the NCAA Tournament.

This time Recker didn't confide in Knight. He wasn't going through that again. Recker waited until Knight left the country on a fishing trip to Cuba, and faxed in his resignation.

Trying to take the high road, Recker didn't say anything bad about Knight or the program, then or later. "This is the toughest decision I have ever made," Recker wrote. "I love the state of Indiana and playing for IU was always my lifelong dream. It is not easy to leave my friends, my family and my home state. I appreciate the opportunity given to me by Coach Knight. However, I have not been satisfied with my development as a player. I blame no one but myself for this and believe my development will best be served in another program."

As always, the departing player was vilified. A "Fuck Recker" banner hung outside an apartment near campus. Recker was said to have handled his departure in a cowardly manner, rather than face Knight.

However, Recker wasn't like the others who had left. He was not only the Hoosiers' leading scorer but their most popular player since Alford and Bailey, and represented years of investment on the part of Hoosier fans.

"Neil Reed became a prima donna, who didn't want to practice and all that stuff," says Rick Bozich, the Louisville *Courier-Journal* columnist and former *Indiana Daily Student* reporter. "This is a kid that played a lot of one season with his injured shoulder in a shoulder brace. He was known as a gritty kid then, but when things went bad, he was a bad guy. I think Knight at that point still had enough of an upper hand and enough strength within the university and around the state that nobody really took it any more seriously than, 'Oh, that's just another kid who's not tough enough to handle Bobby.'

"Recker was a white, athletic, Mr. Indiana Basketball in high school who had committed to IU as a sophomore. After he left the team, there were stories about how Recker didn't want to play defense and Recker was soft and guys on the team didn't like him, and there was one story about how he got caught with a teammate's girlfriend. And all that kind of stuff started coming out, as it always did the last few years when somebody left."

There were no happy endings. Recker transferred to Arizona, but that summer, before school started, he and his girlfriend, Kelly Craig, an IU cheerleader, were involved in an auto accident in Durango, Colorado, when a drunk driver sideswiped the truck they were riding in.

Kelly was paralyzed in her arms and legs. Her brother, Jason, was in a coma. The driver of their car, a 23-year-old friend, was killed. Recker's temporal artery was severed. He survived only because a friend stanched the flow of blood by keeping pressure on the wound. Recker also lost an ear, which was repaired through plastic surgery, and suffered a broken thumb.

After spending two months at Arizona, he would withdraw with Coach Lute Olson's blessing and transfer to Iowa to be closer to home. Olson continued to check in on him, as did Keith Smart, Recker's former teammates, and members of the IU athletic department. But Recker never heard from Knight.

"Luke gave him his heart and soul for two years and he never even as much as got a card," said Recker's mother, Marti. "Don't tell me how he's there for everybody, because he's not."

After several press people asked about it, Knight noted gracelessly that he had called Kelly instead, because her injuries were greater. "He wasn't hurt very badly," Knight told the *Chicago Tribune*'s Rick Morrissey. "What really got to me was the girl and her brother. I tried to call her family. I left word that we called and nobody returned the call. I made the effort. I think the girl and the brother kind of got left out of the whole thing. That's where the tragedy is."

Myles Brand had now been at IU for four years without ever taking Knight to task. Nevertheless, even an administration as tolerant as Brand's saw Recker's departure as an ominous sign.

"I think there was a prevailing feeling amongst the trustees, particularly toward the end of Knight's tenure, that there was a pattern of character assassination for every player that left," says Christopher Simpson. "That was extraordinarily troubling to them. For Reed to leave is one thing. For Collier to leave is another thing. But Luke

Recker was made in the mold of Steve Alford. There's been nothing at Indiana University like Steve Alford until Luke Recker walked into Assembly Hall the first time to put on the uniform. So, for him to leave, I think, shook a lot of people and they believed it's a new day. It's not like it's always been. . . .

"I think it was clearly telling, not only that Luke left but remember how he left. He waited till the coach was in Cuba fishing and he issued a press release. He was long gone before the coach got back onto American soil. And that struck a lot of people, I think—operative phrase being I *think*—as being, 'Oh, man, what's going on?'

"And I know that's what got Robert Abbott looking into this."

Abbot was the producer from CNN/SI who was about to come onto the scene, after which nothing would be the same.

There was no peace to be had around Knight anymore. The Recker controversy had barely died down in June 1999, when Knight was involved in a dispute at a Mexican restaurant during which he was alleged to have choked a 38-year-old Bloomington guitarmaker named Christopher Foster.

Knight had been dining with his wife, Karen, and her two sisters. Foster, who is white, claimed he heard Knight say, "When I have a black player who comes into some money, I tell him, buy your mother a house, and you hang on to the rest of it. Because when one of those people comes into money, they come out of the woodwork."

As they paid their bills, Foster told Knight he was offended by his racist remarks. Knight said they weren't racist. In the ensuing exchange, Foster said Knight grabbed him by the neck, leaving marks and requiring treatment. Karen said her husband tried to walk away. Knight claimed he only pushed Foster out of the way.

It was clear that Foster had instigated the incident, if not what ensued, but Knight wasn't in his gym now. The case was referred to the Monroe County prosecutor to determine whether he should be charged with battery. Knight stewed for 10 days, helping with the investigation through a friend in the Indiana State Police, Sergeant J.

D. Maxwell, who interrogated witnesses at Knight's suggestion. The prosecutor finally announced that Knight wouldn't be charged, but he was still angry, insisting anyone else would have been cleared immediately.

"If the Monroe County prosecutor's office investigated Charles Manson, it still would be undecided," Knight said ruefully at his own press conference. "I'd like to refer to this whole thing as a real Mickey Mouse operation but that would be an insult to Mickey Mouse."

Sergeant Maxwell also appeared at the press conference to issue a testimonial on Knight's behalf, and was suspended for eight days by his superiors for involving himself against orders. Christopher Foster had to stay with friends to get away from threatening phone calls.

Knight fumed at Doninger, who been serving as a liaison with the prosecutor's office. Knight kept telling Doninger to expedite the case, but Doninger kept telling him the prosecutor had to be thorough, lest he look like he was kowtowing to the local celebrity. As far as Knight was concerned, Doninger might as well have been on the prosecutor's staff. Doninger says that they had repaired their relationship since he had suspended Knight in 1993, but this tore it for good.

"Bob was incensed with me over all that," says Doninger. "That was the crowning blow in our relationship. He ended up blaming me for the restaurant incident."

Knight refused to deal further with Doninger, his superior, and began making his arrangements through Steve Downing, his former player who was working in the athletic department, and who now became the de facto athletic director for basketball. Brand and Simpson tacitly endorsed Doninger's demotion, leaving him out of the loop in discussions about the basketball program to avoid angering Knight.

It was a busy offseason. In October, on a grouse-hunting trip in northern Wisconsin, Knight accidentally shot longtime friend Thomas Mikunda in the back and shoulder with his shotgun. Mikunda was hit by 16 pellets and required medical treatment but the wounds weren't life-threatening. Knight was cited for failing to report the incident, as well as for not having a current license, pleaded no contest, and paid a $582 fine.

Knight said his finger had slipped off the safety and hit the trigger accidentally. However, Mikunda subsequently sued him, claiming Knight had shot at a grouse with Mikunda in the line of fire, then had pressured him to give investigators a false account of the incident to avoid legal problems. The suit would be settled out of court, but around the Big Ten that season, students delighted in holding up signs that said, "Don't shoot, Bob."

A few weeks later, at the Big Ten media day in Chicago, Knight visibly snubbed the new Iowa coach, Steve Alford. They sat at adjoining tables without exchanging so much as a hello. When reporters asked Knight about Alford, Knight pointed to the "Indiana" sign on his table and snapped, "Can you guys read that? That's what we're here to talk about."

Alford had shot up the coaching ranks—from Division III Manchester College to Southwest Missouri, where he made the NCAA's Sweet 16 twice, to Iowa—and Knight didn't like hearing that Indiana fans wanted Alford to succeed him. Worse, when Alford was asked about coaching at IU, he not only answered but suggested he would love to. "You know," said Alford, whose ambition belied his boy-next-door appearance, "it is my alma mater."

Completing the bill of indictment, Alford was about to sign the transferring Recker, which to Knight made Iowa a virtual Hoosier government in exile. Wrote the *New York Post*'s Lenn Robbins after Knight's media day snub, "It's a good thing Alford wasn't on that hunting trip."

The Hoosiers started the 1999–2000 season 3–0, with the third game an 81–64 romp over Notre Dame on November 30 in Assembly Hall. The next day Knight fired assistant Ron Felling after listening in on a telephone call between Felling and Dan Dakich, the former IU assistant who was now head coach at Bowling Green.

Felling had been on the IU staff for 12 years, making him Knight's longest-serving assistant. Felling was in his third season with a new title, administrative assistant, although he still sat on the bench and drew the same salary. A bachelor, he made no secret of his fondness for nightlife and women and the debt he owed Knight for hiring him, but he was also considered a sharp coach who knew his Xs and Os.

Knight said he had been in his office about to watch a tape of the

Notre Dame game when he reached for a soft drink, knocked the phone off the hook, and began listening when he recognized the voices of Felling and Dakich.

"I had a glass of ice and Dr. Pepper that was on a table beside the chair that I sat in to look at the tapes," Knight said later in a deposition, taken when Felling sued him. "And I reached across to get that glass of Dr. Pepper and as I did, I bumped the telephone, and didn't even think anything about it until all of a sudden two voices came on the telephone that I recognized to be Felling and Dakich.

"And the first thing I heard was Dakich saying, 'Are you doing anything different in practice?' And Felling said, 'No, we're doing the same old shit, four corners and all that stuff that doesn't do any good at all. But he won't listen to anybody.'

"And then, 'You should have seen that fat fucker come into the locker room with no shirt on and try to show somebody post defense. You know, it just got ridiculous . . .'"

A confrontation ensued in the coaches' lounge between Knight and Felling, with Davis and assistants John Treloar and Pat Knight there, and with Dakich on a speakerphone to establish what Felling had said. Dakich proceeded to confirm Knight's account, convicting Felling, and Knight made Felling's termination official.

According to Felling, Knight then hit him with a forearm shiver that sent him sprawling backwards into a TV set. Knight said he only bumped Felling. However, in Pat Knight's deposition in the Felling suit, he said his father knocked Felling over and he would have done the same thing.

Q: *So you think your father was justified, getting up and knocking Ron back into the TV?*

A: *I do.*

Q: *And if you'd been in your father's shoes, you would have done the same thing?*

A: *Yes. And I probably would have done more.*

Q: *What more would you have done?*

A: *I'd beat the shit out of Ron because I do not put up—I mean, you guys can live in whatever world you live in but I don't think there's anything that should be more dealt severely than disloyalty.*

Felling says Steve Downing came to his apartment to get him to sign a paper saying he had resigned. Felling refused, so IU announced he had been reassigned. The real story wouldn't surface for months, although rumors spread around town and a local talk-show host named Mark Shaw called for an investigation.

The 1999–2000 season went on with no one the wiser. The Hoosiers were 13–2 on January 18 when Iowa came to town. It was Alford's first time back as a coach, and it had been highlighted on everyone's calendar since Knight had snubbed him. Knight had been stewing for three months while Alford acknowledged "the rift" to the press. Alford said he had tried to contact Knight, noting plaintively, "There are things I wish I could talk to him about."

By then, there was some question if Knight would even let Alford in the door. With the whole state waiting to see what happened, Knight walked onto the floor dramatically late, as usual, but not by his normal route; instead he came up behind Alford, put his hands on his shoulders and shook his hand.

IU won, 74–71, raising its record to 14–2. It looked like Knight had defused the situation deftly until he began railing in the postgame press conference, "If Alford wants to sit down and talk with me instead of holding press conferences and talking about a bunch of bullshit, I'll explain things to him!"

Unable to leave it at that, Knight stomped out of the press room but then stomped back in to announce, "Let me tell you one more thing I'm tired of! I had a chance to speak to a total of three coaches! There's seven I didn't speak to! If I've got a chance to speak to someone, I'll speak to them! What about the other six coaches I didn't talk to?'

Then Knight left and returned for a third time to protest, "He's 20 feet away from me and I'm surrounded by people. . . . Why didn't he come speak to me if it's such a goddamned offense?"

The Hoosiers went 10–6 in the Big Ten, their best conference record in four seasons but only good enough for fifth place. The mad whirl continued to the end. After a February 19 loss in Assembly Hall to Ohio State, Knight began raging at the 65-year-old Doninger, and had to be restrained by the team physician, Brad Bomba, a long-time friend of both. Knight acknowledged Doninger had done nothing more than sympathize with him, but he insisted the IU athletic director had no business being in the hall outside the dressing room. Knight claimed he hadn't threatened Doninger and hadn't even raised his voice.

"Well, that last year my relationship with Bob had really, really been strained," says Doninger. "And maybe even Bob said some I-don't-want-you-around type thing. . . . So, that whole last year, when I would go to the locker room after a game, I tried to be very innocuous, okay?

"I was there talking with Brad Bomba and I looked up and there Bob is, coming toward me and walks past me and I said in a very quiet way, 'Coach, that was a tough loss.'

"And he gave me that look that he's got and said, 'How would you know?' Very belligerently. And then walked back and forth in front of me a few times and then said, 'I'm sick and tired of your people not supporting me.' Whatever that meant, and that was also belligerent. I didn't say anything to that, so, at this point, I've said one thing: 'Coach, that was a tough loss.'

"And then he walked back toward the locker room and then back toward me . . . and he said, 'I want you out of here,' and gave me that look.

"And I said, 'Bob, you have no right to say that to me.' Again, I didn't say this belligerently. . . .

"And so he then walked away and then he came toward me and Brad Bomba jumped up and put his shoulder into Bob to keep him from getting to me. And I'm standing there, I don't know what's going to happen. And then Patrick is trying to get to me and another team physician [Dr. Larry Rink] sort of gets between him and me. So, basically, I had two 6-5 guys wanting a piece of me."

Says Pete Obremskey, then an IU trustee and another friend of Knight and Doninger: "If it wasn't for Brad Bomba and Dr. Rink, I believe Knight would have tried to beat Clarence up. . . . If I was the athletic director, I'd have fired the son of a bitch on the spot."

Doninger says he reported the incident to Christopher Simpson and Myles Brand, then talked to Big Ten Commissioner Jim Delaney, after which no one took any action. It was another story that didn't get out but would soon. After 29 turbulent years in which so many things had been kept secret, the day of reckoning was drawing near.

TWELVE

TWILIGHT OF THE HOOSIERS
INDIANA, 2000

The positive need to be weighed against the negatives. He coached the 1984 gold-medal Olympic team and he yelled at a secretary. He has a 98 percent graduation rate and he threw a chair. He's raised millions of dollars, directly or indirectly, for this university and he put his hands on a player. He has a short fuse with reporters and he's won three national championships.

—IU athletic department spokesman
Todd Starowitz, May 11, 2000

The political climate changed. Back when Knight was throwing chairs and doing all these other things, if the president of the university would have fired Bob Knight, I would bet the citizens would have burned the university down and the governor would have led the charge.

And over the years, my peer group—because I'm old enough to have lived through all this crap—just got tired of all the crap.

—IU trustee Stephen Backer

And then, everything changed.

Even after all the recent disappointments, Knight was still unchallenged at IU in the spring of 2000. Turmoil had been a constant in his 29 years but he was dug in deep. Despite the gloomy speculation in the press, he could still get players, having just signed 6-10 Jared Jeffries of Bloomington North, touted as his best recruit since Isiah Thomas. It would take more than some so-so seasons and the departure of a Mr. Basketball like Luke Recker to unseat him. In Indiana, Knight was a king.

Nevertheless, a chain reaction was already under way that would shake his kingdom to its foundations. It had started a year before, in the spring of 1999, when Recker left. That piqued the interest of CNN/SI managing editor Steve Robinson, who called a young producer named Robert Abbott into his office in Atlanta and told him to check out the IU situation.

Abbott had begun trying to interview the parties involved, including the other players who had left, like Neil Reed. Abbott assumed he would put together a piece that would be ready to run to coincide with Midnight Madness in the fall when the teams started practicing again for the 1999–2000 season. The problem was, it didn't seem like a college basketball story. It was more like a Stephen King novel.

"It was extremely difficult," says Abbott, "because no one wanted to talk about Bob Knight. Everyone feared him. Everyone was scared of him. And, as a result, they didn't want to say a word. Nobody wanted to . . . They would start to tell you something and then they would stop. They would kind of get into it and then they would back off and then they'd call you back and say, 'You're not going to ever report that, are you?' And everybody was paranoid, people who you wouldn't even think would be paranoid."

Recker had declined to be involved. Jason Collier said he was through with the subject. He did tell Abbott if he wanted to know what Knight was like, to rent the movie *Full Metal Jacket*, in which a Marine recruit, brutalized by basic training, shoots his drill sergeant and turns his rifle on himself.

Reed wouldn't agree to be interviewed, but he and Abbott stayed in touch, maintaining a dialogue via phone and e-mail. Reed wanted to put IU behind him, but Knight was still trashing him three years later, claiming Reed had been a problem in his year at Southern Mississippi. (People at the school said Reed had fit in well.) Abbott sent a camera crew to Holland, where Reed was playing professionally, to shoot footage of him in case Reed changed his mind.

Midnight Madness came and went and Abbott was still on the case, amid the usual tumult. He was working on his piece throughout the 1999–2000 season while Knight fired Ron Felling, raged at Clarence

Doninger, and brought his team in at 20–7, IU's best overall record in six seasons.

On March 10, the Hoosiers lost in the opening round of the Big Ten Tournament to Illinois, 72–69. Four days later, Abbott's piece ran and their world began to crumble.

The IU administration knew all about Abbott's piece, since he had been trying to interview officials and players, as well as Knight, with no success. The official posture, as usual, was that if Knight wouldn't talk, no one else at Indiana would.

What IU officials didn't know was that Abbott had finally broken through to Reed, who had described the 1997 incident in detail, asserting that Knight had grabbed him by the throat.

"I want to make this real clear because Neil Reed was never out to get Bob Knight," says Abbott. "We were going back and forth and we're talking every couple of days and a few times a week and then, finally, he called me up, actually in Bloomington, and he said, 'I'm ready to do it.'

"And I said, 'Why?'

"And he said, 'Because Bob Knight went after my dad in an article in the *Chicago Tribune*. I'm tired of it because my dad hasn't done anything to Bob Knight. He keeps attacking me and my family. I haven't been there for two years. Why is he attacking me and my family? I'll do this interview.'"

On camera, Reed told Abbott that Knight "came at me with two hands but grabbed me with one hand." He estimated Knight held him for five seconds and said they were separated by Felling and Dan Dakich, the assistants.

"It doesn't matter what people call it," Reed said. "I call it choking, when you put your hands around someone else's throat." Teammate Richard Mandeville corroborated Reed's account to Abbott on camera. A second teammate, Charlie Miller, said he didn't think Knight had choked Reed, "but he did put his hands around him." Reed and Mandeville also said Knight had thrown Myles Brand out of a practice for talking. They described another incident in which Knight had come out of the bathroom with the toilet paper he had just wiped himself with and showed it to his players. As Mandeville put it, "He came out with his pants down around his ankles and just wiped his ass and said, 'This is how you guys are playing.'"

On March 13, the day before it was to air, CNN/SI sent out a release outlining the story to key TV critics, including USA Today's Rudy Martzke, who called Simpson, asking for a comment.

"Catches me off guard," says Simpson. "Out of the office, out of the state, out of the car, and on a hiking trail with my 15-year-old son. And I get a page, 703 number, and I know from my days in D.C. that that's northern Virginia, so I immediately returned the call, and I get on the other end, 'Rudy Martzke, USA Today.'

"And I just went, 'Oh, shit.' I didn't know Martzke but I knew Martzke was the sports TV columnist for the largest newspaper in the country, and the only reason Martzke could possibly be calling me was about my problem.

"And Martzke was very nice. He said, 'Hey, I've got a press release from CNN/SI and let me summarize what it says. They're going to air a piece in 48 hours that has Neil Reed, one of your former players, making three allegations. Number one, that he was physically and mentally abused by Knight, and number two, that he witnessed at practice Brand being cursed out by Knight, and then Knight tossing Brand out of practice.' And number three, what we eventually began to call the ugly toilet-paper incident. And he said, 'I need the university's response.'

"And I said, 'Rudy, I'm in Tennessee, the president's on the West Coast, give me an hour and I'll get back to you with a response.'

"He said, 'Okay, fine.' And I hung up on the cell phone and I just shrugged and dropped my head. My son, David, looked at me, kind of no clue what was going on and he said, 'Hey, is it bad? Dad, is it bad?'

"I said, 'David, you don't have any idea how bad that call was.'"

Simpson called Brand, who insisted Knight had never thrown him out of a practice. They couldn't confirm or deny the other two allegations, and decided to come to Knight's defense. At IU, it was a response ingrained by decades of experience, from the time Knight was photographed with a fistful of Jim Wisman's jersey 24 years before.

The next day, on March 14, IU responded in a press conference held by the athletic department before the CNN/SI story even aired. Meanwhile, Abbott says IU officials worked behind the scenes, trying to kill the story.

"I got called into the office," says Abbott, "and in the office is Jim Walton, the executive vice president of CNN/SI; Steve Robinson, the managing editor; Rick Davis, who is in Standards and Practices at CNN; and the two head legal counsels for CNN. And Jim Walton, whom I'd known for 13 years and had been pretty good friends with for 10 years, asked me, 'Have you ever told anyone that you're out to get Bob Knight fired?'

"I said, 'No.'

"'Have you ever told anyone about what you're doing and you think it may get Bob Knight fired?'

"And I said, 'No.' And they just kept asking me and asking me and asking me and then I finally got pissed off. I said, 'Goddamn it, I haven't lied to you in the 13 years I've worked here.'

"What they told me later was somebody from Indiana had called and, as crazy as it sounds, someone from Indiana said that they're going to hold a press conference at six o'clock saying they have a piece of paper that says I would rather shake Adolf Hitler's hand than Bobby Knight's and that I had signed it. And I am not making this crap up.

"Todd Starowitz—he's the information director for basketball at Indiana—when he introduced the press conference for [IU players Michael] Lewis and [A. J.] Guyton, he stepped to the podium and said something to the effect of, we heard this was going to be a hatchet job, we heard the people they're going to interview, we didn't want to be a part of it and just to let you know, the producer of this piece has had it out for Bob Knight since 1984 when Indiana beat North Carolina in the Final Four. He said that. That was on their web site like the next day as a transcript of the press conference.

"I was at Florida State in 1984. I was a sophomore. I had just quit the golf team. I was more worried about girls and having fun than anything."

The defense at the IU press conference was the standard blanket denial and counterattack on the messenger. Abbott was characterized as biased and out to get Knight; CNN/SI was said to be doing it to derail the Hoosiers on the eve of the NCAA Tournament. "I don't think the timing is an accident," said Lewis, a reserve freshman guard. "It's a blatant attack against Coach and the team."

Brand released a statement denying Knight had ever thrown him out of a practice. In another statement, trainer Tim Garl said, "The allegations Neil Reed described in the press release never occurred. Part of my job responsibilities require that I am at every practice and every game. Therefore, I would have witnessed such events. I can say without a doubt that any events Neil Reed described in the press release never took place."

From Bowling Green, where he was now the coach, Dan Dakich released a statement calling the allegation that he had separated Knight and Reed "totally false."

The CNN/SI piece aired on the night of Tuesday, March 14. It was 15 minutes long and would be generally deemed balanced, noting Knight's 98 percent graduation rate, the spotless reputation of his program, and including IU's assertion that the percentage of players who left was in line with other schools. With no one connected with IU willing to go on camera, Abbott found a former player, Alan Henderson, to speak on Knight's behalf.

However, in Indiana, Abbott's story was taken as another attempt by mean-spirited outsiders to tarnish their hero. Robert Garton, the president pro tempore of the Indiana State Senate, laughed at the allegations, noting, "This isn't ratings month, is it?"

Abbott's piece aired again on Wednesday, March 15. The same night, HBO's *Real Sports* showed a Knight interview with the respected Frank Deford, with footage just shot at an IU practice in which Knight was deliberately taking players by the back of their necks and guiding them into position. Deford stood up, took Knight by the front of the throat and asked, "Did you go like this?"

"I don't remember that," said Knight, in a nondenial denial. "I am sure that I have with kids. I will tell you this, there isn't a thing that I have done with one kid that I haven't done with a lot of other kids. I have no apologies to make whatsoever for anything that I have done in an attempt to motivate kids."

The next day Knight appeared at an NCAA Tournament press conference in Buffalo, New York, where the Hoosiers would open against Pepperdine. In a rambling 22-minute tribute to himself, including allusions to his graduation rate and his gifts to the library, Knight noted, "We're not teaching kids to play canasta. This is a game where kids get bloody noses and get hurt. . . . If my kids left and they weren't successful and they didn't have degrees and were on the bread line or they were selling drugs or were in jail for one thing or another, then I'd really have a lot of questions about just what the hell my methods were all leading to."

As he had with Deford, however, Knight stopped short of a flat denial, conceding it was possible that something like what Reed described had happened. "Sometimes I grab a player," Knight said. "Maybe I grabbed Neil by the shoulder. Maybe I took him by the back of the neck, I don't know."

To a man, the Hoosiers said the CNN/SI story wouldn't be a factor, but it hung over them like a thunderhead. The next day Pepperdine bombed them, 77–57, in the first round of the tournament. Center Kirk Haston sprained his knee early in the game and came out. Guyton, their leader, didn't make a shot from the floor.

"We knew after the allegations came out it was going to be a long week," said Guyton afterward. "Reporters asking us dumb questions about Neil Reed and Richard Mandeville, who have been gone for two or three years."

"What hurts is knowing that assholes like Neil Reed in the world laugh at us for the rest of the year," said Michael Lewis, in a quote the *Indiana Daily Student* published.

However, the IU administration could no longer ignore Reed's allegations. As long as Reed had refused to talk about the incident, Brand didn't have to deal with it. Now that Reed had told the world, Brand had no choice. Still Brand wasn't embarrassed enough to order an independent investigation, which could go wherever it wanted, preferring instead to handle it in-house.

"Well, at the time, the question was, do you do an investigation?"

says Simpson. "Surely, you have to. The minimum, you have to. Who does it? I argued the point, personally, that, remember, Neil Reed left three years ago, it wasn't last week. And when he left, on at least two different occasions if not more, Clarence met with him one-on-one and said, 'Neil, what's going on, what happened, I want you to tell me what happened.' And Mr. Reed never availed himself of those opportunities. . . . Here you've got a guy that left, had the opportunity to tell his story, refused to, and all of a sudden appears out of the blue three years later. And the argument I made, and I can't speak for anybody else, was this does not rise to the level of a special-prosecutor-type situation where you're going to appoint somebody from outside to come in."

At a press conference in Indianapolis, Brand named IU trustees John Walda, a former president of the state bar, and Frederick Eichorn, another prominent attorney, to investigate, calling them "men of impeccable credentials."

"This is Indiana University," said Brand. "There are no sacred cows at Indiana University."

It didn't even fly across the room. After years of determined non-confrontation, there was widespread skepticism about IU's ability to deal with Knight. It was a perception that was shared by some of the other members of the board of trustees, to whom Walda and Eichorn would report.

"Again, you've got to understand what's on the board at the time," says Stephen Backer, an Indianapolis lawyer who had become a trustee in 1998. "We had a number of people on the board who had been on a long time, who over the years were very close with Bob Knight. John Walda was, Fred Eichorn was, Jim Morris was, and Pete Obremskey was and so was Steve Ferguson. He had five guys out of nine who were really close to him. . . .

"I think that they didn't even feel that there was much there until they started investigating. And then all of them did a 180."

Adding to the skepticism, Brand said the investigation would be confined to Reed's allegations. Moreover, Walda, the lead investigator, didn't have "impeccable credentials" at all, as far as this case was concerned. Not only had he and Brand co-authored that 1997 op-ed piece that concluded, "IU is most fortunate to have Knight as our head basketball coach," Walda was already on the record discounting Reed's story, telling the *Indianapolis Star* that "as a lawyer, I would put no stock in old allegations."

Once again, Brand had been unsuccessful in his attempt to demonstrate that IU was bigger than its basketball coach. Still, the story played on two levels, as always. Nationally, it confirmed Knight's image as an unfettered tyrant and IU's as his enabler. In Indiana, where Knight was still widely seen as a hero, Brand's response was seen as reasonable.

Even in Indiana, skepticism was rising as the state began to split in an emotional divide. The Indianapolis papers were taking a tough line, notably *Star* sports columnist Bill Benner, an IU grad who had admired Knight when he was on the beat in the '70s but had become disenchanted after hearing about his attack on Sports Information Director Kit Klingelhoffer. Benner's columns had long angered Hoosier fans, but now their rage was off the charts. Benner said one caller promised to make the *Star's* offices look like the bombed Federal building in Oklahoma City; another caller threatened his mother. Benner told his wife that if Knight was ever fired, they would have to be careful for a while. Wrote the *American Journalism Review*: "Reporters who have covered Kosovo or the Colombian drug cartel might find it hard to imagine peril in covering a college basketball program. They have never lived in Indiana."

IU had circled the wagons around Knight before and it seemed to be working again. Knight was once more in crisis mode, cooperating with Brand and saying he welcomed the investigation. It was still the word of the departed Reed, Mandeville, and Miller, against Knight, Garl, Guyton, Lewis, and IU players from all eras who arose to defend Knight once more.

Now, however, emboldened by Reed's testimony, others began to come forward with their own long-held secrets. Ricky Calloway, who was running a pool-construction company, told the *Houston Chronicle* he had seen Knight punch Steve Alford and slap Darryl Thomas in the mid-'80s. Alford and Thomas quickly denied Calloway's story.

The *Indianapolis Star* reported the argument between Knight and Doninger after the Ohio State game. In Bloomington, an indignant IU spokesman, Todd Starowitz, replied, "I find it unbelievable that an argument between several people would warrant a 20-plus-inch front-page story."

Unhappily for IU, Starowitz was right. The incident with Doninger was about to become the least of Knight's problems.

Doninger was still the athletic director but he was playing little part in the IU defense. Knight had refused to deal with him since their argument. Brand and Simpson had allowed themselves to be persuaded that Doninger was no longer objective when it came to Knight.

"From the time the Neil Reed incident was made public, the biggest mistake we made, without question, was not having Clarence as a key player in all of the decisions," says Simpson. "And he was almost exclusively excluded because we had been told by other administrators that Clarence wasn't objective because of the run-in he had with Coach, and we listened to those people and that was a big mistake. . . . Nobody's reputation was harmed, in my opinion, worse than Clarence's for absolutely no reason."

The problem wasn't just that Doninger deserved better. The problem was that Doninger had been around a long time and knew a lot of things that the administration didn't.

"There had been a rumor that I had heard over some period of time that there was a tape out there that showed an incident between Bob and Neil Reed," Doninger says. "I not only had heard the rumor, I had had people tell me that they had seen it. So there was a powwow with the administration and I was there. You've got to understand, I'm sort of on the outs, at least I think that, and everybody's still pro–Bob Knight in the administration.

"And so I said, 'Now you've got to be careful in what you say because I think there's a tape out there. I haven't seen it, I don't know who's got it, but you have to assume that there's a tape out there and you have to assume that CNN's got it.'

"And I also said, 'I have had at least two people tell me that they were present when Bob cleared the gym, including the president, okay?'

"And so, the next thing I know, the institution is guessing who's got the tape. And they're trying to get the tape. Rather than working through me, they're making all sorts of demands and so on and so forth. So they just royally screwed it up. You can quote me on that.

"[I said] 'Don't get out there and say it didn't happen. The coach says it didn't happen and he's out there. He's already had his press conference and you can tell. He says things like, 'Well, I know sometimes when there are problems I'm teaching, I do this, and when I'm teaching, I do this.' Well, you know there's something. . . .

"Quite frankly," Doninger says, laughing, "I mean, even after I told them you've got to assume there's a tape, I don't think anybody believed me."

There was a tape.

It had become common practice for coaches to videotape practices as well as games. This practice had not only been taped, Knight would later acknowledge having gone back and reviewed it "probably twice after that practice was over."

Three years later, in the spring of 2000, as the IU establishment rallied around Knight, the tape was gone. The word going around was that Ron Felling had taken it after he was fired in November. The Springfield, Illinois, *State Journal-Register* reported that friends of Felling in Lawrenceville, Illinois, where he had once coached, said he had the tape. The Knight people said that Felling had told Steve Downing he had it.

Other people had heard about that tape, too, including Abbott. He had even been allowed to view it while working on his piece, but he won't say who showed it to him. "I made it known that I was interested in it, obviously," says Abbott, "but only if somebody was ready to give it to me."

Three weeks after Abbott's story aired on CNN/SI, the tape showed up in his mail in a plain manila envelope with no return address, no letter, and an Ohio postmark. Abbott played it for his bosses, who were stunned. As far as they were concerned, anyone who had done what Knight did to Reed in their studios would have been fired. Abbott began working on a follow-up piece, built around the tape.

"We had the tape," says Abbott. "We put together the piece. My bosses, Steve Robinson, Jim Walton, want to call Indiana University, notify them we have the tape. . . .

"They wanted to show them the tape. I was 120 percent against it because here's a university that I had, in some ways, been fighting for six months, trying to get to the truth. I didn't think we owed them anything. My bosses thought differently. I also said, 'What if they slap an injunction on us? We could have this tape and not be able to run it.' They didn't believe they would do that. I said, 'I'm not so sure.'

"So, they fly a delegation from IU down to Atlanta. It's Terry Clapacs [IU's vice president of administration], Frederick Eichorn, Christopher Simpson, John Walda. Those four guys come into our offices. They walk in. I'm there with Jim Walton and the managing editor, Steve Robinson. Steve sits there and says, 'You know, we figured we'd invite you down. We have this tape.'

"Simpson kind of cuts him off and says, 'We understand that you have stolen property that belongs to Indiana University.'

"And I'm sitting there going, whoa! And Steve Robinson said, 'We were kind enough to invite you down here. If you want to term this stolen property, if you want to pursue this legally, you can go call your lawyers and I'll walk out the door right now and it'll be out on the air 30 seconds later. We invited you down here. Do you want to look at this tape or do you want to threaten us?'"

A discussion on procedure ensued, with the IU people asking to watch it alone, and Abbott objecting, fearing they would take the tape. They agreed that Abbott would show them the tape, that anything they said while watching it would be off the record, and Abbott would interview them afterward. That left Abbott alone in the room with four men who wished he had never been born.

"So then, Terry Clapacs starts in with me," Abbott says, "saying, 'Have you ever been to Indiana? Have you ever been to a practice? Ever been to a game?'

"And I knew he was just trying to find out what I had done to do this story and things like that so he could find ways to spin it. Like here's a guy who produced a show and he's never been to an Indiana game, never been to a practice. And so he was doing that and I said, 'Everything in here is off the record, so do you want to ask me questions or do you want to watch this tape?'

"And then Christopher Simpson stood up and he said something like, 'I just want to see the tape.' And I said, 'Sit down. I'm here to play the tape. You want to see the tape, sit back in your chair right now.'

"Because they were actually bothering me, to be honest. Because he wanted to see the tape, I wouldn't let him. And I told him, 'You want to watch the tape? Because if not, I'll unplug this machine and walk out with it. Just sit down, I'll play it back as many times as you want. Don't ask me questions, just watch the tape.'"

The IU officials watched it in silence. Afterward, Abbott interviewed Walda on camera. Sounding like a lawyer who had just been hit between the eyes by surprise testimony, Walda said, "The tape does seem to shed some light on the reported incident between Coach Knight and Neil Reed. Now it will be up to us to continue and complete our investigation."

Trying to elicit more than a statement of policy, Abbott says he asked question after question. "I said, 'How would you feel if that was your son there getting choked?'" he says. "And I asked some personal questions to try to get a response out of him, and he just deadpanned every time, 'Well, after viewing the tape, we're going to take it in as part of our investigation.'"

Within hours of the IU delegation's departure from the CNN/SI offices on April 12, 2000, Abbott's second piece aired.

It was the smoking gun. Knight had said he often grabbed players by the back of the neck to guide them into position, but he was shown grabbing Reed by his throat with one hand and holding him, according to the stopwatches, for 2.3 seconds. There was nothing to suggest Knight was positioning Reed since they were at midcourt, facing each other.

Even after millions of people had seen the tape, Knight still made no concession to the actual image, insisting that his hand had only been "attaching to his chest," which was the way the local *Herald-Telephone* referred to it, too. The reaction of Knight's inner circle was not remorse but anger. Downing and Pat Knight publicly identified Felling as the rat who had given Abbott the tape.

"Here's a guy like Felling who steals the tape," Patrick told the *Indianapolis Star*. "He's going around telling people that he's got it. Thirteen years of loyalty to someone and he's pulling that kind of stuff. It makes me sick."

The question at hand wasn't Felling's behavior, however, but Knight's, and the facts in the Reed incident were no longer in dispute. Knight's success, his ideals, and his charismatic personality had given him a godlike credibility in Indiana that was now shaken. The ground gave way under him as the press became more aggressive and began following up old leads.

On April 13, the *Indiana Daily Student* called for Knight's firing in an editorial entitled: "Coach Knight Must Go."

On April 16, the *National Post* of Toronto published excerpts from Butch Carter's forthcoming book, including the accusation that Knight told an unidentified player that he would end up like "all the rest of the niggers in Chicago, including your brothers." The player Carter was referring to, Isiah Thomas, quickly denied Carter's claim.

On May 10, Doninger's secretary, Jeanette Hartgraves, described her two run-ins with Knight to an Indianapolis TV station—the one witnessed by Doninger and another from the '80s, when she worked for Ralph Floyd, and Knight stormed into his office and threw a vase against the wall, spattering her with shards of pottery.

On May 11, the former secretary in the sports information director's office, Terry Cagle, described Knight's attack on Klingelhoffer to another Indianapolis TV station.

The same day, the *Indianapolis Star* reported the IU investigation had widened to include the allegation that Knight had beaten up his son Tim on that 1994 trip to Argentina. Tim acknowledged they had had a "wrestling match" to the paper.

The trustees' investigation was supposed to last until the middle of

June but they suddenly decided to wrap it up a month early. If they were once inclined to discount the CNN/SI allegations, the accumulated weight of the stories they had heard was sobering.

"John and Fred investigated," says trustee Stephen Backer, "and they did a very thorough and a very good investigation and it turned out, I think they were shocked by some of the things that they found out."

Brand was already aware of much of the behavior, like Knight's argument with Doninger and the Jeanette Hartgraves incident, but now he could no longer stay out of the fray. The investigation he himself had launched meant Brand would finally have to confront Knight.

Knight would later insist he had distrusted Brand for years, but as far as anyone else knew, they had always been on cordial terms. Backer remembers them at a game at Ohio State a year before, sitting on the bench, chatting away. "Bob genuinely enjoyed talking to Myles, I think," says Backer, "and you could tell they had a very good relationship."

Now, the university's image was being battered daily and the board of trustees was no longer a bulwark supporting Knight. Even his oldest friends on the board weren't going to the wall for him. Steve Ferguson, a Bloomington attorney, was recusing himself because he had done legal work for Knight. Pete Obremskey would later adopt the same position. There was growing sentiment on the board for firing Knight immediately.

Brand didn't need anyone's consent to fire a university employee. In this case, however, knowing that Hoosier fans would arise and the legislature might follow, he wanted the trustees at his side. That was now assured.

Knight was fishing in the Bahamas, acting unconcerned, telling the press he might even leave IU, as he had once hinted he would go to New Mexico. When he finally realized he was in real trouble this time, he faxed back a statement, apologizing for his behavior, with the usual self-legitimizing elements.

"Practically all of us have some problem to deal with in life," Knight said in his statement. "For some, it's something as simple as meeting people or talking in front of people. My temper problem is a lot more troublesome than those and it's something I've had to deal with for as long as I can remember.

"There are times when my passion for basketball led me into confrontations I could have handled a lot better. I've always been too confrontational, especially when I know I'm right. I'm not very good at just forgetting something and going on and I'm truly sorry about that. I am working on it and I have a helper. I've mentioned before that my wife has posted signs around our house: THE HORSE IS DEAD. GET OFF IT. As hard as that is for me to do, I think I'm getting better because of her and those signs. . . .

"Intense, demand, and temper have been a three-braided rope for me, and I really believe that the first two have been a major reason for the success of our kids and teams. It's my job and determination to temper the third braid. I'll leave it up to our kids to judge if I'm improving."

As the trustees finished, Knight flew home, arriving on Saturday, May 13. The situation had become dire. Doninger says he was told that Ed Williams, a former IU vice president and Knight's long-time friend, and Terry Clapacs actually went to see Knight to tell him he was through.

"The way it was told to me was the trustees basically had recommended that he be terminated," says Doninger, "that a couple of people from the administration, not the president, had gone over to talk to Bob to tell him that that was probably going to happen. And Bob went crazy. . . . They were there to tell him that he was going to be fired. Then he went over and convinced Myles that he should have a second chance."

The meeting with Brand was scheduled for that night. This time Brand didn't come to Knight's office or to a practice or a game on the road. Knight came to the president's Bryan House residence. Brand was set to break the bad news to him but Knight's charisma cut both ways; he was scary when he was angry but irresistible when he was vulnerable. It would take a hard man to terminate a humbled Knight and Brand was moved.

"Before the meeting, I didn't think he could change his behavior," said Brand, a few days later. "I'd never seen him before contrite and apologetic . . . sincere. He made a personal pledge to me to change his behavior. He gave me his personal word and I believe him."

The next day, Sunday, May 14, hundreds of press people waited outside the University Place Hotel in Indianapolis. Inside, Brand met for more than two hours with eight trustees, with Ferguson recusing himself. Brand described Knight's reaction, recommending he be retained. The trustees agreed.

However, no announcement was made that day and the atmosphere remained foreboding. Reporters, hanging on every clue, agreed the trustees had looked grim. In Bloomington, junior guard Dana Fife announced he would leave Indiana if Knight was fired.

The next day, Monday, May 15, in a full-dress press conference in Indianapolis, Brand announced that Knight would stay but with "zero tolerance" for further incidents. Knight would also be suspended for three games and fined $30,000.

Walda presented the report of the trustees' investigation, which stated Brand had not been thrown out of a practice and said they had been unable to substantiate the "soiled paper" incident. "On the final incident," the report said, "the most serious, our videotape analysis confirmed that Neil Reed was grabbed by the neck but was not injured. However, that single action by Coach Knight was clearly inappropriate." The report went on to note, "The review, the first of its kind during Coach Knight's 29-year tenure, also uncovered new information that illustrated a protracted, troubling pattern in which Coach Knight has a problem controlling his anger."

Brand said Knight had apologized to Jeanette Hartgraves and everyone else would get a general apology. Knight, who wasn't present, said in a prepared statement, "I have absolutely no problem with the guidelines. The establishment of effective and proper guidelines can in the long run help me become a better coach."

The irony was that it was true, even if it was late by decades. The problem was that few people were satisfied with "zero tolerance," including Knight.

*   *   *

It was now open season on Myles Brand, who was dealing with irreconcilable constituencies: Knight, the trustees, the academic community, the people of Indiana, and national opinion. Knight diehards thought Brand had been cowed by the media. Everyone else said Brand had been cowed by Knight.

Sports Illustrated ran a picture of Knight's angry face that filled up its entire cover along with the word, "Whitewash!" under which it said: "Indiana Caves, Knight Stays." The *New York Daily News*' Mike Lupica, once a Knight admirer, blasted Brand in a column headlined, "Hoosier Brass Chokes in End." The headline over Harvey Araton's column in the *New York Times* said, "At Indiana, the Toadies Are Shocked." The *Boston Herald*'s Gerry Callahan called Brand "a pathetic little fellow" with the "authority of a Muppet," adding, "Woody Hayes didn't just roll over in his grave. He kicked his way out of his coffin and demanded his job back."

Prominent IU professors denounced Brand. Bruce Cole, distinguished professor of fine arts, said, "The investigation is like the *Titanic* but with even more leaks and poorer planning." Distinguished Professor of Psychology David Pisoni said the image of the university was "irrevocably damaged."

"Well, I can tell you the attitude of the board of trustees," says Obremskey, Knight's friend and former lawyer, as well as a trustee. "Here we had a guy there that was head basketball coach for 29 years. He had by and large been successful, a very successful coach. And he acquitted himself well in terms of dealing with the reputation that he enhanced at Indiana University.

"But there were times when he got out of line but nobody had cracked the whip on him and told him it's not going to happen anymore. So we felt like we had to tell him that, 'Coach, we can't have this.'

"I think under the circumstances it was very appropriate. I mean you can't fire somebody in the organization unless you put them on notice of the fact that what you've been doing for the last 29 years no longer sells."

*   *   *

Two weeks after Brand sentenced him to zero tolerance, Knight returned from a trip to Scotland and sat down with seven handpicked sportswriters. Then he did a separate interview with ESPN's Digger Phelps and Roy Firestone, both of whom Knight had approved. The project was Simpson's brainchild, but due to the volatility of the central figure, he was proceeding with care.

The writers were Dave Kindred, who had retired from daily journalism and was writing columns for the *Sporting News*; Hubert Mizell of the *St. Petersburg Times*; Billy Reed of the Louisville *Courier-Journal*; Bill Gildea of the *Washington Post*; Ursula Reed of the *New York Post*, and Mike Leonard and Lynn Houser from the *Bloomington Herald-Times*. An *Indianapolis Star* reporter was turned away at the door along with one from the Associated Press and another from a local TV station.

Knight was upbeat, insisting in the face of skepticism, even from these long-time insiders, that he could survive under zero tolerance.

"I've got a great plan," Knight said. "Let's have a lottery. Let people bet. Proceeds will go to our library."

He thanked Brand for "sticking his head out and making a decision that many people did not agree with," but dug in his heels as far as taking responsibility for any specific act. "I got a call from Joe Paterno," said Knight. "He says, 'Bob, I've seen that tape of the Neil Reed incident. Watched it over and over. If that is called choking a player, I could probably be convicted of it 200 times a season.'"

Asked about his recent apologies, Knight said, "Let's just say I'm in agreement with all that has been done. I'm ready to just be a basketball coach."

The ESPN interview proceeded along the same lines. The most memorable moment was Firestone's admission that he hadn't seen the Reed videotape, resulting in headlines on TV columns like "ESPN Knight Moves a Joke" (*New York Daily News*) and "Failure to Watch Tape a Knightmare" (*Los Angeles Times*).

Firestone said he had intended to show the tape during the interview as Knight commented on it, but Simpson vetoed that idea. However, if Knight hadn't been grilled, he had said enough to suggest he wasn't the man rolling around in remorse that Brand had described.

"Bob Knight was interviewed by Roy Firestone and denied having told Myles Brand that he apologized or promised to do better," says then-trustee Ray Richardson. "Which goes back to the fact that Knight believed he was bigger than the university. I believe that Bob Knight set out the next day to show that he was the boss. And it started with the Roy Firestone interview."

If IU was looking for signs that the local tiger hadn't changed its stripes, they wouldn't be hard to find.

Thus began the summer of everyone's discontent. The atmosphere was so charged that Murray Sperber, a 59-year-old professor of English and American studies who had been a long-time Knight critic, took a leave of absence and moved to Canada.

Sperber had written a book decrying the influence of big-time college sport in 1990. He was the IU academic the press turned to when it needed a comment on Knight, and he had appeared in Abbott's first CNN/SI story, saying there was "no one in this state and certainly there is no one in this university" who would stand up to Knight. "You want to wipe your ass in front of your team," Sperber said, describing IU policy, "have the toilet paper, Bob." Knight supporters had found Sperber's e-mail address in the course catalogue, and he was now getting so many threats, a dean had offered to post armed guards in his classroom.

When Sperber departed, 165 faculty members petitioned Brand, protesting the administration's inability to protect him. Professor Emeritus of Music Keith Brown returned an official scroll he had been awarded to the president's office to express his disapproval of Knight, noting, "I was very honestly embarrassed to be part of Indiana University."

Knight wasn't any happier. He began taking what he said he saw as precautions to keep himself out of jeopardy. His growing army of skeptics, which now included the administration and the board of trustees, saw his behavior as a way of getting back at IU.

Knight gave up teaching his physical education class. He said he was the last Big Ten coach who did it, so what was the problem?

He boycotted the big alumni summer functions in Indianapolis, Chicago, and Bloomington, angering IU's biggest boosters. He said his lawyer had told him not to go because he would be at risk for doing something that violated zero tolerance.

"Oh, he was very bitter," says Stephen Backer. "He had never been disciplined before, you know. Here's a guy who's gotten away with murder. I mean, he's a wonderful guy but he's gotten away with murder. He had all the power and the presidents shook in their boots. He stood up to a couple of them and won. I think he misjudged this one. . . .

"You could tell, it was like a marriage gone sour. You can tell it isn't going to work because of the attitude of the parties and the bickering and the pettiness and those kinds of things. Well, it kind of started to get into that."

Knight had been given discretion to decide how he would pay his $30,000 fine and to choose the games he would miss. However, when administration officials asked what his plans were, he put them off. In one of those discussions in early summer, he blew up loudly and profanely at the IU counsel, Dorothy Frapwell, and ordered her out of his office.

This incident, too, went unreported and took several months to surface. When it came out, it sounded more like the old days than zero tolerance.

"I know what Dotty said occurred," says Simpson. "She went to his office, talked about a legal matter and the conversation denigrated, he lost his temper, he yelled at her a little bit, used profanity, told her to leave, and she did.

"The involvement I had in that situation is when it was brought to the president's attention by Dotty. Dotty didn't want to pursue it. She didn't want to file a complaint or make an issue of it because Dotty is a very, very good lawyer and a very good university employee. She'd been around the institution for 20 years or 25 years and she understood there was a bad side to Knight and she happened to see it one time in 25 years. But her job was to handle legal affairs for the university, not to make an issue out of Knight losing his temper. . . .

"At the time that that occurred, there were several troubling things.

One, his refusal to do some key alumni events. He also, and he told me on one occasion, maybe more than one, one for sure . . . he was also refusing to tell the university which three games he would sit out, and how he was going to pay the $30,000 fine.

"So, that doesn't sound like a team player to me. And in that context, he had this run-in with Dotty, but Dotty's the chief counsel for the university. She had had tough run-ins with a lot of people for a lot of years and she knew that came with the territory. It was not a big issue to her. The whole pattern was troubling, but there was not one individual event that you would say triggers zero tolerance, or whatever."

Everyone could see where this was headed, but there was no turning it around. Obremskey, still friendly with Knight, tried to talk to him about his attitude one day that summer while playing golf, and they wound up in each other's faces.

"Knight's attitude about it was not good," says Obremskey. "It was not good and it was not going to work, given his attitude. Something was going to occur. It didn't make any difference what it was, whether it's because he wouldn't go to an alumni function or wouldn't do this or he wouldn't do that. He asked me if he should quit, and I'm embarrassed to say that I didn't tell him, 'Yeah, you ought to quit.'

"I wish he would have. I liked Knight. I liked that he was able to remain at Indiana University. He's terribly successful. I wanted the guy to go out with a blaze of glory. But it wasn't going to happen. I had a nose to nose and a toes to toes over it. . . .

"Well, he'd blown me off at that golf outing we had, and I didn't think it was appropriate. And the kind of guy I am, I'd just keep talking to him on the golf course, and we had a very frank and direct discussion about it and I told him how I felt. And he told me how he felt and he asked me if I wanted him to quit and I said, 'No, I hope you don't quit.' Should have said he should quit.

"And he thinks that way now, too. He thinks he should have quit, and I agree with him."

However, school was out, literally, at IU. Brand and Knight were gone much of the summer. The trustees met only briefly, to install new officers.

"The month of July, Brand was at his home in Oregon the entire month," says Simpson. "The first of August, Knight left and went to Russia for three weeks fishing. So the two protagonists, or antagonists, or a combination of the two, were gone from the first of July till about the third week in August. When they both landed back on the IU planet, things began to go south very rapidly."

Simpson says he saw Knight a lot that summer and breaks it into two periods, before Knight went to Russia in August, when he was trying to figure out how to make it work, and after he returned, when his mood turned dark.

"We played golf together that summer, meaning middle of June to August, we played golf together three, four, five times, just the two of us," says Simpson. ". . . There's a buddy of his that had a place, a private lake, owned some land that had a lake on it about 40 miles west of Bloomington. My daughter and I went there and fished with Knight a couple of times. So, I did fish with him a couple of times, played golf with him three, four times. We had dinner once or twice.

"And during the summer, I did not discern any change in his attitude at all. He left, to my recollection, the first of August to go to Russia, fly fishing. He was gone about three weeks. So, up until that point, I didn't discern any change in his attitude at all.

"Playing golf one day, just the two of us, he told me how he'd figured it out. And he said, 'My only concern about zero tolerance'—or he didn't use that phrase—'My only concern about living within these guidelines or sanctions is how I deal with media, because you know I don't particularly like a lot of the media.'

"So, the way Knight had figured out how to handle it . . . is that he had talked to Don Fischer [IU play-by-play announcer, who hosted Knight's call-in show] and Bob Hammel. He had talked to them and they had agreed that after every game in the upcoming season that, instead of Knight going out and talking to the media, that Fischer and Hammel would come into the locker room and they would interview Knight as reporters and then they would just feed that out to all the media. And the media would all use it because you either use that or you get nothing. . . .

"When he got back from Russia in late August, early September, the first time I was with him again, his attitude had changed. It had worsened. It was almost like he had rethought the sanctions and reasons behind them and now he didn't agree with it as he did back in May, June, and July.

"And I don't know what precipitated that, but it was very distinct. And I was with him in September three, four, five times is my recollection and every time I was with him, I said, 'Coach, if you give the trustees a reason to fire you, they're going to fire your ass, okay? They're in a corner now. They've laid down these guidelines and you've agreed to them. They've drawn a line in the sand. Should you cross the line, they don't have any choice but to fire you. So, we need to be sure as we move into fall and talk about how you deal with the media, etc., that we do so in a manner that keeps you well beyond that danger zone.'"

Knight was drawing his own line in the sand. When Brand announced "zero tolerance," he stipulated, and Knight agreed, that he would respect the chain of command. However, when Doninger wrote Knight, asking to meet so they could make a fresh start, Knight refused.

"I think what happened is he had to plead for his job," says Doninger, "and now he sits back and says, 'Wait a minute. Now it's over, I'm Bob Knight. Why did I have to do that?' And then at that point, he turned on everybody. He turned on Pete Obremskey. He turned on Myles. He turned on Christopher Simpson. He turned on everybody. And some of his friends in Bloomington came to me and said, 'What's with him? Well, tell him, Bob, you can't do that.'

"It just didn't end. . . . I mean, this was building all summer long. Everybody knew it was."

That included Knight. He thought the administration was gunning for him, ready to take him down for the slightest mistake. "Every day it just got worse and worse with me," he wrote in his autobiography. "I was sorry. As much as anything I was sorry that I was still there.

"The months between May and September were at best for me an uneasy truce. . . . I told Karen several times the season didn't concern me; I didn't know if I could get to October."

Simpson says he was with Knight on September 6, the day before the incident that brought everything to a head, and Knight was upset.

"He called me that morning, said, 'I got two of my freshmen working out this afternoon, come over and watch,'" Simpson says. "So I went over there and it was Knight and Hammel, who sat up in the stands. And Knight was clearly very agitated. . . .

"And I remember telling him in front of Hammel, saying, 'Coach, what I'm hearing is you won't tell the university when you will sit out the games or how you're going to pay the fines and please remember, if you give these guys on the board a reason to fire you, they will fire your ass. Please remember that.'

"Hammel was standing there. And he [Knight] was just clearly agitated over the whole thing. His demeanor had gone south."

Kent Harvey was a freshman in his first week at IU on September 7, 2000, the wrong day to stumble into the path of the wrong man.

Harvey, his two brothers, and two friends were walking out of the lobby of Assembly Hall after buying football tickets when he saw Knight coming in and said, "Hey, Knight, what's up?" Harvey said Knight grabbed him by the arm and said, "Show me some fucking respect. I'm older than you." Knight said he only took Harvey by the elbow, didn't use profanity, and "lectured the kid on manners and civility."

It wasn't one of the most outrageous things Knight had ever done, but it would no longer take anything momentous to end his IU career. Anything could do it if it got on the news.

Harvey was one of triplets who lived with their mother and stepfather, Mark Shaw, a local lawyer and author who had written eight books, served as a trial analyst for ESPN and USA Today, and appeared on Good Morning, America and Entertainment Tonight. Until July of that year, he had also hosted a local radio sports talk show.

The Harvey boys attended Knight's basketball camp when they

were nine. Shaw had never met Knight, but said he had twice written-him, offering to ghostwrite his autobiography. Knight replied politely both times, according to Shaw, saying if he ever did one, it would be with Hammel. Shaw claimed he had been middle of the road on Knight, but got tough on him the preceding December, questioning Felling's disappearance. Even then, Shaw said he invited Knight to come on his show and that Knight declined but sent Shaw a polite note.

Shaw would be accused of self-promotion, but he didn't go straight to the press the day of the incident. Instead, he called Simpson, who had once been a guest on his show.

"He said, 'Are you ready to test zero tolerance?'" says Simpson. "And I said, 'No, I'm going to work out, have a quiet afternoon, I hope.'

"He said, 'Well, the coach has just'—and I don't remember his words, grabbed my son or assaulted my son, I don't remember which he said. My immediate thought was, 'My God, 36,000 students, the coach has to grab Mark Shaw's son?'"

It wasn't until the next day, Friday, September 8, that Simpson got a call from ESPN's Andy Katz asking about the incident, which Simpson confirmed. After that, it was like dominos falling. The administration already had a crisis-response team ready. Brand, who was in South Bend, had Dorothy Frapwell call Shaw and tell him to report the incident to the campus police, who would determine what had happened.

Knight held his own press conference Friday night, with props and corroborating witnesses. He had a blackboard on which he diagrammed the layout of the Assembly Hall lobby, pointing out which door he used and which door was broken. Assistant Coach Mike Davis, who had been there, said Knight had neither cursed nor raised his voice.

"You might understand," said Knight, "I hope you'll understand, this very thing, the reason why I'm not teaching a class, it's the reason I'm not doing the Tip-Off Luncheon, it's the reason why I'm not going to put myself in a position where this kind of thing can happen." Knight also claimed not to know what zero tolerance meant, insisting, "Nobody's been able to give me a definition."

It was too late for semantics. Brand returned to campus that night, met with his staff at Bryan House and had them call the trustees and ask them to come to campus the next day.

"Basically, we got a preliminary summary of what the police had learned," says Simpson, "and what they had learned was the kid's walking in, he says, 'Hey, Knight, what's up?' Knight grabs him. The kid contends he was assaulted. Knight said, 'I was correcting his rude manners.' So, the only dispute is the severity of the grab.

"In the university environment today, you don't ever put your hand on a student for any reason, period. And particularly when you're under the scrutiny Knight was under, you never touch a student. And, as I told the president that night . . . 'You don't have any choice. You drew a line in the sand back in May saying, you can't assault students, you can't abuse students, and now you have him in September grabbing a student who contends he's been assaulted. If you do not react very aggressively towards this, then it's clear what you said back in May is irrelevant and has no teeth to it at all. This is not a gray area, this is black and white. And I don't think you have any choice but to react very sternly toward Knight.'

"And that's what he did."

The next day, Brand began meeting with the trustees at Bryan House, deliberately talking to them four at a time to get around a state law prohibiting secret sessions if a majority of the members was present.

"I got a call on Friday from someone who said, 'Myles Brand wants to talk with you Saturday morning at, I don't know, ten o'clock, at his residence,'" says Ray Richardson. "And I said, 'I'll be there.' And I walked in, there were three other trustees, out of a total of nine, as you probably know. And we had a discussion. And all three of the other trustees, all four of us, again, we didn't vote, but all four of us were expressing our opinion. All four of us were recommending dismissal."

That night Brand talked to Knight by telephone. Knight said he was leaving the next morning to go fishing in Canada, as he had previously planned. When Brand asked him to stay in town, Knight said no.

"I was there when the conversation occurred and I heard half the conversation, Brand's side," says Simpson. "I couldn't hear what Knight said. And I heard Brand say specifically, 'Bob, I don't think you ought to leave the country on your trip. This is very serious. You need to stay in town.'

"And what Brand told me after the conversation was Knight said, 'No, I'm going,' and that was kind of the way they ended."

Brand would later call it "gross insubordination." The white-haired former professor of philosophy was fuming.

"When Myles Brand called me on Saturday night, he was pissed," says Pete Obremskey. "Woke me up. How'd you like to tell your boss you can't come in and talk to him for some reason because you're going fishing? What would happen to you?

"We were worn out. Trustees were worn out. The university was worn out. Knight, whether he wants to admit it or not, was worn out. The whole process needed to end. You just had to understand it was more than a bunch of specific incidents. It was the culture of it all, the atmosphere and the breakdown in a lot of different areas for a lot of different reasons. And finally, it ain't worth it.

"Kind of like Richard Nixon when he finally decided he had to resign and even the people who were his most ardent supporters decided that, 'Much as I love you, Mr. Nixon, I'm going to vote against you in the Senate, to impeach you, because the United States of America is a lot more important than my love and admiration for you.'

"All this was just building, building, building, building, building. It was kind of like a volcano that ultimately is going to have to erupt and, either the coach was going to bring it to a head by quitting or the university was going to bring it to a head. Because the university's too big and too complex a place to worry about a basketball coach all day, every day."

Early Sunday morning, Knight called Brand from Canada. Brand gave him the option of resigning. In a 10-minute conversation, Knight refused and tried once more to talk Brand into letting him stay. "Coach did say he did not believe he did anything wrong," said Brand. "He did try to change my mind. . . . He talked of his success at IU and that he would try harder in the future."

It was just like old times except for one thing: Brand told Knight he was fired.

"Knight called Brand about 7:00 A.M. on Sunday," says Simpson. "Brand called me about 7:50 A.M. at home and said, 'The coach called me.' And what he told me was, he said, 'Bob, you're being dismissed effective immediately as basketball coach.'

"And he called me to tell me what he had told the coach, and he said, 'How should we announce it publicly?'"

Brand made the announcement at an afternoon press conference in Indianapolis. "It was the ethical and moral thing to do to give him one last chance," said Brand. "The fact is that, having given Coach Knight one last opportunity, he failed to take advantage of it."

For those asserting their confusion with zero tolerance, Brand read the definition, as set down on May 15: "Any verifiable, inappropriate, physical contact in the future with players, members of the university community or others in connection with his employment at IU will be cause for immediate termination."

Brand then proceeded to lay out a bill of indictment that went back almost to May 15. "There have been many instances in the past 17 weeks," Brand said, "in which Coach Knight has behaved and acted in a way that is both defiant and hostile. These actions illustrate a very troubling pattern of inappropriate behavior that makes clear that Coach Knight has no desire, as he personally promised me, to live within the zero tolerance guidelines we set on May 15."

Knight flew back to Bloomington that day and went straight to Assembly Hall to meet with his players for a teary good-bye. Meanwhile, a crowd estimated at between 2,000 and 4,000 students gathered in front of Kilroy's, a local tavern, and marched to Bryan House, Brand's residence, chanting "We want Bobby!" "Fuck Myles Brand!" and "Die, Harvey, die!" Flyers were circulated with Harvey's face above the words, "Wanted: Dead." An effigy of Brand was burned.

Bloomington police responded with riot gear, emergency vehicles, and dogs. Brand had stayed in Indianapolis, but a ring of state policemen in Smokey the Bear hats circled Bryan House. A student was handcuffed to a jeep in Brand's driveway.

The students marched to Showalter Fountain where some plunged in. To chants of "Tits for Knight!" several coeds bared their breasts. To chants of "Fish! Fish! Fish!" students pried several of the 1,500-pound iron dolphin statues off their moorings. They then carried one of the statues to Assembly Hall, a mile away, and left it in the doorway. "An offering of sorts," wrote Jason Vest, reporting for Salon.

Police tried vainly to get the crowd to disperse at Assembly Hall. Finally, Knight came out and talked to the students through a loudspeaker the police gave him, saying he appreciated their support ("There's nobody who's ever coached that's appreciated the student support as I have") and would meet with as many of them as possible to tell his side of the story ("I think you'll be very interested in hearing it"). Then he asked them to go home, and they did.

Damage was estimated at $30,000. Several students were arrested. A policeman was hospitalized after he was injured by pepper spray. "Overall," said IU Police Department spokesman Lieutenant Jerry Minger, "the group was fairly ruly."

Two days later, Knight spoke to a crowd of students estimated at 6,000 in newspaper accounts (and at 15,000 by Knight), in Dunn Meadow, next to the Student Union. Since the school wasn't going to coordinate the event, it was done jointly by the *Daily Student* and the Zeta Beta Tau fraternity. The crowd began gathering at 3:30 in the afternoon, and by five the meadow was covered. Seventeen TV trucks were lined up around it. At 6:30, Knight finally arrived, like a rock star, with his wife, Karen, to chants of "Bob-by! Bob-by!" Dressed in a blue checked sport shirt, wearing no red, Knight looked tired rather than defiant, as did Karen. At one point, she gave him a kiss and put her head on his shoulder.

Knight later wrote that, as he stood there, looking out over the thousands in the meadow, he thought "*This administration and these trustees will never collectively have done anything in the span of time connected with Indiana University that will be rewarded with anything close to the appreciation these kids are showing me.*

"Sure I choked up and so did Karen standing beside me. . . .

"If that was my last view and my last memory of Indiana University, it was the one that will stay in my mind as long as I live."

Simpson would later say that Doninger was the biggest loser. To be sure, Doninger, a lifelong Hoosier who once played for Branch Mc-Cracken and was a Hall of Fame bike rider in Bloomington's famed Little 500, was treated badly, forced into retirement a year later, and booed at games. In the worst moment of all, he was booed at a ceremony honoring IU's All-Century team, where Kent Benson got on the microphone and announced, "To President Brand, to Clarence Doninger, to the board of trustees, we are human and we err. To those who did err and those who did handle the firing of Coach Knight, it's not the firing, it's the way it was handled." Nevertheless, in the end Doninger came out looking like what he always had been, a loyal and respected IU employee.

The biggest loser was Knight, who went into exile with this final sad reminder of how much IU meant to him.

The same night, Knight did a one-on-one interview with ESPN, conducted by Jeremy Schaap. ESPN had been criticized the preceding spring for letting Knight pick his interviewers. When he asked for Phelps once more, the network came back with a choice of Dan Patrick, Bob Ley, or Schaap.

Knight had a warm relationship with Jeremy's father, Dick, and chose Jeremy. Nevertheless, ESPN had put Jeremy on the list because he wouldn't be intimidated.

Asked why he had so much as touched Harvey, Knight said he would do it again "to teach him about manners." However, when Schaap noted that Harvey had been advised by police to leave town, Knight tried to let him off the hook. "This was a kid like I was," said Knight, "caught in some circumstances. . . . I would certainly hope that anything that would be as untoward as what you've just mentioned would cease very quickly."

The interview was most memorable for the way it ended, with Knight complaining Schaap was cutting him off. Knight then took advantage of the situation to teach Schaap about manners, too. Before the show, Knight had met at his home with Phelps, Isiah Thomas, and Bob Hammel, putting together a list of talking points. One was that Pat Knight was, as Knight told Schaap, "the real victim in this whole thing." Knight was in the process of explaining why when Schaap cut in, trying to get the subject back to him.

SCHAAP: *He—*

KNIGHT: *Let me finish, Jeremy.*

SCHAAP: *But Coach—*

KNIGHT: *He's the victim in this.*

SCHAAP: *Yeah, but—*

KNIGHT: *Pat is the victim in this.*

SCHAAP: *He is the victim but if you would have abided by the rules, would he have been the victim? Would he still have his job?*

KNIGHT: *I don't think I had any chance to abide by the rules.*

SCHAAP: *Why not?*

KNIGHT: *Let's get back to Pat, okay? Now, with Pat and our situation where it was, now we have to find another place. But, again, before you interrupted me, what I—and you have a real faculty for doing that.*

SCHAAP: *Thank you.*

KNIGHT: *No, I don't think it's anything to be real proud of yourself.*

SCHAAP: *I'm sorry.*

KNIGHT: *I talked about Pat—*

SCHAAP: *Bob, we came here to do an interview. I'm asking you questions.*

KNIGHT: *Well, let me finish the answer. Is that okay, Jeremy, is that fair enough? Have I interrupted your questions yet?*

SCHAAP: *Yes.*

KNIGHT: *No, I haven't. You've interrupted my answers with your questions and then I've tried to get back so let me finish.*

SCHAAP: *Please continue.*

KNIGHT: *You've got a long way to go to be as good as your dad. You better keep that in mind.*

SCHAAP: *I'll keep that in mind. What's next? What do you do this year?*

KNIGHT: *Oh, I don't know. I may go fishing tomorrow. I may work on my of-*

fense tomorrow. I may go look at some tapes tomorrow. There's never a
day goes by that I don't work in basketball. And I'll continue to do that.

Knight refused to shake Schaap's hand afterward. It was an object
lesson in why zero tolerance hadn't worked.

"Bob Knight had to know how to comply with zero tolerance," says
then-trustee Ray Richardson, "and that is he had to know that all he
had to do was stop being a jerk. Try being a decent guy. Try showing respect to others and just be a decent guy."

Knight told his assistants that if they left and couldn't find jobs, he would
pay their salaries out of his own pocket, a generous offer. What he really
meant was, he wanted them to leave too. However, when Mike Davis
was offered the head coaching job, he accepted, and John Treloar, the
other assistant, chose to stay on his staff. That ended the Knight–Davis
relationship. They were never in contact after that.

The players, who were threatening to leave en masse, were molli-
fied by the selection of Davis. Dane Fife said Knight advised him to
transfer and announced that he would, as did touted freshman A. J.
Moye. However, Fife and Moye both changed their minds, and in
Davis's second season they went to the NCAA Finals. It was the first
time the Hoosiers had been beyond the second round in eight years.

Brand, hailed as the man who finally stood up to Knight, was named
president of the NCAA in the fall of 2002. Nevertheless, there was a
question of just how courageous he had been.

"Myles, true to where he'd been all along, stayed with him [Knight],
which is the irony of all this," says Doninger. "The NCAA, that committee, they think they're getting a guy that stood up to him. That's the
irony of this."

"Look what he went through for the year afterward," says Stephen
Backer, defending Brand. "It was pretty gruesome. I mean, he was booed
at games, he was threatened. It was not a happy situation. It did take a
lot of courage to do it and to stand up finally. It should have been done
20 years ago but since it wasn't, somebody had to do it. And it did take a

lot of courage. You can be second-guessed, you can be questioned. I mean, it'll always be controversial and there'll always be people who love Bob Knight."

Brand had spent five years staying out of Knight's way. Besides the Reed allegations in 1997, Brand knew about the incidents with Jeanette Hartgraves in 1999 and Doninger in 2000. However, Brand didn't even investigate officially until Abbott's first CNN/SI report forced his hand.

Nor was Brand's investigation getting anywhere before the practice tape aired in Abbott's second piece. Without that tape, Knight might have gone on to coach many more years at IU.

Even after seeing the tape and announcing zero tolerance, Brand would all but concede that Knight had been violating it almost from the moment he proclaimed it.

Nevertheless, Brand did fire Knight. It was easy for outsiders to look down at Brand and the trustees, but as Pete Obremskey said, "None of them know Knight. None of them have been around Knight."

To Knight, it wasn't remarkable that Brand and the trustees supported him for so long. What shocked him was that in the end, as he saw it, they sold him out.

Knight doesn't "spin," he introduces an entire alternate reality. He acknowledged reviewing the Reed tape in a 2002 deposition he gave when Felling sued him, but insisted it proved *his* point.

Q: *You've seen the Neil Reed tape?*
A: *I've seen it.*
Q: *Describe for me what happened that day.*
A: *The Neil Reed—I obviously touched Neil Reed on the chest. It was said that I choked him with both hands, that an assistant coach had to pull me off. The tape immediately shows that neither of those two things happened. In fact, Felling is the coach in the tape, and Felling just glances and walks right on, if you've seen the tape. There certainly was no choking at all. I've put my hand on a lot of kids to either pat them on the back, stop a kid, put a kid in position. . . .*

Q: *The tape clearly shows that when you touch Reed, his head jerks back suddenly. . . .*

A: *Okay, you don't know whether he jerks his head back because he sees my hand coming at him, or because of the force of my hand attaching to his chest . . .*

Knight would always claim he hadn't choked Reed, which would require two hands. However, Reed had always said that Knight had used one hand. Knight's defense was nothing more than a disagreement about what constituted "choking."

There were never any misunderstandings in Knight's version of events. He insisted on his own interpretation, condemning everyone who was involved in his dismissal or who didn't back him to the end. To Knight, it was all betrayal.

In his book, Knight wrote that Brand had used Knight for his own purposes, to enhance his own image as academic reformer.

Knight called Doninger "the most incompetent and least trustworthy man I've ever met in sports, a very small man in all respects, other than size."

Knight wrote that Doninger's associate director, Mary Ann Rohleder, was "the most vindictive person I've seen in an athletic department in 35 years," and that she had told Steve Downing that she would "do everything she could do to get me fired, a year before it happened."

Felling, who was with Knight for 12 years, making him his longest-serving assistant, was someone "I never should have hired and should have fired years before."

Knight wrote about a meeting with trustees Walda and Eichorn, two more old friends, after which his wife, Karen, called them the "two most disgusting people I've ever had to sit through."

Knight wrote that his friend and lawyer, Obremskey, customarily came to games and practices with bags of things for him to sign, but recused himself "in the critical hours when he could have countered spurious charges with his own personal knowledge and experience."

Simpson "never in any way fooled me. The term I used for him almost from the start was 'double agent.'"

They were the people Knight had spent 29 years with in Indiana. He had fished with them, played golf with them, eaten with them. They considered themselves his friends, until he decided otherwise.

"Come to my house," says Simpson. "I'll be glad to show you the pictures of him teaching my 12-year-old daughter to fly fish, or the three of us fishing out on the lake together, just the three of us. . . . I'm sorry if that's the way he feels because I remember the guy when he taught my daughter to fly fish or he and I used to play golf together and talk about great figures in history. There's a great side to Knight that I will always respect and admire."

Years before, Knight's friend Dave Kindred, then at the Louisville *Courier-Journal*, had noted the George Patton quote on Knight's office wall, warning how "loyal friends" would do "their hypocritical God-damndest to trip you, blacken you and break your spirit."

Kindred had remarked, "Pretty dark."

And Knight had replied, "And true."

"I thought then and I think now," Kindred wrote in May 2000, after Brand's warning but before Knight's fall, "that a life believing that of your friends would be a life spent in conflicts, real and imagined."

For 29 years at Indiana the conflicts were real enough. Knight went out with everything he had always said he wanted, true to himself, and acknowledging no authority above him. The shame was that he aimed so low.

THIRTEEN

THE LION IN LUBBOCK
TEXAS TECH, 2001–

Peace is going to be a hell of a letdown.

—General George S. Patton

Six weeks after he was fired, for the first time since 1962 and the presidency of John F. Kennedy, the college basketball season started without Bob Knight.

From the moment Myles Brand fired him in the fall of 2000, Knight began planning to come back, informing his IU players he would coach again as he said good-bye to them. Nevertheless, the dismaying truth was he was 60 years old, he had been at Indiana for most of his adult life, and wasn't sure he could start over now. Worst of all, he wasn't even sure anyone wanted him to.

Of course, all his friends said he would get offers, and later he would say he had always known he would. At the time, however, he was worried. As he wrote in *Knight: My Story*, whenever someone assured him he would be in demand, he thought, "They don't *know* that. They can't."

The 2000–2001 season was about to begin and no jobs would open up until it was over, a depressing fact of life Knight regarded as his business and no one else's. In his autobiography, which is notable for its stoicism, he concedes it was a difficult time, then devotes the next 25 pages to accounts of fishing with President George H. W. Bush, shooting birds in Spain with King Juan Carlos, taking Karen to see Oklahoma and Florida State in the Orange Bowl for the national title, various golf excursions, and a trip to Florida to visit Tony LaRussa at the Cardinals' training camp.

However, under the wrong circumstances Knight could vent anguish like a geyser. On October 14, when the college teams began practicing, he drove up to Akron University where his son Pat was an assistant coach, with Lawrence Grobel, who was interviewing him for *Playboy*. The *Playboy* interview had a no-holds-barred format, but Knight had done one before in 1984. He and Grobel were in their second session as Knight drove to Dayton to pick up his friend Don Donoher en route. Knight had just answered questions about Clarence Doninger, zero tolerance, and Kent Harvey, when Grobel noted that Mark Shaw had said Knight shouldn't have been fired.

"Jesus Christ!" Knight exploded, according to Grobel, banging the steering wheel with his fist. "Jesus Christ! This is bullshit! I'm not here for a fucking inquisition! And if that's what this is, then get the fuck out and hitchhike home! The fucking stepfather was a fucking goddamn fucking asshole from the word goddamn go! He fucking lied and he lied and he lied! Jesus Christ! I mean, this is my fucking life we're talking about. My fucking heart was ripped out by this goddamn bullshit!"

Grobel wrote that they then drove in silence for two minutes but Knight calmed down and the interview resumed. They picked up Donoher, who asked what kind of story they were working on.

"I'm not really sure," says Knight. "There is a question whether he will live long enough for this article to see the fucking light of day. You know that movie, *A Bridge Too Far*? That's what happened to Larry this morning but it was *A Question Too Far*. I think to a small degree I may have overreacted."

They continued to Akron, watched the practice, and took Pat to dinner before heading back. Donoher took over for the drive back to Dayton. Knight rode in front with one of Grobel's tape recorders and Grobel sat in back with his other one. Knight explained why he fired the starter's pistol at Russ Brown and described the incident with the LSU fan, insisting other coaches did similar things that the press ignored.

"So," said Grobel, "the question comes back, why you?"

KNIGHT: *You know, forget this whole thing. Do whatever the fuck you want to do with this. I don't think you understand that I don't need to go through*

this kind of bullshit. [Throws tape recorder into the back seat.] I'm not
trying to defend myself. I don't give a fuck what you write. You come here
and bring up all the bullshit that's happened to me over the years and why?
This whole thing has been ridiculous. You think I've enjoyed this bullshit?
Going through this crap? Like I have to defend myself. [Slight pause.]
Give me your two tape recorders.

PLAYBOY: *No, Coach, I'm not going to do that.*

KNIGHT: *Give me the tape recorders.*

PLAYBOY: *I can't.*

KNIGHT: *Stop the car, Don. [He turns around, his knees on the seat, his head*
now inches from mine, as he grabs my wrists, trying to get my bag with
the tape recorders in it. "Pull over!" he orders Donoher, who keeps driving.
"I want him out of here. And I want those goddamn tapes!" "You don't
want to do this," I say. "Calm down, Bob," Donoher says, still concen-
trating on the road. "Sit down."

According to Grobel, Knight calmed down. When they dropped
Donoher in Dayton, Grobel volunteered to take a cab back to Bloomington but Knight told him, "Get in the car, I'll take you." Grobel says
he extended his hand and Knight shook it.

"You don't understand," [Knight told Grobel]. "You can't under-
stand. How would you like to have your whole world taken from
you for no good reason? Today was the first time in 38 years where
I attended a practice without having a team. For 29 years, I did
things for Indiana. I raised $5 million for a library, I established two
professorial chairs and when I left, there was no thanks. Not a
word. I'm selling my house, moving to Phoenix. I don't know if I'll
ever get another coaching job. I never made more than $230,000 at
Indiana and when they hire some new coach, it will cost them be-
tween $600,000 and a million."

He begins laying out his woes. How someone at the Mexican
restaurant where we had eaten the night before had goaded him and
abused him and took it to court and it took nine days before the
judge threw out the case. How the university lied and spun stories

about him. He never threw a vase at the athletic director's secre-
tary; she wasn't even in the room when that happened. And he
didn't call her a fucking bitch but he said he didn't like her acting like
a bitch. And about Neil Reed: Did I know that Knight asked his
players whether they wanted Reed on the team and they voted him
off, eight to zero, with one abstention? And Reed went to another
program and the coach there said he didn't belong. Did I know any
of that? How come we never hear of these things, only him?

"I don't think anyone you've ever interviewed has been more
forthright and straightforward as I have with the questions you've
asked," he says.

"That's why I didn't want to let you destroy my tapes," I say.

"You can put the machines back on. I won't do that."

The interview resumed again and ended amicably, with Knight saying he hoped to work for "people I really like and respect, who feel the
same way about me. I want better final memories than I have right now."

Grobel called it "the ride of my life." Even for Knight, it was up
there.

The Knights moved to Phoenix that winter but didn't buy a home. Bob
didn't know what lay ahead and seemed cut loose, not only from Indiana but the principles he had lived by. After a lifetime of railing about
betting, he now became a tout for an online betting site, Sandbox.com,
predicting outcomes of NCAA Tournament games.

In March, just before the 2001 tournament started, he came home
and found a message from an old friend, Texas Tech athletic director
Gerald Myers, a former coach who had served on his Pan-Am staff in
1979. Myers needed a coach to replace outgoing James Dickey and was
thrilled at the thought of having a chance to hire such a giant.

On March 5, Myers met Knight in Florida, bringing Texas Tech
President David Schmidly with him. Schmidly, an avid fisherman, and
Knight hit it right off. Ten days later, Knight and Karen arrived in Lub-
bock for a three-day visit, amid fanfare worthy of a movie star.

The Knights were as thrilled with Lubbock as Lubbock was with them. Knight later said he had been sitting down with officials from another school when Karen, who was behind them, began shaking her head no. Knight said his wife, the native Oklahoman, told him, "No place in America will understand you better than West Texas."

It was as if it were meant to be. The arena was on Indiana Avenue. The school colors were scarlet and black, so Knight could still wear his red sweaters. Knight, who had been a Red Rider at Orrville High, would now be a Red Raider. An editorial cartoon in the *Avalanche-Journal* showed the heavens parting and angels ushering him into the spotlight over the caption, "And Bob came unto the Plains to Saveth Men's Round-ball. And it was Good. Amen."

Knight, still irresistible after all these years, assured Schmidly that his time away had given him a new perspective. Schmidly didn't ask for any behavior clauses in Knight's contract and airily dismissed press concerns, insisting he knew of nothing Knight had done at Indiana that would have gotten him fired at Texas Tech. (Schmidly said grabbing Neil Reed's throat was only a "single incident.") Schmidly claimed to have interviewed 100 people who knew Knight but was only vaguely familiar with the Reed tape and saw no need to watch it. When 60 members of the faculty signed a petitition protesting the hiring, Schmidly placated them in a meeting, promising he would be personally responsible for Knight's behavior.

On March 23, 2001, Myers announced Knight's hiring at a rally in United Spirit Arena, attended by a raucous crowd of 7,500. Knight delighted them, making the Texas Tech "Guns up" salute with both hands. When Myers presented him with a red sweater vest, Knight said, "This is without a doubt the most comfortable red sweater I've had in six years."

A press conference followed, but with reporters in from around the nation, Knight invited the crowd to stay, encouraging his new fans to let the press know what they thought of its questions. When a reporter tried to ask a follow-up question, Knight declined. When the reporter persisted, Knight asked the crowd, "How many of you want to hear a follow-up from this guy?" The crowd booed.

Be it ever so humble, or unfamiliar, there was no place like home.

*   *   *

Indiana was the state in which Dr. James Naismith said basketball grew up. Texas was more like the state in which football grew up. Odessa, immortalized in *Friday Night Lights* as the home of the Permian High School Panthers, where parents put little footballs in babies' cribs, was only 150 miles to the south.

Lubbock was far out on the West Texas plains, closer to Albuquerque, New Mexico, than Dallas. It gave the world '50s rocker Buddy Holly, but it also produced country singer Mac Davis, who wrote of growing up thinking, "happiness was Lubbock in my rearview mirror."

"It's kind of, well, not Mayberry, but the people are kind of like that," said Pat, who came with his father as assistant and associate head coach. "No one bothers you. They'll come up and talk to you about the game but they don't want to know why you didn't go into the post or why this and why that. . . . We're kind of out in the middle of nowhere. We only have one newspaper. You don't hear much about Dad. He kind of likes that."

Nevertheless, it wasn't the windblown truckstop the press made it out to be as it dramatized Knight's fall from grace. With a population of 200,000, it was more than three times the size of Bloomington's 65,000. Nor was Knight bringing the cowpokes a new game they had never heard of. Texas Tech had a new 15,000-seat arena and had been in the NCAA's Sweet 16 more recently than Knight had, in 1996. The Raiders went 30–2 that season and forward Darvin Ham won them more fame by shattering a backboard in their tourney win over North Carolina. Ham and teammate Tony Battle went to the NBA.

Unfortunately, with big-time athletes came trouble. An NCAA investigation subsequently unearthed an array of violations, including "free bail bonding and legal services" provided to student-athletes. Texas Tech forfeited its 1996 tournament wins, had its scholarships limited, and endured four losing seasons in a row, spiraling down to the 9–19 record just posted by Dickey. Attendance in two-year-old United Spirit Arena was running below that of the Lady Raiders, who were still the local stars after winning the 1993 NCAA title with Sheryl

Swoopes. In celebration, the Lubbock *Avalanche-Journal* put out its first special edition since Pearl Harbor. As a local bumper sticker put it, TEXAS TECH—WHERE MEN ARE MEN AND WOMEN ARE CHAMPIONS.

Under normal circumstances, Texas Tech would have had a better chance of hiring Pat Knight than Bob. New Mexico, which had pursued Bob in 1988, was a perennial power in a basketball hotbed and had offered him a king's ransom. Texas Tech was the runt of the Big 12 and Myers could only offer a $250,000 salary, below the conference average, although Knight was promised another $500,000 from various sources.

Even if times had changed and lots of Texas kids played basketball, Knight wouldn't have his pick of them, as he had at Indiana. The University of Texas dominated the state in all things and the Longhorns, along with Kansas, Oklahoma, and Oklahoma State, dominated Big 12 basketball.

In his darkest days at IU, Knight could still attract top prospects from around the nation when he felt like trying. At Texas Tech, he was limited, no matter how hard he tried. Pat said that when they called out-of-state recruits, they often had to tell them where they were located and what conference they were in.

Nothing showed how far down the food chain Knight had dropped than the first blue-chip prospect he pursued, 6-8, 250-pound Sean May of Bloomington North, the son of Scott, who remained one of Knight's archloyalists. Scott got his son to take a look at Texas Tech, but it was only a courtesy visit late in the process.

Sean had been considered a lock for IU with his former high-school teammate Jared Jeffries there. Sean also played in high school alongside Mike Davis, Jr., the son of the Hoosier coach, and was over at their house all the time. However, after leaving Lubbock, Sean made the surprise announcement that he'd go to North Carolina, prompting speculation back home in Indiana as to just what Knight had told him.

"Scott said he took Sean down to Lubbock because he owed Coach Knight a chance," says the Louisville *Courier-Journal*'s Rick Bozich. "Scott said, 'Hey, I'll get him down here. You've got to convince him to stay here or come here. That's on you, Coach. I'll get him here and you go from there. I'm going to give everybody the same opportunity.'

"But, in the end, supposedly it was a compromise choice, in that he wasn't going to go to Texas Tech because that would be probably not the best thing for his basketball career. And he wasn't going to stay at Indiana because I'm sure that would piss the Knight loyalists off. So, he went to Carolina and supposedly Phil Ford was some kind of a factor because Phil Ford and Scott May were friends from the '76 Olympic team. And Phil Ford assured him that if he came to Carolina that he would look after his son."

Scott May said it had nothing to do with who was mad at whom. "This isn't about the rift between Coach and Myles Brand or the rift between Coach and the university," said Scott. "This is about my kid."

At a certain point, when the entire attention of the media is turned upon him, a celebrity becomes a cartoon, and Knight had passed that point. In his first season at Texas Tech, ESPN presented its TV movie of *A Season on the Brink*, although after weeks of promotion, it arrived with the impact of a feather. In the lead role, Brian Dennehy was more like a panda in a red sweater than a grizzly bear like Knight. "All credit to Brian Dennehy, you can't act like Bobby Knight," says former Hoosier Mark Haymore. "Bobby Knight can't act like Bobby Knight. You just have to be around him when something happens, man."

Knight wasn't a cartoon. He was flesh and blood, he felt pain, and he had regrets, even if he hid it.

"I'll tell you what's amazing," Pat said. "He always talks to me about not making the same mistakes he did. 'Be careful, watch your language. Don't do what I did early on. You have a good rapport with guys, you enjoy talking, keep that up. Don't fall into the same traps.'"

If nothing else, a year off had shown Knight how much he loved coaching. Everyone, from Karen to the press people who passed through Lubbock that season, said it had changed him. Indeed, Knight appeared calmer during games. He even opened his practices to the public and the press in his first season.

He began getting over some of his old grudges. Pete Newell said John Wooden wrote Knight a nice letter and Knight responded with one of his own. Knight consented to give John Feinstein, whom he once called "a pimp and a whore," an interview for his book on Red Auerbach.

The most painful feud of all, with Mike Krzyzewski, ended. It had started when Knight snubbed him at the 1992 Final Four but Krzyzewski broke the ice in 2001, asking Knight to present him at his Hall of Fame induction. Nevertheless, their days as surrogate father and son were over for good. "My relationship has been basically that with most players, it's a player–coach relationship," Knight told ESPN Classic for a 2005 profile on Krzyzewski. "It's not pal to pal. It's not buddy to buddy. I think maybe we went apart. It'll never be as close as we were in the beginning."

As usual, it was Knight, who insisted he hadn't changed when everyone was saying he had. "Somebody made the comment the other day, 'It sounds like Bob's changed,'" Knight said. "And Gerald [Myers] said, 'Bob hasn't changed. The environment, the people around him have changed. He's the same guy I knew 30 years ago. I don't want him to change.'"

Knight's first meeting with his new players after taking the job that spring was at seven on a Saturday morning, where he laid out the new dress and hair codes. Freshman Andre Emmett, who had braids with beads in them, said his introduction to Knight was "short, straight and matter of fact. I drove home to Dallas, went to a barbershop and cut it all off."

Eight days after Knight took the job, a three-paragraph press release announced that three returning players, including starting point guard Jamal Brown, had been kicked off the team. According to one of the players, they had been late several times but no more details were forthcoming. "We're not going to say anything beyond what's been said," said Myers. "They're not going to be on the team next year."

That left only four scholarship players from the previous season's 9–19 team, who would be joined by one scholarship freshman, two junior college players, two freshman walk-ons, and two seniors who were given scholarships. That fall, when practice began with Midnight Madness, Knight said only, "We have a chance to be competitive."

Knight was never better than when he had something to prove and he had never had more to prove in his life. As he said before his Texas Tech debut, a victory at home over William & Mary, "I feel like the Earps, going to Tombstone."

Tombstone shaped right up. The Red Raiders won 16 of their first 20 games, beating conference powers Oklahoma and Oklahoma State. Attendance jumped to 13,500 a game. Students billing themselves "the General's troops" wore World War II helmets. Fund-raising zoomed as Knight appeared in rallies throughout Texas—and some in Indiana.

The Raiders finished the regular season 21–7, third in the Big 12. However, they fell in the first round of the NCAA Tournament to Southern Illinois, coached by former Gene Keady assistant Bruce Weber, who said his old boss told him, "Don't let that SOB beat you."

If anyone doubted him—and many had in the pile-on that followed his firing—Knight could still coach. A *Time* magazine essay titled "How College Basketball Left Bobby Knight Behind," had gone so far as to assert: "Truth is, Knight was never a great coach. He was a good coach of often underrated players."

The truth was, in the proper frame of mind, Knight was capable of things that awed his peers. "I can't say this enough, " said retired Texas–El Paso Coach Don Haskins of that first season in Texas Tech. "His team didn't overachieve. It over, *over*achieved."

Ironically, that was the spring IU came back, too, as the unheralded Mike Davis led the unheralded Hoosiers to the NCAA finals. After a 6–5 start, with Davis looking overmatched in his second season, the Hoosiers warmed up in conference play, and caught fire as a No. 5 seed in the tournament, stunning Krzyzewski's No. 1–seeded Blue Devils in the South regional, then beating Kent State to advance to the Final Four in Atlanta.

It was the season Indiana needed to move beyond Knight. For Knight, however, there was no moving beyond Indiana. His bitterness was like a black hole in space, sucking everyone around him into it.

Knight had had no contact with Davis since the night he offered to pay Davis' $95,000 salary out of his own pocket if he left with him. Instead, Davis had taken Knight's job when it was offered to him and the relationship deteriorated from there. When Davis was deposed for the Ron Felling suit in 2002, he was asked if Knight was a bully and replied, "Yes." Asked if Knight's coaching style was always appropriate, Davis answered, "No . . . I mean, if we were sitting here now and you said something he didn't like, he would go off and scream and yell and curse at you."

In Knight's autobiography, which came out during the tournament, he wrote that he'd been fired just as he was about to lead the Hoosiers back to greatness, adding he had thought they even had a chance to win the NCAA title. This was audacious and not just because Knight had won only two tournament games in his last six seasons at Indiana. It wasn't a gifted team aside from the 6-11 Jeffries, who said he came to IU as much for Davis as for Knight.

The Hoosiers were such underdogs, it became a joke. At the Final Four, Dane Fife observed that teammate Kyle Hornsby had tripped 632 times in his career, not in games but just walking around. "We're probably the last team that you'd look at, athletically," said Hornsby.

In the Final Four, the Hoosiers faced highly favored Oklahoma. Before the game, Pat Knight called Davis "a backstabber." Pat and Steve Downing, who was now at Texas Tech, each said they would root for Oklahoma.

It turned into a firestorm in Indiana. Todd Leary, Pat's former teammate and close friend (Pat was in his wedding), and now the color commentator on IU broadcasts, told the *Indianapolis Star*'s Terry Hutchens, "If Bob Knight would just send a telegram to Indiana University and congratulate all those kids for what they've accomplished, he would be loved by 99 percent of the people in the state of Indiana. But we all know that will never happen. I don't know why I keep thinking Coach Knight will take the high road because he never does. . . .

"If Coach Knight was still coaching his style at IU, these guys would be sitting home this week watching basketball, just like the guys at Texas Tech are doing. Tom Coverdale would never have played this role under Coach Knight and Jared Jeffries wouldn't still be here. And everything else under the sun would be different."

Pat Knight had been in Pat Graham's wedding, too, but Graham was also quoted in the story, although he wasn't as outspoken as Leary. Nevertheless, two days before the Oklahoma game, Graham got a call from Pat, who accused him and Leary of not being loyal.

"I thought, 'Unloyal?'" says Graham. "I mean, I can remember sitting in that locker room in Miami, crying my balls off. . . . I can remember how much I cared for the man and I remember respecting him. I was crying because I'd just cost him a game, I felt. And then, all of a sudden his son's telling me I'm not loyal and I think, 'God, come on.' Some of us guys would have done anything to play up there and play for him again, and to have everything kind of work its way around to where now there's a lot of resentment, now there's a lot of people that hate people . . . It's just, I mean, it's like a soap opera. . . .

"His [Patrick's] comment was, 'I can't believe two former players and two former friends would do this to me.'

"And I said back to him, I said, 'If this is the way it's going to end, if this is the way our friendship is going to end, I hope you can sleep at fucking night.'

"And he went, 'I fucking won't have a problem.' And he went, click. That's the way it ended. I love Pat Knight to death and he hasn't spoken to me and he says he'll never speak to me again and all this bullshit. . . . I'm an Indiana basketball fan and I still love the man [Bob Knight] but, hey, this is who I'm rooting for. I'm not ever going to root for Texas Tech. I didn't get anything from Texas Tech. And I'm not a part of that cult that just thinks this man walks on water."

That was that. When Pat Knight was married in Indianapolis shortly thereafter, neither Leary nor Graham was invited. As Graham notes, Leary lived about 15 minutes from the church.

The entire state was torn. When *Knight: My Story* came out that spring, Knight did a signing at a Barnes & Noble in Bloomington, where an estimated 1,000 people stood in line. In Indianapolis, Knight's first wife, Nancy, ran a store selling Texas Tech gear. Graham and Leary say two of Knight's former Hoosier players, whom they won't name, sent them form letters, soliciting donations to Texas Tech.

Knight had never been litigious or motivated by money at IU, giving his six-figure Adidas stipend to the university annually, calling it "pimp money." After being fired, however, he spent years pursuing redress against IU in the Indiana courts. Despite a severance package that paid him $425,000 annually for 10 years, he contended he was owed more for the income he lost. When a Monroe County judge ruled in favor of IU, Knight appealed before finally dropping it. Then he filed another suit against the university, seeking to have IU pay his legal fees.

More suits involving Knight rattled around the Indiana court system. A group of 46 loyalists sued IU, contending Brand had deliberately skirted the law against closed meetings when five or more trustees were present by meeting with them in groups of four, before firing Knight. A Clark Superior Court judge ruled in favor of the university. Felling's $1 million suit against Knight was settled, with Felling getting a token $25,000, which still must have felt like too much to Knight.

If Knight's old life was gone, his new one had its own challenges. Texas Tech went to a new level, winning 20 games in each of his first three seasons. That was wonderful for the Red Raiders but only standard for Knight, who was used to competing for conference titles as a warmup before competing for national titles.

In Knight's second season, the Red Raiders went 22–13 but didn't get an NCAA bid, settling for a third-place finish in the NIT. It was so disappointing, he announced he was giving back his $250,000 salary.

It had some of the old turbulence, too. Before the February 17 game at Texas, one of the most important of the season for Red Raider fans, Knight benched Andre Emmett, the team's star, and reserve Nick Valdez for oversleeping and missing a walk-through. It was reminiscent of Indiana's 1985 game at Illinois, where Knight benched four starters against the favored Illini. The Red Raiders were 4–7 in conference play and the Longhorns were No. 3 in the nation. Texas Tech lost, 77–65, but Knight praised his players. "We didn't have somebody we had to make up for on defense every time down the floor," he said. "From my standpoint, it was a team I enjoyed watching."

Knight said his players had voted unanimously to bench Emmett and Valdez. Asked to elaborate, Knight exploded. "I said all that's going to be said about it," he stormed. "It's none of your fucking business beyond what I've said, period. Let's not worry about someone that didn't deserve to play. I've said all I'm going to say, period."

In another unbecoming scene reminiscent of IU, two of Knight's players chimed in, attacking Emmett and Valdez. "They didn't deserve to play after what they did against Oklahoma," said senior Will Chavis. "We didn't want them to play and we voted them not to play."

This time, there were complications. Knight circulated a two-page document outlining Valdez' confidential disciplinary history in a meeting with 20 local business leaders. Knight said they were "people who needed to know." Some of the information had nothing to do with Valdez' basketball career and, as the *Avalanche-Journal* reported, constituted a possible violation of a Federal privacy law, although no charges were ever filed.

Valdez quit but Emmett accepted his punishment—500 sprints the length of the court and back—and returned to the team. When Emmett complained in the course of completing his work-parole program, Knight doubled his sentence, and then tripled it.

"I felt like I was running for nothing," says Emmett. "It was supposed to be 500. So I ran the five and it was 500 more. So that made a thousand. So he said, 'Five hundred more.' I was like, 'Hold on.'

"Took me three and a half days and on the fourth or the fifth day we had a game so I was in the ice tub for a couple days. . . . I would start maybe 5 o'clock in the morning until my 8 o'clock class. Came back in the afternoon for practice, ran until about 9 o'clock at night, went home, started out over again. He had two guys there counting, making sure I got every last one of 'em.

"After my first 500, I felt like I was on my way out. I was trying to go home but my family and my supporting cast, they told me, 'Stick in there, don't let nothing stop you from doing what you do.'

"After that I kept my mouth closed and I ran the next thousand without saying a word."

In the 2003–4 season, Knight's third at Texas Tech, the Raiders went 23–11 and advanced to the second round of the NCAA Tournament before losing a close game to No. 1–ranked St. Joseph's, 70–65. Unfortunately, like several of Knight's seasons at IU, this one would not be remembered for anything that happened on the court.

In December, Texas Tech was to play Iowa in Knight's first meeting with Steve Alford since 2000. It was nationally televised and good exposure but meant an obligatory review of their rift. Knight wasn't having any of it. A few days before the game, he blew up in the midst of an interview with the *Dallas Morning News'* Brian Davis, who says Knight grabbed his tape recorder out of his hands and demanded he erase Knight's remarks. The day of the game, Knight, sitting with Alford for a joint interview, went off on ESPN's Fran Fraschilla, the former St. John's and New Mexico coach, who merely asked if they wanted to put the issue to rest.

"Let me answer that," said Knight. "You know, this is an absolute crock of bullshit. You know, you fucking people in the news media, all of you fuckers, dwell on some negative piece of bullshit like that. And I don't know how Steve feels about it but it fucking pisses me off and you don't have to bleep one single fucking word of this. . . . So all of you media people can go fuck yourselves when it comes to something like that. Now, I don't know if Steve has anything to add to that or not."

Predictably, Steve did not. ESPN aired the interview, although with bleeps. The Red Raiders, who were in the midst of a 16–2 start, won the game, 65–59.

Close losses to Texas and Oklahoma State dropped them to 16–4 but they were still ranked 19th in the nation on February 2, when Knight and Gerald Myers went to lunch at a fashionable downtown grocery store called Market Street. Knight was at the salad bar when Texas Tech Chancellor David Smith came up to him. After that, in a familiar pattern, the stories diverged wildly.

Knight said Smith congratulated him on the way he handled himself in the Texas game when he ordered students to stop their rude chants at the Longhorns. Knight said he answered, "David, as long as I've been here for the most part . . . I think I've done pretty well."

"I go around to fix my salad," said Knight. "He came at me pretty hard, saying 'You've got issues, what are they?' Right then is where I think I was at fault. I should have just shook my head, walked away, and did a lot of other things and I didn't. I went on to tell him what one of those issues was and it went back and forth a little bit. But the one thing there was, I absolutely did not instigate anything."

Smith, a physician of moderate size and frame, said he had been talking to Myers, saying how much he appreciated Knight's approach, when Myers suggested he tell Knight. In a report for university use, Smith wrote, "As I approached Mr. Knight, I placed my hand on his shoulder, kidded him about eating healthy and stated that, 'Most of us only hear the negatives, it is important that sometimes someone re- members to express the positives.' I expressed the same sentiment that I did with Gerald Myers that despite some tough losses, I especially wanted to commend him on how he had handled the last few weeks and in particular the student section at the University of Texas game.'

"His demeanor and habitus changed drastically. With a red face, his response was curt and angry as he responded, 'I always handle things well and have always handled things well. . . .' He walked about two or three steps to my left with a very angry look, tried to place more salad in his takeout tray, obviously upset and shaking when I asked, 'What seems to be the problem? I only wanted to commend you and provide some positive feedback. . . .'

"He became even more agitated, stating that I was always misinter- preting him just like his actions in the locker room last year when he abruptly walked away from me in front of Gerald Myers. The response was clearly disconnected from the original conversation and at first con- fused me. I did finally understand that he was now responding to an episode last year that occurred in the Tech locker room. Knight trying to rationalize his response stated that last year he was only straightening his collar and that I over reacted to his actions at the time and misrep- resented them. (This locker-room episode occurred prior to the Texas A&M game immediately followed by the University of Texas game when Andre Emmett and Nick Valdez were not awakened for practice and a media furor occurred where I stated to the media when no other university officials were available for comment . . . 'We would look into this event.')

"I responded that Gerald Myers (still to my right) was also in the locker room and that he had a similar impression and was so upset by Knight's action towards me that he immediately followed me to my suite to apologize in front of several witnesses. Knight's response (in a very loud voice) was in essence, 'He did not!'

"Knight then began a very angry and confrontational outburst in public directed at me. He stated almost in a scream, I always misinterpret comments and that I called him a 'liar,' apparently because I had contradicted his version of the locker room encounter. He repeated yelling, 'I am not a liar!' At this point, he was red faced, physically confrontational and the entire area of the busy lunch crowd was watching. . . .

"I chose to walk away out of the store. Just steps past the checkout counter, I turned around to see Bob Knight charging up behind me furious with fists clenched and confronted me before I could leave the store. I did not engage him in the store. Once, in the parking lot, he continued to yell at me that I had called him a 'liar.' . . . Gerald tried to pull Coach Knight away by his shoulder somewhat unsuccessfully."

Smith said Knight and Myers drove away, with Knight at the wheel of his tan Lincoln, but that Myers then got out of the car "and appeared to be yelling at Coach Knight." According to Smith, Knight then got out and ran after Myers, abandoning the car with the driver's side door open in the middle of the street, before getting back in and driving off in pursuit of Myers, trying to persuade him to get back in the car.

The next day, Texas Tech officials went into high-level talks to decide Knight's fate. Meanwhile, Lubbock Mayor Marc McDougal, an avid Red Raider fan, appeared on a talk radio show, calling for the community to rally around Knight by filling up United Spirit Arena for that night's game against Baylor. Asked later about the propriety of his remarks, McDougal insisted he wasn't taking sides. "Certainly, if there's a situation between him and the chancellor, I'd like to see it resolved," said the mayor. "Let the chancellor go about raising money for the university and let Coach Knight coach basketball."

Knight got a standing ovation from a crowd of 9,835 before the game. After the Red Raiders won, he gave his version of events but this wouldn't be one of his set-piece defenses with corroborating testimony from whoever he was with. Myers didn't say a word in Knight's defense and the available evidence supported Smith's version. Unnamed witnesses told the *Avalanche-Journal* that Knight and Smith had been talking quietly before Knight began yelling, "Are you calling me a liar?" and said that Knight followed Smith after he walked away. They also corroborated Smith's description of Myers jumping out of Knight's car and Knight jumping out to pursue him, leaving his car in the street.

The university released a copy of a letter Myers wrote to Knight, officially reprimanding him. "Bob, from this day forward you must avoid these kind of incidents," Myers wrote, "and any further behavior of this type either public or private is unacceptable and will result in severe actions."

However, no apology was offered or demanded. A statement from Knight was released, saying only, "I regret that the situation turned out the way it did. I look forward to finishing this season in a strong fashion and I am glad the situation is behind me so that I can return to the business of coaching."

As the IU administration once had, Texas Tech officials negotiated Knight's sentence with him. The *Avalanche-Journal*'s Patrick Gonzalez reported that Knight had been asked to sign a letter accepting a three-game suspension but had refused. Knight confirmed that the discussion had taken place.

"I will tell you that suspension was a thing that was talked about and I told Gerald I would not agree to that," Knight said after the Baylor game. "I would not think that was fair. . . . I have thoroughly enjoyed it here and so has my wife and we decided if that's the way it went with the suspension, I would go through every means possible to fight that. But I would have stayed through the suspension simply because I feel so strongly about this situation, this community, and these kids."

Having decided on a reprimand, rather than a suspension, which would incur Knight's displeasure and perhaps even his resignation, university officials tried to put the incident behind them as fast as possible. Smith declined to discuss it; his written account surfaced only after the

Avalanche-Journal obtained it with an open-records request. Myers said the whole thing had been a "misunderstanding."

Once again, there was a question of who was bigger, Knight or the school. Only the school had changed.

The 2003–4 season ended with that spring's 70–65 loss to top-ranked St. Joseph's in the NCAA Tournament, and an uncertain future loomed before Knight's Red Raiders.

In his first three seasons at IU, Knight had won two Big Ten titles and gone to the Final Four. After three seasons at Texas Tech, Knight was 68–33 but Emmett, the leading scorer in Big 12 history, had just left, and there was no one of his stature on the horizon.

Knight had a well-heeled personal following in town, but the excitement around his program had died down. He was still the darling of the business community, which lavished its support on him. Knight, who had predicted the IU administration would deck Assembly Hall in advertisements after he left (incorrectly, it turned out) was now a walking advertisement, himself. With two Adidas logos on his shirt lapel and an O'Reilly Auto Parts logo on his chest, he looked like a NASCAR driver.

However, attendance had dropped back under 10,000 a game, 2,000 below that of the Lady Raiders. Before the 2004–5 season, the indefatigable Pat Knight spoke at fraternities and dorms all over campus, encouraging students to turn out, something no IU assistant could ever have imagined.

The Ohio State job came open that summer and, despite decades-long estrangement from his alma mater, Knight was interested.

He had never forgiven the Buckeyes for firing Fred Taylor in 1976. Taylor got over it, but Knight didn't, refusing Taylor's invitation to return to Columbus in 1985 to celebrate the anniversary of their 1960 NCAA title. However, after Knight was fired at IU, he softened, saying he regretted not pursuing the Buckeye job when it became open three years before.

Now, after years of struggle and a scandal that had just consumed

Coach Jim O'Brien, there was a groundswell of support for Knight among Buckeye alumni. Knight made no comment and claimed afterward he never talked to anyone, but behind the scenes, the action was frenetic. His assistants began looking at Ohio State tapes and putting their own recruits on hold.

Two weeks later, Ohio State athletic director Andy Geiger, under media criticism for even considering it, called Knight to say he would go in another direction.

"We're glad this is over," Pat Knight told ESPN.com's Andy Katz. "The reason we didn't call our recruits until Thursday was we knew what the first question would be and we didn't have an answer. Now that it is, we haven't missed a beat and we'll be right back at it. . . .

"The more he thought about it, it was becoming less of an easy decision. Yes, Ohio State is his alma mater but it would have been a hard decision. In Columbus, he would have been back in the media spotlight. Breaking the record [Dean Smith's 879 victories] will mean more to him here than it would at Ohio State because these people gave him a shot when he was down and out. They offered him a job when he was out for a year."

Knight had been negotiating an extension with Texas Tech; however, only after Ohio State moved past him did he sign it.

Expectations were minimal in the fall of 2004. The preseason consensus had the Red Raiders in the bottom half of the conference so it was another of Knight's surprises when he went to a three-guard lineup, finished the regular season ranked No. 16 in the nation at 18–9, and reached the finals of the Big 12 Tournament. Senior guard Ronald Ross, a one-time walk-on, led them in scoring, but they were a model of balance with four players in double figures.

Seeded No. 6 in the NCAA Tournament, they put away UCLA, moving into a second-round matchup with the No. 3 seed, Gonzaga, a small school from Spokane, Washington, but a perennial power. As expected, the Zags went up by 13 points in the second half, but the Red Raiders came back to win, 71–69, going ahead to stay on Ross' three-pointer with 1:06 left.

Knight, who had barely celebrated any of his three NCAA titles, was visibly moved by this win. When the game ended, he told Pat to go up in the stands and bring Karen down. She was already crying when she reached the floor, and continued to weep as she hugged her husband around the midsection while he did a TV interview. In the most tender gesture he had ever made on national television, Knight cradled Karen's head in his shoulder.

By now, Knight fairly idealized Karen. He no longer said she knew enough basketball to carry on an intelligent conversation with Pete Newell. Now, he said, "If I pick three or four people who know the most about basketball, she and Pete Newell would be my first two choices. I just wanted to thank her for all the help she's given me preparing for this game."

The era of good feeling lasted for several hours, until Knight did an interview with Chet Coppock of Sporting News Radio, a former Indianapolis on-air personality, who asked the wrong question. With the Hoosiers coming off a bad season amid speculation Mike Davis would be fired, Coppock asked about it and Knight vented his bitterness yet again.

"They created that for themselves," said Knight. "The guy that's coaching there is a guy that I told Pat we were going to replace at the end of the season." Knight went on to blast the IU administration again and say the athletic director "didn't know his ass from third base."

The next day, as if answering Knight, IU announced Davis would remain.

Knight and his players were on a cloud for the next five days, before their third-round game against West Virginia in Albuquerque. It was only 320 miles from Lubbock and the Pit on the New Mexico campus was filled with Red Raider fans. The Mountaineers didn't look unbeatable. They were dark horses, themselves, No. 7 seeds who had just upset second-seeded Wake Forest. In a bracket with no great teams, Knight even seemed to have a chance to return to the Final Four for the first time since 1992, when he had also come through Albuquerque.

The run-up to the game was another Bob Knight Festival. At a press conference, he told Ross to say he was really "a latter-day Santa Claus," and when it was Knight's turn at the mike, he asked, "Do you want to hear my ho, ho, ho?" After the NCAA forbade him to drink out of his O'Reilly Auto Parts cup at press conferences, Knight, the one-time scourge of NCAA commercialism, brought it anyway, announcing, "First of all, I'm really happy to be here with my O'Reilly Auto Parts cup." Stories went out, saying Knight had *really* mellowed this time.

The dream died against West Virginia. The Red Raiders fell behind by 10 points, came back to go ahead in the second half, and trailed 62–60 in the closing seconds when several tip-ins that would have tied it bounced around the rim. In the ensuing scramble, the ball was headed out of bounds off a West Virginia player, but the Mountaineers' Patrick Beilin got it, leaped in the air, and called time out before coming down with :30 left. The Raiders had to foul, Kevin Pittsnogle made two free throws with :17 left and West Virginia won, 65–60.

"I told our players after the game that they'll look back on this game and they'll feel like they made mistakes," said Knight, which was his way of saying it had been their game to win. "But I think if they can look at the total picture and see what all happened from beginning to end, they should feel very proud of themselves for what they were able to accomplish this year." It was his way of saying he was as surprised and as pleased as anyone else.

It wasn't paradise, but it was home.

In fall 2005, Bob Knight, now a 65-year-old enfant terrible, began practice with his team, as he had every autumn but one since he graduated from Ohio State in 1962. Knight had three starters back from his Sweet 16 team, with Dean Smith's 879 career victories dead ahead, 25 ahead of Knight's 854.

His life was quieter, if not quiet. Patrick, now his associate head coach, was an ideal buffer between his father and his players, the referees, and the press. There were no reported incidents of head-butts, kicks, or chokes, however inadvertent or instructional. His best players weren't leaving one after another, as they had at the end at IU.

However, Knight was still Knight. In 2005, when Andre Emmett, by then a member of the Memphis Grizzlies, heard a replay of Knight's blood-curdling 1992 diatribe at Indiana, the one that that lasted one minute and 14 seconds with 15 "fucks" and 16 first-person references, he said it was the same Bob Knight who had coached him.

"I think it's one of those things you have to live through, to see for yourself," says Emmett. "I've never really met anybody to this date who broke down the game of basketball as well as he did. He's beyond coaching. He's a teacher of the game. He was tremendous. And then, how his style works, it was very different for me but it made me a tougher person. . . .

"From the outside, it may have looked like that [that he was mellowing] but from the inside, I mean he was always intense. He was always the same old Coach Knight. My three years with him, he was pretty much the same. Actually, he picked it up each year."

Nevertheless, there was no doubt Knight had found a comfort zone. Many of his old retainers like Steve Downing and his IU secretary, Mary Ann Davis, were with him in the athletic department. The sports information director was Clair Bee's son-in-law. Knight's sons and their wives were near, as was his grandson, Tim's boy.

Pete Newell, living outside San Diego in his 90s, remained Knight's mentor of mentors, visiting Lubbock when he could, talking to him by phone weekly. Newell says that when the three coaches—he, Bob, and Karen—get to talking about the Red Raiders, it's often he and Karen on one side, trying to tell Bob that some player he expects more from is really okay.

"He's more relaxed," says Newell. "He's more accessible too. . . . I do think he's at peace now much more. He'll never be totally at peace and that's him."

For a man who seemed doomed to drive himself into a bitter retirement, this would be a happy ending. Of course, whether it's more glory that awaits, another fall, or both, his story isn't over.

ACKNOWLEDGMENTS

Anyone hoping to understand Bob Knight is indebted to John Feinstein for *A Season on the Brink*; to John Flynn of the Louisville *Courier-Journal*, an old confidant from Knight's early days at Army who wrote the first great profile of Knight; to Bruce Newman, who as an IU student wrote a wonderful profile of Knight for the campus paper before going on to *Sports Illustrated*; to *SI*'s Frank Deford for his memorable "The Rabbit Hunter"; and to Knight's intimates—Dave Kindred, Tom Cushman, Pete Axthem, Hubert Mitzell, and Billy Reed—for their columns over the years.

We're also thankful to Knight himself for *Knight: My Story*; to Steve Alford, the author of *Playing for Knight*; to Isiah Thomas, the author of *The Fundamentals*; to Jack Isenhour, the author of *Same Knight, Different Channel*; and to Phil Berger, the author of *Knight Fall*, for the insights and background their books provided.

Knight declined our requests to interview him. However, we're deeply thankful to the people who were so generous with their time and memories: Robert Abbott, Tom Abernathy, Dr. James Anderson, Stephen Backer, Dick Barnes, Roy Bates, Taylor Bell, Ira Berkow, Larry Bird, Uwe Blab, Pauline Boop, Rick Bozich, Delray Brooks, Dale Brown, Russ Brown, Loren Buckner, Terry Cagle, Ricky Calloway, James Capshew, P. J. Carlesimo, John Carlson, Dean Chance, Connie Chung, Doug Clevenger, Don Cox, Billy Cunningham, Vernon Curie, Tom Cushman, Dan Dakich, Gus Dielens, Clarence Doninger, Norman Douglas, Tim Dudich, Wayne Duke, John Duren, Jim Dutcher,

Bill Dwyre, Robert Eakle, Gary Eiber, Andre Emmett, Chuck Fattore, Rick Ford, Paul Franke, Tim Franklin, Bill Frieder, Lawrence Funderburke, Gary Gearhart, Peter Gelling, Mike Giomi, Jack Graff, Pat Graham, Steve Green, Ken Gros Louis, Glen Grunwald, Mike Gyovai, Joe B. Hall, Kathy Harmon, Beth Harris, Warner Harper, Kirk Haston, Mark Haymore, Jud Heathcote, Joe Hillman, Marv Homan, Richie Hoyt, Terry Hutchens, Phil Isenbarger, John Kamstra, Frank Kendrick, Kaye Kessler, Dave Kindred, Bob Kinney, Joe Kleine, Jon Koncak, Joe Kosciusko, Richard Lapchick, John Laskowski, Chris Lawson, Todd Leary, Ronnie Lester, Mike Littwin, Mike Lord, Kevin Mackey, Kyle Macy, Jon Mikula, Tom Miller, Mark Montieth, Gus Mueller, Dr. Bob Murphy, Hayden Murray, Dick Nagy, Lynn Nance, Pete Newell, Bruce Newman, Lori Nickel, Howard Nourse, Mel Nowell, Pete Obremskey, Mike O'Koren, Johnny Orr, Dick Otte, Dr. James Oxley, Scott Pearlson, Sam Perkins, Whitney Pope, Rance Pugmire, Wayne Radford, Dick Rhoads, Phil Richards, Ray Richardson, Steve Risley, John Ritter, Joe Roberts, Alvin Robertson, Steve Robinson, Rick Roway, Tom Rucker, Jeremy Schaap, Danny Schantz, Dan Schrage, Billy Schutsky, Dave Shepherd, Bob Shonk, Bill Shunkwiler, Larry Siegfried, Christopher Simpson, Dave Skibinski, Norm Sloan, Keith Smart, Kohn Smith, Cooper Speaks, Stan Sutton, George Taliaferro, Loren Tate, Barry Temkin, Isiah Thomas, Wayman Tisdale, Frank Truitt, Jeff Turner, Landon Turner, Larry Vucovich, General Sam Walker, Gordon White, Sherron Wilkerson, Frank Wilson, Jim Wisman, and Courtney Witte.

Our thanks to our talented agent, David Black, and our gracious editor, Jack Sallay. Thanks also to Jeffrey Neuman for nurturing the book in its early stages and reading the manuscript later on.

Above all, my deepest thanks to my wife, Mary Kay, and our three daughters, Emma, Hannah, and Grace, for blessing me with their tenderness and love.

—*Steve Delsohn*

*   *   *

I'd like to thank Steve Delsohn, who got me into the book business in general and this project in particular. And, as usual, thank you to my beloved Loretta and Emily.

—*Mark Heisler*

ABOUT THE AUTHORS

Steve Delsohn is a correspondent for ESPN TV. His previous books include *Talking Irish: The Oral History of Notre Dame Football*; *True Blue: The Dramatic History of the Los Angeles Dodgers, Told by the Men Who Lived It*; *Out of Bounds* (coauthored with NFL great Jim Brown); and *The Fire Inside: Firefighters Talk About Their Lives*. He lives with his wife and three children in Thousand Oaks, California.

Mark Heisler covers the NBA for the *Los Angeles Times*. His previous books include *The Lives of Riley*, *Madmen's Ball*, and *They Shoot Coaches, Don't They?* He lives with his wife and daughter in Northridge, California.